THE GUIDE TO ETHNIC MONTREAL

The Guide to

ETHNIC
ASIAN
BLACK
CHINESE
EUROPEAN
GREEK
ITALIAN
JEWISH
LATIN
MIDDLE
EASTERN
MONTREAL

Barry Lazar & Tamsin Douglas

1992

Published with the assistance of The Canada Council and the
Multiculturalism Programs Branch of Multiculturalism and
Citizenship Canada.

Cover art and design: Paul Lavoie
Cover art direction: J.W. Stewart
Walking tour maps: Rita Bauer
Book design & imaging: ECW Type & Art
Printing: Imprimerie d'Édition Marquis Ltée

CANADIAN CATALOGUING IN PUBLICATION DATA

Lazar, Barry
    The guide to ethnic Montreal

ISBN 1-55065-030-0

1. Montréal (Quebec) — Population — Ethnic groups.
2. Montréal (Quebec) — Description and travel.
I. Douglas, Tamsin   II. Title.

FC2947.9.A1L39 1992   971.4'28'004   C92-090272-3
F1054.5.M89A25 1992

VÉHICULE PRESS

P.O.B. 125, Place du Parc Station, Montreal, Quebec, Canada H2W 2M9

Distributed in Canada by GENERAL PUBLISHING CO. LIMITED,
and in the United States by BOOKSLINGER INC. (St. Paul, MN)
and INLAND BOOK COMPANY (East Haven, CT).

Printed in Canada on acid-free paper.

CONTENTS

CHINESE MONTREAL

History 99.

Festivals 107, Organizations 108, Media 112.

Restaurants and Clubs 112, Food Sources 121, Shops and Services 122, Walking Tour 125, Books and Films 133.

EUROPEAN MONTREAL

History 135.

Baltic (Estonian, Latvian, & Lithuanian) 138, Bulgarian 139, Czechoslovakian 140, Dutch 140, German 142, Hungarian 144, Polish 145, Romanian 147, Ukrainian 147, Yugoslav 151. Restaurants and Clubs 152, Food Sources 155, Shops and Services 158, Ukrainian Walking Tour 158.

GREEK MONTREAL

History 165.

Organizations 168, Media 171, Books and Films 172.

Restaurant and Clubs 172, Food Sources 173, Shops and Services 175, Walking Tour 175.

ITALIAN MONTREAL

History 183.

Organizations 190, Media 194.

Restaurants and Clubs 194, Food Sources 198, Shops and Services 200, Walking Tour 203, Some Books, a Play and a Film 210.

JEWISH MONTREAL

History 213.

Organizations 218, Media 225, Books and Films 227.

Restaurants and Clubs 228, Food Sources 232, Shops and Services 234, Walking Tour 235.

INTRODUCTION

Dear Reader,

You may be thinking, "Who is this book for?" Well, it's for Montrealers who want a different perspective on their hometown. It is also for visitors who already know that Montreal is one of the world's great French cities but wish to find out more about the city's other languages and cultures. It's for shoppers and eaters who are looking for something beyond the ordinary. But most of all, THE GUIDE TO ETHNIC MONTREAL is for the urban explorer in all of us — a cultural passport to Montreal's growing ethnic communities.

There are many excellent books about English and French Canadians (and the Welsh, Scots, and Irish) — this is not one of them. THE GUIDE TO ETHNIC MONTREAL is about the dozens of ethnic communities and million or so Montrealers with roots in other countries.

We've compiled unusual walking and driving tours through parts of Montreal seldom travelled by tourist buses. We've made notes on more than 500 clubs, restaurants, shops, and community organizations. We've added information about holidays and celebrations, why people came to Montreal, and where they chose to live.

We're proud that the publication of THE GUIDE TO ETHNIC MONTREAL received the approval & support of **Célébrations Montréal 1642–1992** the organizing committee for Montreal's 350th birthday.

You can stand here in the bookstore and read it all now; but better yet, take THE GUIDE TO ETHNIC MONTREAL outside and let the city open itself up to you. Chances are you're in a part of "Ethnic Montreal" right now.

Barry Lazar and Tamsin Douglas
Montreal, May 1992

P.S.   We would appreciate your comments and suggestions. You can reach us through our publisher: Véhicule Press, P.O.B. 125, Place du Parc Station, Montréal, Québec, H2W 2M9.

GENERAL INFORMATION

For general tourist information call 873-2015 in Montreal. If you are out-of-town call 1-800-363-7777 weekdays from 9:00 a.m. to 5:00 p.m. You can also write the Greater Montréal Convention and Tourism Bureau, 1555 Peel St., Suite 600, Montréal, Québec, H3A 1X6, or Tourisme Québec, P.O. Box 20,000, Québec (Québec), Canada G1K 7X2.

If you are arriving by air, check out information booths at Dorval and Mirabel International Airports. And there are information booths in Old Montreal at 174 Notre Dame E. (near Place Jacques Cartier), and downtown at 1001 Square-Dorchester (between Peel and Metcalfe streets). Office hours vary with the location and season.

The downtown and Old Montreal offices are particularly worth-while visiting for general information and maps. The small, free *Tourist Guide to Montreal* is useful for first-time visitors to the city.

GETTING TO MONTREAL

By car

Montreal is an eight hour car drive from New York City and about six hours from Boston or Toronto along major highways. Distances and speed limits are in kilometres. 1000 kilometres is 600 miles. 100 kilometres per hour is 60 miles an hour. Call 873-4121 for highway and travel conditions in French or English.

Drivers take note: radar detectors are forbidden in Quebec, even if they are turned off; and right hand turns on red lights are not permitted.

By bus

The bus station for all long distance bus routes is the Voyageur Terminal (Berri-UQAM Métro station), 505 boul. de Maisonneuve E. (842-2281).

By train

Amtrack (1-800-426-8725) and VIA Rail (871-1331) trains arrive downtown at Central Station (Bonaventure Métro station), 935 de La Gauchetière W.

By air

Almost all North American flights land at, and depart from, Dorval International Airport (633-3105), about a half-hour drive from downtown Montreal. Taxis charge about $20.00 for the trip while limousines cost $31.50 There is a bus to downtown hotels for $8.50. If you are not in a rush and don't have much luggage, take local bus number 104 for $1.60. It goes to the nearby Dorval train station. Ask for a transfer and take the 204 bus to Lionel-Groulx Métro station.

Mirabel International Airport (476-3010) is for flights from outside North America and is about an hour's drive from the city. Taxis charge about $45.00 and limousines $62.50. The Aéroport bus costs $11.00 and travels between Mirabel and downtown with stops at Central Station and the Voyageur Bus Terminal.

GETTING AROUND IN THE CITY

St-Laurent boulevard divides Montreal into east and west. (For example, there is a 1000 Sherbrooke St. E. and a 1000 Sherbrooke St. W.) On north-south streets, building numbers increase as you go north with even numbers on the west or left hand-side. Don't be surprised if you're walking up St-Laurent and see the sun set. The island is at an angle because there is a bend in the St-Lawrence river and the points of the compass are used more for convenience.

Montreal's downtown area is long but narrow. It stretches about seven kilometers (two and a half miles) from Atwater avenue on the west to rue St-Denis in the east; and spreads south about four long blocks from Sherbrooke to René-Lévesque boulevard. It is a dense, exciting area; bars don't close until 3:00 a.m. and Montrealers love to cruise the streets. Early morning traffic jams are not unusual!

Montreal has an excellent Métro (subway) and bus system. Public transportation generally shuts down between 1:00 a.m. and

5:30 a.m., although a few major bus routes run throughout the night. Call AUTOBUS (288-6287) for help, in French or English, to get to a particular destination. Buses must be boarded with exact change or a ticket. A single fare is $1.60 and a strip of 6 tickets costs $6.50 which can be purchased in some stores, pharmacies, and all Métro stations. Transfers to another bus or Métro are free but transfer tickets must be obtained when the fare is paid.

It's easy to get a taxi in Montreal, either flagging one at the curb or phoning for pickup at the door. Rates start at $2.15 adding $0.95 for each kilometre.

WHEN YOU USE THIS BOOK

All addresses in THE GUIDE TO ETHNIC MONTREAL are in the City of Montreal unless another municipality is mentioned. Except as noted, all phone numbers are local — in the 514 area code.

We have done our best to confirm that stores, shops, and organizations are still in business as we go to press, however, Montreal's fame as a dynamic city means that many small shops and restaurants change hands every year. Please call first.

RESTAURANTS

Each chapter lists several local restaurants which cater to their community but are still accessible to those outside their community. We look for places with good cooking, perhaps an original touch to the menu or decor, and a staff which goes out of its way to make a newcomer comfortable. Good cheap places are prized. We've found many that excite us and pray that they will stay open long enough to develop a clientele.

$ indicates that a lunch or dinner should cost under $10 (without taxes, tips, or wine).

$$ is under $25, and $$$ above that.

"BYOB" identifies a restaurant in which diners can bring *their own* wine or beer. Quebec-bottled domestic and imported wine can be purchased in a *dépanneur* or corner store. For a wider selection you must go to a Société des alcools du Québec (SAQ) outlet, a government-run liquor store.

Major credit cards accepted are noted: AMEX (American Express), DINERS (Diner's Club), EN-ROUTE, MC (Mastercard), and VISA. Hours often vary with the seasons, so please call ahead.

WALKING TOURS

Walking tours take between one and two hours. We recommend going slowly, even indulgently, so we have tried to include places for a quick espresso, a smoked meat or empañada or whatever looks good along the way. While the walks are detailed tours, they are intended to be aids to your own explorations. You can always stroll off the path for a while and come back to the tour. Most start and end near a Métro Station.

The driving tour of Middle Eastern Montreal has several stops. (Remember to take off your shoes in the Mosque.)

DEMOGRAPHICS

THE ETHNIC GUIDE TO MONTREAL is not a study in statistics, but when a community's size is mentioned, we've taken our figures from the most recent available census (1986). Canadians are permitted to choose more than one ethnicity in the census and frequently do. The figures should not be read as a statement of the size of any ethnic group as much as an indication of how many Montrealers consider themselves to be part of that community.

THE MULTICULTURAL VULTURE

Interested in a little inter-ethnic dabbling? Montreal has lots of inexpensive community courses. You can learn Spanish, Italian or Hebrew, do some Japanese flower arranging, try out the latest Chilean wine, and get refreshingly pounded with a Swedish massage. Dozens of courses begin each September and January and are listed in the free publication *Les loisirs au coeur de votre quartier* (872-6211).

L'autre Montréal Bus Tours (521-7802) is a non-profit organization that takes groups of at least 20 people on a tour through major ethnic neighbourhoods. Tour guides speak French, English and Spanish and can modify the itinerary to meet the interests of a particular group.

Le Bureau Interculturel de Montréal (BIM), City Hall, 275 Notre-Dame E. (872-6133) is a city office linking municipal government and Montreal's more than 80 ethnic communities. BIM also tries to sensitize city authorities to minority needs and cultures while at the same time informing ethnic groups of the city services available to them. The staff know a lot about Montreal's cultural communities and organizations.

The **Cinémathèque de Montréal**, at 880 Roy E. (872-3680) is a rental library (that also rents projectors). It's open most afternoons and has a broad range of mostly older films on other countries.

The **Cinémathèque Québécoise**, 335 de Maisonneuve E. (842-9763) specializes in foreign feature films which can be viewed in the Centre Documentation (or rent the small but sumptuous theatre for your own Fellini festival).

The **National Film Board Library**, 200 René Lévesque W. in Place Guy Favreau (283-4823), rents hundreds of its films, documentaries and animated cartoons on video and 16mm (but does not rent film projectors or VCRs).

FESTIVALS

Montrealers have an affable approach to the word "festival." There seems to be a festival of movies, music, or theatre almost weekly and local restaurants regularly feature "festivals" of smoked meat, spaghetti, and even draft beer! Still, we do have several annual events that are real festivities which every visitor should enjoy.

ALCAN FESTIVAL INTERNATIONAL DE JAZZ DE MON-TREAL (871-1881). From July 1–12 Montreal hosts jazz and blues performers from all over the world. The big name draws perform in the large venues and in some local clubs but most of the 300 or so outdoor concerts are free, on downtown streets between Bleury and St-Denis.

BENSON AND HEDGES INTERNATIONAL FIREWORKS FES-TIVAL (June to early August) (342-9010) is the best and brightest of its kind in the world. Pyrotechnic professionals from a dozen countries mount incredible displays on Saturday nights in June and Sunday nights in July and August. The shows begin after dusk and the best seats are at the La Ronde amusement park on Ile Ste-Hélène, however, the view is almost as good (and free) from the Montreal side of the river, not far from the Frontenac Métro station.

FESTIVAL OF THE AMERICAS (842-8599). In late spring, Montrealers are treated to two weeks of a dozen or so new plays by groups from off-Broadway to out of the Andes.

FOLKLORE CANADA INTERNATIONAL (524-8552). Director Guy Landry keeps in touch with community cultural groups throughout the country, while getting ready for July's 10 day Festival Mondial de Folklore de Drummondville.

INTERNATIONAL NEW DANCE FESTIVAL (287-1423). In early fall, leading companies from around the world perform at venues throughout the city. Several afternoon shows are free.

INTERNATIONAL NEW CINEMA AND VIDEO (843-4725). Canada's oldest international film and video festival is held in October. This is a major showcase for filmmakers working out of the mainstream and is a particularly good opportunity for seeing Third World and non-traditional films.

JUST FOR LAUGHS (845-3155). At the end of July, Montreal hosts the world's largest humour festival. It's ten days of multi-comedian gala concerts, special shows and scores of mimes and jokers in the streets.

MONTREAL WORLD FILM FESTIVAL (848-3883) in late August is a fortnight of world-class film and often the only chance to see an incredible range of recently-made foreign films. Get a schedule and plan ahead; there is way too much to see.

ORGANIZATIONS AND SERVICES

The **Alliances des Communautés Culturelles pour l'Égalité dans la Santé et les Services Sociaux** (ACCESS), 3680 Jeanne-Mance (842-6891) is an umbrella organization to help community groups gain access to the public health and social services network.

Association Multi-ethnique pour l'Integration des personnes Handicapées du Québec, 91 St. Zotique E. (272-0680) lobbies on behalf of the disabled and provides services and assistance in many languages.

Canadian Council of Christians and Jews, 1450 City Councillors (987-9501) brings together different religious and cultural groups.

Centre de Recherches Actions sur les Relations Raciales (CRARR), 3465 Côte des Neiges (939-3342) studies race relations in Quebec.

Fiesta Smolash Productions, 5027A Plamondon (FAX: 342-6696). Chinese shadow theatre entertainers, organ-grinders, Caribbean steel bands, Flamenco artists, Yemenite folk dancers — over a hundred dance groups, singers and musicians,

The Intercultural Institute of Montreal, 4917 St-Urbain (288-7229) offers programs in intercultural education and training, promotes research on people's rights and cultural identity, and acts as a network to foster greater understanding between Montrealers.

La Ligue Antifasciste Mondiale (LAM) (1-800-INFO-LAM) helps people who have suffered discrimination and monitors the activities of local racist organizations.

New Acropolis, 1631 St-Denis (848-0553) is part of an international organization. Members meet regularly to discuss Western and Eastern philosophies.

Rassemblement pour l'Amitié Mondiale, (842-6999) brings together people with different cultural backgrounds to combat racism.

The Thomas More Institute, 2333 Sherbrooke W. (935-9585) teaches through discussion. Recent courses have included histories of Ukrainian, Scottish, Spanish, and Irish communities and some unusual cultural programmes like "How to be Japanese" and "How to be Chinese."

The downtown **YMCA**, 1440 Drummond (849-8393) is the first abode for many refugees who are often housed here and hang out in the Y's cafeteria. It's a great place to chat with newcomers and you can stay for hours over a cup of coffee. The Y is also known for its language programs in Greek, Japanese, Italian, Portuguese, Russian, and Spanish.

Substantial studies of Quebec's ethnic communities are published by the **Institut québécois de recherche sur la culture**, 14 rue Haldimand, Québec G1R 4N4 (418-643-4965). The Canadian Historical Association at 395 Wellington Street, Ottawa, K1A 0N3, publishes short histories on many Canadian ethnic groups.

MEDIA

Several free magazines and newspapers are good sources for community information and events. *Images* is a bimonthly intercultural magazine with reviews and articles in French and English emphasizing the city's ethnic communities. The English-language city tabloid, *The Mirror* is published weekly and has regular features on city politics and race-relations as well as news about new clubs and restaurants and complete entertainment listings. It's French-language counterpart, *Voir* also has good entertainment information but has more book reviews and articles on culture.

Montreal has several multi-ethnic radio stations. The oldest is the mainstream CFMB 1410-AM (483-2362). Radio-Centre-Ville CINQ 102.3-FM (495-2597) is the longest-established community-run station, with several programs produced for different communities each day. McGill University's CKUT 90.3-FM (398-6787) and the Université de Montréal's CISM 89.3-FM (343-7511) both have multi-cultural community and music programs.

Ethnic communities produce their own programs for channel 24 on cable television. Schedules are available from CFCF Cable (277-7133) or Vidéotron (282-1001).

ASIAN MONTREAL

POPULATION: 90,000

MAJOR COMMUNITIES: Brossard, Villeray, Côte-des-Neiges, Ville-St-Laurent, Cartierville.

SHOPPING AND FOOD: Victoria and Van Horne, Poirier Street in Ville St-Laurent, Chinatown (Boulevard St-Laurent and La Gauchetière).

Asians account for sixty percent of the world's population, and since 1984, half of all immigrants to Quebec. Ethnic Chinese form the largest part of Montreal's Asian community. For a tour of Chinatown and more information about that community, see CHINESE MONTREAL, page 99.

Much of Montreal's Asian community has roots in western Canada where, more than a hundred years ago, Chinese, Sikhs, and Japanese immigrated as labourers to build railways, and work on farms and in mines and forests.

With the Canadian Pacific Railroad completed, Asian immigration was discouraged. Chinese wanting to come to Canada had to pay a fee — a "head tax." This practice ended only when the federal government decided that, except for rare cases, *no* Chinese or Japanese could enter the country. This legislation lasted for over a generation, ending only after WWII.

Asians who did enter from other countries found further official discrimination. They were lumped together as "Orientals" and only allowed to enter if they had $250, a financial requirement not demanded of Europeans. After anti-Asian riots in Vancouver in 1907, Asians lost their right to vote in local and federal elections in British Columbia and Alberta. Legislation was also passed to ensure they could not be hired for public service jobs or work on government projects.

Even as late as 1952, immigration officers had authority to stop anyone from entering Canada because of nationality, ethnic group and "peculiar customs, habits, or modes of life." Attitudes began changing after WWII. Canada was growing and needed teachers, scientists, researchers, engineers, and other professionals. Well-educated Asians, particularly from English-speaking Common-wealth countries like India, found Canada could be a welcome home.

In 1962, the federal government officially ended its policies of discriminating by the race or country of the prospective immi-grant. Hundreds of thousands from India and Pakistan found work in Canada as nurses and other professionals, skilled workers, labourers, and domestics.

The 1975 withdrawal of American forces from Vietnam pre-cipitated a massive evacuation from Vietnam, Laos and Cambodia. Many refugees came to Quebec which continues to attract over 10,000 Asians a year.

While each community has its own festivals there are many common celebrations. In mid-winter, the Festival of Saraswati, the Hindu Goddess of Learning is honoured by Bangladeshis, Sri Lankans and others. Spring is the time for the New Year according to Cambodian, Laotian and Thai lunar calendars and a ceremony and feast are held at the **Kymer Society Pagoda** at 7188 de Nancy (735-6901). In the Fall, there is a four day Autumn religious and cultural festival. Call **The South Asian Centre** (842-2330) or **NACOI** (845-3722) for more information.

Another joint event is the Asian Soccer Cup, held in August in Marcel Laurin Park, Ville St. Laurent. Teams from the Vietnamese, Cambodian, Korean, Japanese, and Laotian communities compete.

Serai means "resting place" in Persian as well as "I will be" ("Je serai," in French). The local publication under the same name, bridges several cultures with articles on Quebec politics and Asian culture.

■■ CRICKET

Cricket gets lousy press. It's probably the names of those positions that put us off: Silly mid-on, silly mid-off, 3rd slip, gully, backward short leg, and a half dozen more. All you need to know is that there are eleven players out there. One of them is called the bowler and he or she throws the ball. The others try to catch it when it's hit by the opposing team's hitters. They're called batsmen.

The baseball similarity ends here. These guys don't use gloves. The cricket ball is smaller, harder and heavier than a baseball and gets thrown over 80 kmh. And those scores! When was the last time you were at a ball game where someone got 100 runs batted in? Aussies, Pakistanis, Gujartis, Trinidadians, Guyanians — everyone knows cricket. In 1990, Quebec won the Canadian cricket championship. Here's what to watch for. There are always two batters on the field. One of them protects a set of pins which the bowler tries to knock over. The batters must run past each other to score. No strikes, no balls and no foul-tips. The bowler throws the ball half-a-dozen times and then everyone changes position on the field. Don't understand something? Just ask. This is a very sociable sport. You've got plenty of time to draw on a beer and have a chat with someone who knows what's going on. Short games last up to six hours, serious ones go two or three days. Bring a lawn chair. Take a snooze. Half the players do. Life doesn't have to be frenetic. Enjoy the soca and Indian film music coming out of the beat boxes. This is the real game of summer. And remember, the home team serves lunch.

Quebec Cricket Federation (367-1281), May to September, 36 teams, two leagues.

Teesri Duniya (488-9994) is a multi-racial theatre group under the cajoling inspiration of writer and director Rahul Varma. The plays are by and about minorities in Montreal. Recent productions include "Land where the Trees Talk," "The Great Celestial Cow," "Job Stealer," and "Isolated Incident."

BANGLADESHI

Bangladesh, one of the world's poorest countries, squeezes four times the population of Canada into an area slightly larger than Newfoundland. It sinks into a shallow delta of the Indian Ocean and was devastated by floods in 1987 and a typhoon in 1991. Global warming may raise the level of the world's oceans and make Bangladeshis the world's first environmental refugees.

Bangladesh was part of Pakistan until 1971. It formally became an Islamic republic in 1988 and tensions are high between Muslims, Hindus, Christians and Buddhists. Some Bangladesh men (teachers, businessmen and professionals) arrived in the 1960s, however, most of the community came to Canada in the past ten years as refugees. Many in this group are unskilled: the women find work in the garment industry and the men also work with cleaning companies and in restaurants. Those more established live on the South Shore and the West Island while newcomers have settled downtown, in Parc-Extension, and in Côte-des-Neiges.

Image of Bangladesh is a locally-produced program on cable TV. December 16 is Bangladesh's Independence Day.

JAPANESE

Japanese men have been in Canada since the 1870s but their wives couldn't immigrate until 1907. Through much of this century,

Japanese Canadians were not allowed to vote, join the armed forces or have government jobs, consequently educated Japanese Canadians usually found professional work within their community.

On December 7, 1941 Japan attacked the American naval base at Pearl Harbour. The next day Britain and the U.S.A. declared war on Japan. Canada invoked the War Measures Act and Japanese-Canadians were declared enemy aliens. They were forced from their homes and sent to internment camps. The government later claimed it did this to protect the Japanese, however, their property was never returned and it took almost 50 years before they received any compensation or an official apology.

During and after WWII, many Japanese were relocated throughout Canada. A few hundred came to Montreal and spread throughout the city. Inter-marriage increased, and children spoke little Japanese at home. The local community remains small but active with about 2,100 people, many of whom live in Westmount, NDG, and Outremont.

Buddhism, which originated in India, is one of the principal religions of Japan. Montreal's **Buddhist Temple**, at 5250 St-Urbain (273-7921), is lead by Rev. Takamichi. In September, the church's community bazaar is a great opportunity to try Japanese delicacies and meet Japanese Montrealers. In 1984, the Japanese community planted trees on René-Lévesque boulevard, from St-Urbain to Papineau, in honour of the visit of Kyoto's Buddhist leader Lord Abbot Koshin Ohtani.

The Montreal **Japanese United Church** (271-6206) is at 8120 Champagneur St. and **St. Paul Ibaraki Church** (725-1215) is the community's Catholic church at 8155 Rousselot St.

Japanese Canadian Cultural Centre (728-1996, 728-5580) is also located at 8155 Rousselot. The centre, established in 1975 to support the national Japanese Redress Movement on wartime internment, has evolved into a cultural education association with 7,000 books in Japanese, English and French, translation services and help for travellers to Japan. Members and staff also help Japanese actors and actresses find work in corporate promotions and films.

Japanese Montrealers have a wealth of culture to share and many people who are eager to teach. For information on local activities call the **Japanese Canadian Cultural Centre** (728-1996) or the *Montreal Bulletin* (481-6795) a local publication on community events.

Arashi Daiko (351-9554). The name means "drumming up a storm" and this traditional Japanese group performs at cultural events throughout the city.

Club Go (932-7446). This deceptively simple game takes a lifetime to master. It's closest western equivalent is chess or maybe three-dimensional tic-tac-toe.

Ikebana is the traditional Japanese art of flower arranging. Dawson College and several of the city's Maisons de la Culture offer courses; local instructors include Mrs. Mayeda (462-2741) and Mrs. Watanabe (279-7552).

Japan–Canada Society (721-0052, 326-4815) was set up 32 years ago to promote understanding between non-Japanese and Japanese. Its monthly activities include visits to Japanese restaurants.

Montreal **Japanese Language Centre** (849-1550, 273-9015). For over 15 years, the Language Centre has given Japanese language lessons to children (its specialty) and adults. Sessions, which cost about $75, start in February and September at Marymont High school, 1500 Côte St. Luc.

Japanese Garden at the **Montreal Botanical Gardens**, 4101 Sherbrooke E. (872-1400). Daily from 9:00 a.m. to 18:00 p.m. This lovely garden was designed by Ken Nakajima, one of the world's top landscape architects. It has 15,000 plants surrounding ponds and brooks in a tranquil setting, a peaceful Zen garden, a pavilion modeled on a traditional Japanese home, a tea room, an art gallery, and one of the world's finest collections of Bonsai (the oriental art of growing trees in miniature forms).

Judo, the pre-eminent Japanese martial art and Olympic sport, is purely defensive and turns an opponent's power against himself. Montreal has one of the country's best Judo academies — **Shidokan** at 5345 de Maisonneuve W., (486-1818, 481-2424).

Origami Hidaiko Sinto (670-2903) teaches the art of paperfolding to small groups and in schools.

Shodo (488-2607). Japanese calligraphy is taught by Mrs. Okata.

Urasanke Montreal (747-6153). Mrs. Kagemori instructs students on how to perform a traditional Japanese tea ceremony. The course consists of four sessions at $20.00 each on Sunday or Monday afternoons. If you're not sure about committing to four sessions you are welcome to observe a class before making a decision.

The NFB's *My Floating World* is a film about the delightful work of local artist Miyuki Tanobe.

KAMPUCHIAN (CAMBODIAN)

Cambodia, a country of about 7 million people, is surrounded by Thailand, Laos, Vietnam and has a short coastline on the South China Sea. The country's origins are part of a 2000-year-old legend telling the story of how a man from the Indian village of Kampuja travelled to the golden land (Cambodia) and married a Khmer princess. In the 13th century the empire covered Thailand (Siam), Cambodia, Laos, and southern Vietnam, but then gradually lost its territories and power, becoming a French protectorate from 1863 to 1953.

Since then, Cambodia's history has been a nightmare of blood. Norodom Sihanouk tried to keep the country neutral during the war in Vietnam but lost to the pro-American Lol Noi in 1970 and was in turn forced out by Pol Pot's Marxist Khmer Rouge. Pol Pot renamed the country Kampuchea and modeled it on the rural society of 12th century Khmer. In an insane purification process, the Khmer Rouge slaughtered over one million ethnic Chinese, Moslems, and Vietnamese as well as doctors, academics, monks, and people with glasses (the mark of an intellectual!).

In 1978, Vietnam invaded the country and still controls the capital, but no one group leads the country. Efforts to bring peace to the country have been hampered by fears of the Khmer Rouge. Since 1975, over 20,000 Cambodians have come to Canada and almost half of them live in Montreal.

Cambodia is a rural society with a strong family network. In Montreal, many have tried to recreate that village life around local temples and neighbourhoods. Many apartment buildings have several Cambodian families and reflect a friendly community feeling as smells of fish, ginger and garlic waft through the corridors and people freely wander about.

The weekly cable TV program is called *Voix du Cambodge*. A pagoda in Côte-des-Neiges is maintained by the **Société Bouddhiste Khmêre**, 7188 de Nancy (735-6901) and lead by the Vénérable Hok Savann. The **Communauté Khmère du Canada**, 7107 St-Denis (277-0493) is a national organization, based in Montreal, that helps newcomers adapt, sponsors local cultural events and has traditional Cambodian dance classes.

KOREAN

Korean Montrealers are almost all from the Republic of (South) Korea rather than the Democratic People's Republic of (North) Korea. The countries, once known as the Hermit Kingdom, were united. However Russian and American forces divided the country into pro-communist and pro-American countries in 1945.

During the late 1950s, teachers, doctors, nurses and students began emigrating to Montreal and Korean workers, without professional training, arrived in the 1970s. Wealthy Koreans are now being wooed by a Canadian government which believes Asian entrepreneurs can increase our trade with Pacific countries. There is some scepticism in the community as to whether this policy is actually working.

Koreans have just about cornered the corner store business in Montreal. According to the Montreal's Korean Businessman's Association, many recently arrived Koreans don't speak English and French well enough for other jobs. The stores are easy to operate and profitable when the whole family shares the long hours. A large Korean community is developing in Lasalle and Notre Dame de Grâce.

Buddhism, Confucianism and Christianity are all common religions in Korea. In Montreal, the **Korean United Church** is at 5964 Notre-Dame-de-Grâce (484-1338) officiated by Rev. Han Gookbay. Church services are in Korean. The church also has a Korean Language school for children, a seniors group, and a group to help newcomers. The Korean Catholic mission is at **Assomption-de-Marie**, 668 Courcelle (989-9816).

The Korean Businessman's Association, 2425 boul. Grand (481-9577) represents small entrepreneurs and has over 300 members. **The Korean Community Association**, 2125 boul. Grand (397-1420) sponsors Liberation Day (August 15) and rents a soccer field for community games and celebrations.

LAOTIAN

Laos' history has been dominated by civil war. In this century it's had political stability only as a French protectorate. After the

Vietnam war ended in 1975, the Vietnamese-supported Pathet Lao took over the country and most of Montreal's several thousand Laotians arrived shortly after.

In Montreal, many work in factories making clothes or electronic goods. There are growing communities in Côte-des-Neiges, Ville Saint-Laurent, and Longueuil. Rue du Laos, in the Mile-End district of Montreal, has cooperative housing for Indo-Chinese refugees.

Lao Canada, 6338 Victoria helps new arrivals adapt to Quebec society and deal with immigration officials. The community newspaper is *Journal Lao Canada,* 4730 Barclay. *Voix du Laos* is seen weekly on cable TV.

PAKISTANI

The local Pakistani community barely existed before immigration regulations changed in 1962 but has grown to several thousand people. Many are professionals who had planned on staying only a couple of years but became permanent residents and citizens.

Almost all Pakistanis are Moslem (Arabs introduced Islam to the area in the 8th century) and most of Montreal's Pakistani community attend mosques under the direction of Muslims from the Middle East and North Africa.

Pakistan's official languages are Urdu and English but many also speak Punjabi, Sindhi, Pushta and Baluchi. August 14 is Independence Day and commemorates the partition of India in 1947.

The Pakistan Association of Quebec (344-1756) holds cultural events and works on behalf of Pakistanis in Montreal.

◆ ◆ ◆

PHILIPPINO

The Philippines are a broad swath of islands, about a third as long as Canada, off the south-east coast of Asia. Negritos first settled there over 30,000 years ago when the islands were still connected to Asia. Others integrated with them: Indonesians who sailed from Southwest Asia, Malays who brought the alphabet and later on Islam, Hindus who influenced literature and clothing, Chinese and Arabic traders, the Spanish in the 16th century, the Dutch in the 17th century and the Americans in this century. The Philippines became a republic in 1946. In 1972, President Marcos declared martial law and remained in power until 1986 when Corazon Aquino won a bitterly-contested election.

In the mid-1960s Philippinos began coming to Canada. Most immigrants were professionals, particularly doctors and nurses, who had studied in the United States and encouraged others to come as Marcos became increasingly repressive. Since 1982 prospective immigrants have been able to enter Canada as domestic servants. Doctors, lawyers and architects have left their families to work here as domestics, often claiming less education and more housework experience than they really have, just to get into this country. The Philippino community is one of the few in Montreal with many more women than men.

An Independence Festival of the Philippines is held on the Saturday closest to June 12th. The parade proceeds from Kent Park to Mackenzie King Park in Côte-des-Neiges.

Utang Na Loob means "reciprocity" and, for Philippinos, all favours must be returned. At it's grandest, this may involve a lifetime of debts and gratitude, so the traditionally-minded rarely act without considering that not being able to reciprocate may mean a curse or losing face.

By the way, is it Philippino or Filipino? The Philippines were named after King Philip II of Spain but the Philippino language of

Tagalog does not have the letter "F." In using English or French, we are transliterating the sound and therefore both "Ph" and "F" versions are accepted.

The National Council of Canadian Philipinos, 5139 Décarie (369-2200) represents the community to government and works on behalf of domestics, and doctors and nurses who have not received permission to practice in Quebec. The **United Filipino Homemakers Club of Quebec**, 4420 Kent (342-4825) informs domestic workers of their rights and negotiates disputes between domestics and government agencies. **The Filipino Benevolent and Scholarship Society of Quebec** (747-7859) has over 1,000 members. It holds memorial services for those with relatives in the Philippines and visits Filipino invalids here and annually awards a bursaries to several local students.

Pinoy Express (Radio Filipino) is on CINQ 102.5-FM alternate Saturdays at 2:00 p.m. The *Asian Leader*, 20 Roy St. E. (844-8768) covers community events and has correspondents in Manila and New York.

Filipana Dance Troupe (365-7568) is a troupe of young people which performs traditional Filipino dancing; see them during June 12th Independence Day festivities.

SOUTH ASIAN

South Asians have roots in India, Pakistan, Bangladesh and other Indo-Asian countries. India, the homeland of most Canadian South Asians, has almost a billion people, 25 states and 16 major languages. It is the world's largest democracy and its dominant religions include Hindu, Moslem, Christian and Sikh.

The first immigrants to Canada were Indian Sikh men from Punjab. They came around 1900 to work in British Columbia but, with the continental railway finished, white workers feared that these new immigrants would take jobs away. Whites pressured government to impose special taxes and restrictions to keep the Sikhs out.

One convoluted regulation actually forced prospective immigrants to make a continuous journey from their country of birth. This didn't pose much of a problem for the British who got on the boat at Liverpool and stepped off at Halifax, Quebec City or Montreal. However, the only ships coming directly from India were Canadian and it was almost impossible to get passage on them. Before this policy, in 1908, 2,600 people immigrated from India; the next year, only six people came.

However, this still left almost 5,000 Sikh men here and Ottawa actually considered "transporting Hindoos to British Honduras . . . with a view to the settlement there of the unemployed Hindoos now living in British Columbia." In 1914, a group of men set out on their own "continuous journey" from India. They chartered the ship *Komogatu Maru* but it was not allowed into Vancouver harbour and forced to return with all prospective immigrants on board.

The first contemporary South Asian Montrealers were nurses, teachers, academics, and professionals. They came in the 1960s and the community has grown to about 20,000 people. It remains largely professional and middle class. Recent immigrants from Gujarat in India are skilled workers and many live on Mountain Sights and in the Victoria / Van Horne areas of Côte-des-Neiges.

Northerners and southerners see themselves differently; within the community, those from the north are described as entrepreneurs, more likely to open up shops and restaurants. People from the south tend to be more conservative and go into professions. This may partly explain why there are so few south Indian restaurants in Montreal.

The *sindhur* is the red dot many Indian women wear in the middle of their foreheads. It symbolizes purity within marriage and its name derives from one of the rivers which flow into the

Punjab. The *sindhur* is applied like makeup, on the forehead, and has traditionally been worn only by married women. Recently, however, it has become a fashion accent for single women who may purchase *sindhurs* as sheets of multi-coloured dots to colour-coordinate with saris for festive occasions.

The **National Association of Canadians with Origins in India** (NACOI), 1500 Stanley, (845-3722) acts on behalf of a diverse local community of Hindis, Zoroastrians, Goans, Malays, Tamils and Bengalis. NACOI was instrumental in creating a chair of Hindu studies at McGill University and Montreal's Mahatma Gandhi Memorial Park at Van Horne and Hudson streets. It is now trying to build a large community centre, the Bharat Bhavan — Indian Building.

The **South Asian Women's Community Centre**, 3600 Hôtel de Ville (842-2330) works with newcomers from India, Pakistan, Bangladesh and Sri Lanka. It helps women deal with social service, refugee and immigrant settlement programs, and gives support to battered women, has language courses, job training, and job search programs.

The **Cercles des femmes du Québec d'origine Indienne**, 84 Easton, Montreal West (484-3918) helps women immigrants adapt. Women find the transition to a new society especially brutal and are often expected to look after the family, find a way to bring in extra money, and create a haven of cultural cosiness. This group gives counselling and translation services, assertiveness training, and workshops on the law, health and finance.

The **Hindi Association of Quebec** (620-6161, 336-2337) has language schools and cultural programs in Brossard, Ville Saint-Laurent, and Pointe Claire.

Kala Bharati, 3410 Sherbrooke E. (522-9239) is an internationally acclaimed professional dance troupe performing the Indian discipline known as Bharata Natyam. Dr. Mamata Niyogi-

Nakra, the troupe's director, regularly directs performances throughout Quebec.

The multilingual bi-monthly *Pragati*, (481-7445) has international cricket news, squash and soccer scores, political reporting from India, an engaging matrimonial column, and plenty of esoteric trivia. Where else would you read that yoga may cure asthma or that an Indian engineer has etched 515 letters on a grain of rice?

Patrikais, published by the Indo-Canadian Community of Montreal's **Fondation Kala Bharati** (522-9239). This newsletter tries to keep French speaking Quebecers informed about cultural activities in the Indo-Canadian community.

The radio program *Sound of India* is heard Thursday's on CFMB 1410-AM from 11 to 12 midnight. Cable television shows include *Hello India*, Saturday from 11:00 a.m. to 12:45 p.m. followed by the interview program "Bon."

Hinduism, the religion of most South Asian Montrealers, has three main concepts: Karma (fate), Dharma (religious duty), and Varna (caste or societal obligations). Many Hindu families keep a small shrine at home. The Goddess Saraswati, the symbol of learning, knowledge and fine arts, is popular with female teenagers.

In India, Hindu children learn by oral repetition, chanting with parents and grandparents. At the Hindu temple, they would be familiar with the texts, join in and be accepted. In Canada, there is neither the time to learn, nor the generations to teach and it has become common to learn a simple mantra or regularly chant the name of a guru (who tend to have more authority here than they might in India).

The main **Hindu Mission**, at 955 Bellechasse E. (270-5557), has services Sundays at 1:00 p.m. The Pandit (priest) is Sata Raman. The Festival of Holi (which means 'very pious') is celebrated in February or March and includes a religious service, a feast and dancing. Deepavali (or "Deep") symbolizes good over evil through

Lord Krishna's victory over the oppressive monarch Naraka. It is celebrated on November 4 in 1992, according to the lunar calendar.

Krishna is one of the Hindu deities. His teachings are described in the *Bhagavad-Gita* (The Song of God). Admired for selfless action, he is often portrayed as a handsome young man playing the flute. A sect has developed around Lord Krishna, under the International Society for Krishna Consciousness. The **Temple Sri Radha-Manohar** (Temple Hare Krishna) is at 1626 Pie IX Blvd (521-1301).

The Sikh religion began in the 1500s as a dissenting Hindu sect and passed through a leadership of ten Gurus ending in 1699. An independent Sikh state existed in the 1800s until British annexation in 1849. Sikh means disciple; the religion is monotheistic and does not recognize a caste system. There are several Sikh sects. Baptized Sikhs adhere to the "five K's." These are Keshas (uncut hair), Kangha (a comb), Kara (a steel bracelet) Krachha (under shorts) and the Kirpan (a sword or ceremonial dagger).

The Gudwara (Sikh temple) includes a community kitchen for devotees, pilgrims and visitors. The **Sikh Temple Association** is at 1090 St-Joseph Blvd in Lachine (634-3301).

SRI LANKAN AND TAMIL

Sri Lanka is an island country off the coast of India. Around 500 B.C., Buddhist Singhalese came from Northern India and conquered the country. Their descendants still form the majority while about twenty percent are Tamil speaking with roots in southern India. At various times, Portuguese, Dutch and British have all occupied this country, known as Ceylon, which became the Republic of Sri Lanka in 1972.

Singhalese and Tamils have been in a civil war since 1986. More than 10,000 have died and most of Montreal's Sri Lankans are Tamil refugees. Sri Lankan Tamils are usually Catholic, Indian Tamils are usually Hindu.

The **World Tamil Movement** (735-9984) produces local radio and TV programs. There is an information news line in English (739-0602) about events in Sri Lanka.

Eelam Tamil Association of Quebec, 4680 Van Horne (342-3861) is concerned with the welfare of the Tamil community and organizes community celebrations, language classes, and counselling for refugees. The Association also publishes a bi-monthly magazine about the Tamil situation in Sri Lanka. During April, the Tamil New Year, the organization hires a hall for a secular celebration that's worth going to just for the food. This is a time to start afresh: new clothes, new jobs, even new relationships. Titpongal (Thanksgiving) is in January and, in October, Nava Rathi (The 'Nine Days' Festival) celebrates Hindu gods of education, health, and wealth.

Welcome to Canada is an NFB film about the rescue of Tamil refugees off the coast of Newfoundland in 1986.

TIBETAN

This small community often holds events to publicize that Tibet has been under Chinese rule since the mid-1950s. Until China suppressed religion, 20% of Tibetan men were monks. Tibetans follow Buddhist Lamaism headed by the Dalai Lama. The **Tibetan Cultural Association** (487-0665) lobbies for human rights in Tibet. In February, the Tibetan New Year is celebrated with dancing, singing and a community feast. July 7 is the Dalai Lama's birthday and is often celebrated on Montreal's St. Helen's Island.

VIETNAMESE

Vietnamese live throughout the Montreal area but mostly in Côte-des-Neiges, Longueuil, and Brossard. A few North Vietnamese are clustered around Querbes Street.

The Vietnamese were a distinct people by 200 B.C. They were conquered by China in 111 B.C. and drove the occupiers out in 939 A.D. Various Vietnamese dynasties ruled until France captured Saigon in 1859. During WWII, Vietnam was conquered by the Japanese and then became embattled in a civil war between Communists in the north and an American-supported anti-Communist government in the south. The war formally ended in 1954, with Vietnam divided into two countries, but fighting continued and American troops became involved in 1964. Following a major offensive, North Vietnamese forces reached Saigon in 1975, uniting the country.

The first Vietnamese Quebecers were university students who settled here after their studies were finished. They were followed by professionals, doctors, pharmacists, lawyers, manufacturers, and army officers. In 1978, Canada began accepting Vietnamese refugees and over a hundred thousand arrived including Montreal's most notorious Vietnamese immigrant, General Dang Van Quang. He was accused of torture in Vietnam and making a fortune in illegal drugs during the war.

The largest wave of refugees came in the late 1970s as Vietnam battled Cambodia. Many chose to come to Canada where they could be citizens after three years. As well, from Canada, unlike the United States, they could correspond with and send money back to family in Vietnam.

Few families made it here intact and the community has suffered because of this instability. Young adults have become forced to be responsible for their families long before they would do so in Vietnam. As well, those who have arrived in Montreal since 1980 must learn French. Although older generations in Vietnam had learned French, there has been little second-language education under the Communist regime.

Before 1975, most local Vietnamese were connected to either the nationalist-oriented Vietnamese Association of Montreal or the Union of Vietnamese in Canada, a Communist-oriented organization which replaced the Association of Vietnamese Patriots. The community is divided among several groups supporting or disaffected with the current communist regime in Vietnam.

Service des Interprètes Auprès des Réfugies Indochinois (SIARI), 4661 Van Horne (738-4763) helps Chinese, Laotian, Vietnamese, and Cambodian newcomers to deal with life in Québec, find housing, and help established institutions and groups understand the traditions and concerns of Asian refugees.

Most Vietnamese belong to the Tam Giao (Three Ways) tradition of Buddhism which blends Confucian ethics, ancestor worship, Taoist cosmology and Buddhist rituals. Many homes, businesses and shops have a small shrine. Montreal has several Vietnamese pagodas for services, weddings and community festivals, and activities for young people and the elderly. The largest is **Hôi Phât Giào Quan âm** at 3781 de Courtrai (735-9425).

About 2,500 Montreal Vietnamese are Catholics and the Vietnamese parish is **Saints-Martyr-du-Vietnam** at 500 Mt-Royal E. (598-9648).

There are also a few religions specific to Vietnam. Lên Dông is an ancient spirit cult in which women act as mediums. The cosmopolitan Cao Dai Faith, which began near Saigon in the 1920s, combines elements of Taoism, Confucianism, Buddhism, Catholicism and European Spiritualism. The **Cao Dai Temple**, at 5371 Bourret (739-0615) has Vietnamese language courses for children, musical recitals, poetry readings and runs a vegetarian food booth at the annual Vietnamese New Year celebrations.

The **Vietnamese Buddhist Association of Canada**, 306

2nd St., St. Lambert, (671-3402) is a family oriented group which attracts older, religious Vietnamese. Activities take place around the first and fifteenth day of each month (based on the lunar calendar). This group meets at the **Liên-Hoa** pagoda, 715 Provencher, Brossard (672-7498)

1992 is 2535 in the Buddhist calendar. Many holidays follow a lunar cycle including Tet, the Vietnamese New Year. It is celebrated in January or February and has become a joyous public festival now held at Complèxe Desjardins or the Convention Centre — Palais des Congrès.

■■ LÌEN'S STORY

My name is Lìen. I came to Montreal six months ago with my son and husband. We came from Winnipeg where the church had sent us ten years ago, when we left Vietnam. We are from Saigon. My parents are still there. I was a social worker in Vietnam and I worked in Winnipeg as one, too. But, since I don't speak French, I now work as a waitress. Everyone says "you are from Vietnam, why don't you speak French?" I am 34 years old. They don't understand that French was not compulsory for my generation. The Americans were there. I studied French and English too, but I don't remember much after ten years in Winnipeg. I want to learn French, but I work eleven hours a day. My son is learning French and Spanish at school. At home we speak Vietnamese. One customer came into the restaurant. He said "If you do not speak French the next time I come, I will never eat here." I told him to come back in six months and I would serve him in French. We are trying so hard. I just wish some people would be more patient.

March 2 is The Celebration of the Trung Sisters. Two thousand years ago, when Vietnam was ruled by China, the Trung sisters led the Vietnamese in a revolt. The **Vietnamese Women's Organization** (733-8250) has information about where the festival is celebrated in Montreal each year.

May 9 is the birth of Buddha and is celebrated at all pagodas. There is often a vegetarian feast at the **Quam Pagoda**, 3781 Ave. de Courtrai (735-9425) but reservations are necessary.

Other holidays celebrated at the pagodas include: a celebration in April for King Hung Vuong, mythical creator of Vietnam; the Vulan Festival (Parents Day) in late summer to honour those who died without children to pray for them; and the Day of the Children which coincides with the Chinese Autumn moon festival. This day is the most popular after Têt, with Vietnamese games, special dishes for children and a lion dance. Those outside the community are encouraged to participate and can get more information from the **Communauté Vietnamienne** (340-9630).

The Vietnamese community has several politically oriented publications. These include *Dât Viêt* (Land of Vietnam) published by the pro-Communist Union of Vietnamese; *Dân Quyên* (Rights of Citizens) a monthly-anti-Communist magazine; *Dân Tõc* (The People), a bi-monthly, student oriented, non-Communist journal; *Liên-Hoa* (Lotus), a Buddhist bi-monthly, and *Phuc-Vu* (Serve) published by the Vietnamese Protestant Church. *Focus Viet-Nam* is in French, English and Vietnamese and was created in 1990 as a journal for the Vietnamese pro-democracy movement. "Télé-Vietnam" is seen weekly on cable television.

The NFB film *Les Boat People 10 ans après* is about Montreal's Vietnamese community in 1986.

◆ ◆ ◆

RESTAURANTS AND CLUBS

$ indicates that a lunch or dinner should cost under $10 (without taxes, tips, or wine). $$ is under $25 and $$$ above that. Credit cards accepted are listed. "BYOB" means you can bring your own wine. Hours often vary with the seasons so please call ahead.

Some Asian restaurants may serve a few Laotian dishes. Laotian food is similar to Thai. It's spicy with lots of soup, fish and vegetable dishes. Laotian rice is sweet and sticky and is often eaten with the fingers.

ALIWAN
5137B Decarie, Fri–Sun 8:00 p.m. — 3:00 a.m. (482-3556)
■ Irregularly open, this Philippino dance club draws a young crowd with mostly North American-style music.

BUKAHARA $$ VISA MC
2100 Crescent (289-9808)
■ Exceptional Pakistani-style restaurant featuring tandoor cooking exclusively. No cutlery, just yard-long loafs of Nan or other flat-breads to wrap around succulent chunks of meat, fish, or "tandoored" vegetables. An impressive show as everything, including the breads, are cooked to order in the tandoor kitchen which juts into the dining area. The menu is small, the setting elegant.

CHAO PHRAYA $$ AMEX EN-ROUTE MC VISA
50 Laurier W. (272-5339) and 4088 St-Denis (843-4194)
■ There's a fresh snap of lemon grass and peanut sauce in the air. The food is excellent and the service outstanding. A great place to seduce the newcomer to Thai cooking. Spicy dishes (the double chili pepper designation on the menu) are fairly mild. Don't worry. Enjoy. Order Kam Poy Swan (deep fried stuffed crab claws) with a bottle of Thai Signha beer when you sit down. Take your time with the menu. Haven't had a bad dish yet.

CHEZ MAI $ MC VISA
6637 Côte des Neiges (731-1558)

■ The owners are from Saigon and serve dishes they feel reflect that city's cooking such as crispy noodles, Imperial soup with shrimp, chicken and coriander, and spring rolls you roll yourself with chicken, beef or grilled ground shrimp on sugar cane. At lunch there is a list of predictable specials like Tonkinese soup and chicken brochettes. Ask to see the full menu which has several inexpensive dishes. Jasmine tea combines perfectly with the sweet and crumbly Bánh Dàu Xanh (bean sprout cookie) for dessert.

CRISTAL DE SAIGON $
1068 St-Laurent (875-4275)

■ Grab a table near the window and eat while watching the bustle outside. This is one of the oldest Vietnamese restaurants, the food is good value and nicely presented. Nothing fancy but lots of chicken, pork, and beef soups and tasty imperial rolls. Quick and friendly service.

HOAI HU'O'NG $ AMEX MC VISA
5485 Victoria Ave. (738-6610)

■ Luncheon specials are good value with chicken brochettes, large bowls of Tonkinese-style soups and several inexpensive noodle dishes, but generally uninspired Vietnamese cooking. Service is halting but amiable and the place is pleasant, particularly on warmer days when there is a sizeable terraced eating area outside.

HOANG OANH $
2876 Goyer (737-2109)

■ Vietnamese Ph'o tài or "soupe tonkin saignant" comes with lots of thinly sliced rare cooked beef and mounds of long rice noodles in an unusual tasting broth that hints at cinnamon, sugar and onions. Leave room for delicate Imperial rolls. Finish off with a café filtre su'a dà made with a small amount of concentrated milk in the bottom of the glass, espresso coffee and lots of ice.

KOREA HOUSE RESTAURANT $$ VISA MC
4950 Queen Mary (733-7823)

■ Korean cooking is simple but spicy with lots of garlic and chilies. Korea House is recommended by many in the community. The barbecued meats are cooked at your table. The Narkjibokum (octopus with red & green peppers, hot peppers, onions, carrots, mushrooms) has a gingery tomato sauce flavour with a spiciness that builds after the first few bites. Tjajangmyuh (noodles, diced beef, carrots, zucchini, mushrooms, green pepper, onions in a light tasting bean sauce) is a mouthful, but less spicy. Choose wisely since the portions are fairly big and many dishes include salads, several side dishes and lots of Korean kimchee (fiery pickled cabbage).

NATARAJ $$ (at Sherbrooke and Ste-Catherine locations)
VISA MC AMEX
5860 Sherbrooke W. (489-4936), 1639 Ste-Catherine W. (938-1345), and 3961 St-Denis (499-3977)

■ Good lunch and a better Indian dinner buffet with vegetable curries, onion bhaja, lamb curry, butter chicken, tandoori chicken and spinach with fresh paneer cheese. Several salads plus very spicy homemade pickled carrots with onion seeds. The nan bread has yogurt and coriander mixed into the dough before baking and is among best in the city. Sweet lassi, a drink made with yogurt and fruit, is substantial enough to forego dessert.

NISHIYAMA $$$ VISA MC AMEX EN-ROUTE
4022 St. Catherine W. (932-1968)

■ A varied menu includes Japanese basics such as yakitori (grilled dishes), sushi (sticky rice with a topping of fish and vegetables) and other Japanese fare; but here's a chance to try unusual dishes, such as diced eggplant and chicken, that are usually only served at home. Co-owner Mari Toyoda can put together special menus (for Buddhists, vegans, or seafood aficionados) with two days notice.

NEW PUNJAB $ VISA MC AMEX
4026A Ste-Catherine W. (932-9440)

■ A small, family run Indian restaurant with no parking, slow service, ample portions and good cooking. Ignore the buffet and stick to the menu. The vegetable curries can be a little oily, particularly the eggplant. The Vegetarian Thali special has enough for two. The home-made pickled lemons are outstanding.

ONG CA CAN $$ VISA MC
6230 Côte-des-Neiges (735-4179)

■ One of several good but similar Vietnamese restaurants in the Côte-des-Neiges area. Aside from standard soups, try spicy shrimp on a bed of lemon grass and hot peppers or a side order of vegetables in a fiery shrimp sauce.

PALAIS DE BANGKOK $$ VISA MC AMEX
1242 Mackay (939-2817)

■ Simple but elegant decor with good, occasionally excellent food. Look for seafood dishes marked as specialties, such as scallops in a spicy shrimp sauce. The chef has a deft touch with fresh lemon grass and galangal (a piney-tasting Thai ginger-like root), although purists may find the dishes just miss that superlative Thai snap. Service is superb. Trust the staff, if you aren't sure what to order.

PATTAYA $$ EN-ROUTE MC VISA
1235 Guy 933-9949

■ The chef left for Chao Phraya, on Laurier, about two years ago and this Thai restaurant has slipped a bit but is still quite good. Frog legs in garlic, chicken with fried basil, and squid salad are all worth trying. Soups and the ubiquitous Thad Pai noodles are excellent. Portions are small in Thai cooking. Dishes with green chilis are often the hottest and Thais usually eat fresh fruit after a meal. Sweets are eaten as snacks and desserts on menus are a western influence.

▮▮ TAMING THE FIRE

*We were sitting in the **Mogol**, an Indian restaurant at 5868 Sherbrooke W. (481-1486). There were a dozen small dishes sitting in front of us, appetizers for Harry. A meal and a half for me. Harry is a vindaloo kind of guy, likes it hot and spicy. At the Mogol, that's very, very, very hot and spicy. I'm more a madras man myself — sort of mid-range heat. I had my usual array of fire-quenchers: beer to put out the flame, a loaf of soft nan to munch between spoonfuls of curries, some cool cucumber-yogurt raita dip and a chilled sweet drink called lassi. Harry smiled and ordered a cup of water "hot enough to make tea."*

"Learned it from a Sri Lankan," he said. "Best remedy in the world. The heat in the food comes from peppers. They get reduced to pepper oil in the cooking. That oil coats your tongue and burns. What you want is something to lift off the oil. Hot water does it every time."

The food at the Mogol was doing its usual wonders. I was glowing just fine but felt a little bloated from the three beer and two nans. Harry wiped his forehead and sipped some hot water. Then his eyes took on a nasty glint as he bit into a fresh chili pepper. "It cleans the mouth right out," he said, "makes that next spoonful taste even better."

PHO CHIEU TIM $ BYOB
433 Belanger E. (277-5093)
▮ Shop on St-Hubert and browse in the area; then, take a Tonkinese soup break. Phô Chieu Tim's broth is tastier than most and comes with a dozen combinations of meat, seafood and vegetables.

The soup comes in three sizes of bowls, medium is plenty. Add a handful of fresh basil and bean sprouts, and a little chili sauce. Superb.

"Pho" in a restaurant name refers to Vietnam's Tonkinese soup. Tonkin soup has beef base. Southern restaurants serve Cochin soup which has a fish and pork base. Every restaurant has its own version. There may be some fresh coriander on the side, a couple of handfuls

∎∎ HOT STUFF

Here are ten condiments to spice up your food. This is a personal selection ranging from tepid to torrid. On this scale Dijon-style mustard would get a !!! Anything beyond that is for serious capsicum lovers only. Hey, what do we know? Make your own comparisons. Send us the results. The publisher, authors, and anyone who gave you this book disclaim any responsibility.

! *Möllers Mustard Sauce (Swedish)*

!! *Crosse & Blackwell Seafood Cocktail Sauce (Waspish)*

!!! *The Original Jufran "Pam-pa-gana" Banana Sauce (Philippino)*

!!!! *Mrs. Whyte's Prepared Horseradish (Jewish)*

!!!!! *Caribbean Choice Lime Anchar (Bajan)*

!!!!!! *Tabasco Brand Pepper Sauce (Cajan)*

!!!!!!! *Lan Chi Garlic Paste with Chili (Chinese)*

!!!!!!!! *Túóng ót tói Viet-nam Chili Garlic Sauce (Vietnamese)*

!!!!!!!!! *Harissa (Middle-Eastern)*

!!!!!!!!!! *Matouk's West Indian Style Hot Calypso Sauce (Positively ragin')*

of bean sprouts, and a selection of vinegary, spicy sauces. This is soup for slurping, not sipping; a meal by itself.

Vietnamese Imperial rolls usually come on a plate with a fresh vegetable such as cucumber. Take a piece of the vegetable and a slice of the roll and dip them into the fish sauce. Vegetables are supposed to increase your appetite.

PIQUE ASSIETTE $ AMEX DINERS EN-ROUTE MC VISA
2051 Ste-Catherine W. (932-7141)

■ There's more than Indian fare, but the crowd seems to roll in for the luncheon Indian buffet. It has a dozen or so filling but mediocre dishes: tandoori chicken, rice, nan bread, assorted vegetable and meat dishes. Nice setting, unhurried eating. The kind of place where young execs take out-of-town clients and the uncommitted go on first dates.

LA PORTE D'ASIE $$ AMEX MC VISA
2127 Bleury (842-0301)

■ A nice Vietnamese restaurant with a few unusual touches such as apple juice instead of water, small but tasty Imperial rolls, and brightly painted oriental scenes on the crockery. The usual soups (Tonkinese, crab and asparagus) are good. Good main dishes include chicken with rice noodles and greens and a moderately spicy shrimp and vegetables.

PUSHAP $ AMEX MC VISA (at Gouin location only)
5195 Paré (737-4527) and 11999 Gouin W. in Pierrefonds (683-0556)

■ These two small, family-run Punjabi vegetarian restaurants have excellent curries, bhajas (vegetable tidbits fried in a batter), and sensational home-made sweets. The thali daily special has two vegetable curries, rice and freshly made bread. The Paré place is better for take-out. The restaurant on Gouin is larger and has a luncheon buffet and banquet facilities. Although the Paré location serves no alcoholic beverages, the restaurant on Gouin is now licensed to serve wine and British beer on tap.

TAGORE $$ AMEX VISA
4653 boul. St-Laurent (987-7646)

■ The two brothers who run this restaurant named it after the Indian poet and social philosopher, Rabindranath Tagore (1861-1941). Standard (for Montreal) north-east Indian fare, with good tandoor dishes. Tasty dishes include dahl soup (lemony pureed lentils), vegetables such as sag aloo (spinach, potato, green pepper and tomato), and onion bhaji with three sauces. The dining room is pleasant and the service quite good: a nice place in an increasingly trendy part of town.

THAILANDE $$ AMEX DINERS MC VISA
88 Bernard W. (271-6733)

■ Thai salads, soups, fish, chicken, pork, beef and noodle dishes. Specials include several dishes for two people. You'll be asked whether you would like your food spicy hot or just so-so. Medium spicy is pretty easy to take; however the Kaeng Khiao Wan Kai (small chunks of chicken in a curry sauce) was scorching. The incongruity of flavours makes Thai food special. Good asparagus and crab soup with lemon grass and tasty fried fish cakes with peanut sauce.

WOODLAND $$ AMEX EN-ROUTE MC VISA
1241 Guy (933-1553)

■ One of the few places serving southern Indian food. Curries are excellent and there is a good selection of vegetarian dishes. There are several unusual dishes such as masala dosas (vegetable and potato filled pancakes) and idli — a steamed rice and lentil cake that's dipped into spicy curries. Coriander, ginger, and coconut give South Indian food some of its distinct flavour. Samplers can try several dishes from the snack section of the menu.

FOOD SOURCES

Many Asian stores sell Halal meat. This may be lamb or beef, but not pork. The meat has been killed quickly according to Moslem ritual. The method of slaughter is similar to the Jewish koshering of meat.

ALIMENTS IMPORTES DU MONDE ENTIER INC. / WORLD WIDE IMPORTS, Plaza Côte-des-Neiges (733-1463). Breads, condiments, herbs, spices, cheeses, marinades, and exotic vegetables for a dozen cuisines.

ALEXANDRE, 3594 Barclay (737-0612) and 908 Jean Talon W. (278-2994). Sri Lankan, East and West Indian groceries, flat loaves of nan bread, chutneys, curry and other spices from Sri Lanka as well as coconut oil, which is commonly used in Sri Lankan cooking.

ASIA, 530 Ogilvy (274-9766). Worth a stop if you are in the area. There is a large selection of Indian videos, rice in bulk, fresh vegetables and Halal (Islamic approved) meat.

COOKING WITH THOMAS ROBSON (287-7529). Here is a classically trained chef whose real love is Asian cooking. Mr. Robson teaches Indian and Thai cooking techniques, guides dim-sum tours through Chinatown, and conducts Asian dinner seminars at local restaurants.

EPICERIE CENTRALE DES PHILLIPINES, 4605 Van Horne (731-0629). A good store for interesting browsing with Philippino food, imported videos, blocks of congealed molasses and a delightful Hot Banana sauce that's a tangy change from North American ketchup.

EXOTIC FOODS MONTREAL, 6695 Victoria (738-9775). Fresh and packaged foods from Asia, Southeast Asia and the Caribbean. Their meat counter regularly stocks cows feet, pigs knuckles and tongue.

HUNGVIET, 5617 Côte-des-Neiges (731-4877). Good basics and interesting exotica like Philippine button cookies and Chinese salted duck eggs.

KIM HOUR, 4777 Van Horne (731-5203). Foods from around the Orient including Laos, China, Thailand, Korea and Vietnam with sauces, spices, different types of vermicelli, fish and meats, vegetables and candies.

KIM PHAT, 3588 Goyer (737-2383) and 1057 St-Laurent (874-0129). Asian products with a large selection of imported noodles, spices, and canned goods. They are particularly good for Thai cooking supplies and the frozen food section has lots of fish and noodle combinations. Their jewellery counter has unusual rings and pendants with Chinese characters.

KIRUBA, 7244 St-Hubert (273-3589). A compact Indian grocery store run by Sri Lankans. The staff is helpful and it's one of the few places that sell pan, a superb digestive made with natural flavourings wrapped in a fresh betel leaf. It's an acquired taste, but then so is Rolaids.

LANE-XANG, 6430 Victoria (733-7816). Imported Thai products such as woven grass rice holders for carrying cooked rice, or a picnic lunch of fresh spring rolls stuffed with vegetables and seafood.

MADINA, 17 Ontario E. (849-0009). Good samosa pastries and sweets, pan (prepared bitter or sweet, as you like), curry powders, coriander, cardamon, pickles, spicy and sweet chutneys, meat and rice. Of course, with good food, you could pick up a good Indian movie, since more films are made in India than anywhere else in the world. Madina has several thousand in stock in eight languages. Many have French or English subtitles. Shakil, who works behind the counter, claims many are released here before they're available in India.

MANILA 20 Roy St. (844-8768). Lemon grass, yucca, sheets of fried pork skins, jars of pickled mud fish (similar to catfish), blocks of molasses and lots of bottled sauces. There's also a small selection of gift items and cooking utensils such as kawalis, the Philippino frying pan similar to a Chinese wok. Ask Armando Villpando, the manager, for assistance.

MARCHE DUPUIS, 5493 Victoria (733-6616). Indian grocery where you can also get your VCR or stereo serviced. Chapatis, yams and other tubers, canned goods from India.

MIYAMOTO, 382 Victoria, Westmount (481-1952). This is a one-stop mini-Japanese department store with rice paper, artists' supplies, lacquered chopsticks, porcelain chopstick holders, electric rice cookers, rolls of sushi to go, stacks of rami (noodle soups), sauces and imported cookies. The wasabi crackers have a dash of green horseradish and pack a surprising kick.

PHNOM PENH, 5505 Victoria (343-4321). A wonderful Asian grocery store with a huge selection of imported foods, rice, noodles, canned goods, fresh vegetables, meat, and fish.

SHAVIT, 6334 Victoria (739-4403). South Asian groceries and spices, white yams, yellow yams and more yams. Some interesting treats such as sugar-coated fennel candy.

TAN NAM 1090 St-Laurent (876-1139). Thai foods, rice, sauces, traditional looking dishware and small gift items.

TANDOORI STYLE BAKERY, 1615 Newman crescent, Dorval (636-5258). A full range of Indian breads such as flat nans, puffy pooris, and flaky parathas as well as wheat-flour tortillas.

THUAN PHAT, 6025 Victoria (735-9563). Vietnamese, Chinese and Thai foods.

U CAN BUY, 5692 Victoria (345-8622). Indian grocery and video store with several kinds of rice, spices, nan, and chutneys.

VINH HING, 939 Decarie, Ville St-Laurent (748-7014). Small bakery with a half dozen tables for dessert and coffee. Fresh crusty baguettes, French and oriental pastries including custard bread, pineapple buns, and an excellent Vietnamese submarine sandwich.

VICTORIA ORIENTAL, 6324 Victoria (737-4715). An Indian grocery store in the Côte-des-Neiges area. There are lots of varieties of masalas (spice mixtures), imported dahl (lentils), cooking oils, vegetables, and different kinds of rice. Ask for Kishor's help in putting together some of the unusual spice mixtures called for in many Indian recipes.

Ville Saint-Laurent has several stores and restaurants on Poirier Street, between Laurentian and Decarie. Foods from Laos, Cambodia, Vietnam and China are stocked and served. If you want to try cooking Tonkin soup at home, try **Epicerie Orient Poirier** at 1693 Poirier (748-1160). Owner Albert Leung can help the wary put together an authentic meal.

SHOPS AND SERVICES

BANG AUTOBUS, (845-5630, 945-3886). $60 return-fare by bus to the Trump Casino in Atlantic City, New Jersey; leaves Montreal Friday nights at 11:30 and is back in here by 9 Sunday morning.

DRAGON LE FAUBOURG, 1616 St. Catherine W. (932-1634). Small, established store on the mezzanine level of Le Faubourg. Lots of imported handbags and clothing: dresses, kimonos and children's clothes in silk and rayon.

LEELA MUSIC HOUSE, 16040 Ste-Croix, Pierrefonds (620-1419) imports classical Indian instruments such as harmoniums, sitars, and tablas, also classes in Indian classical singing and music.

LUEN TAI, 3812 boul. St. Laurent (982-2512). Fabrics and silks imported from Japan and help in making kimonos.

ORIENTALE, 2075 St. Denis (849-4385). Scarves in beautiful paisley patterns, hand-made jewellery in metal and wood and other knick-knacks from India.

BOUTIQUE PRAGNA, 6342 Victoria Ave. (739-9786). Printed fabrics from India and Pakistan for Sarees and traditional clothing such as Salwar Kameez (a long tunic worn over loose pants).

FLEURISTE D'ART FLORALE DE MONTREAL, 5475 av. Victoria (739-7152). Japanese and European flower arrangements and instruction in Ikebana (Japanese flower arranging).

HERITAGE ASIATIQUE INC., 364 Victoria, Westmount (369-1256). The Sanjotos, who run this small shop, are from Singapore. They travel to the Far East regularly but most of their gift items are from China. The jewellery and lace tablecloths are a cut above what you might find in a foreign exchange department store, such as the Friendship Stores of China, and there are usually several exquisite pieces worth looking at.

K.L. VIDEO, 823 Decarie, Ville St-Laurent. Thai videos and music cassettes.

MAISON DE L'ORIENT QUEEN ELIZABETH HOTEL, 900 boul René-Lévesque W. (861-5254). Lots of kitsch, but also nice kimonos. Gift items include teapot sets from China and Japan, and inlaid mother-of-pearl touch-tone phones from Korea.

PHILORNOVE VIDEO CLUB, 5708 Victoria (739-5806). Philippino (some with English sub-titles) and North American videos. Information on Philippino cultural events, dances and dinners.

SAIGON VIDEO 5477 av. Victoria (733-4320). Asian and North American videos.

ASIAN WALK

Start at Plamondon Métro
End at Vietnamese pagoda Hôi Phât Giào Quan,
  3781 de Courtrai

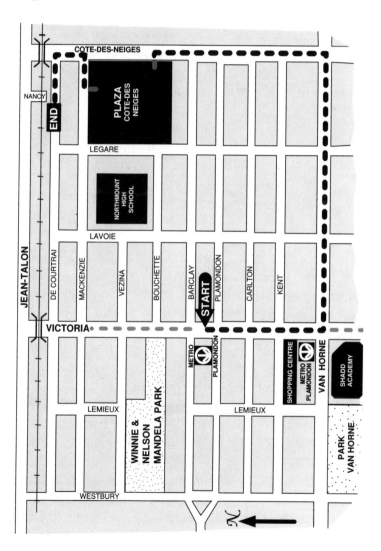

The Plamondon Métro station has two entrances: at Barclay and Van Horne. START at the Barclay street side of the Plamondon Métro.

Unlike other walking tours in *The Guide to Ethnic Montreal*, this is not a detailed exploration of one ethnic community. Rather, it neatly brings together much of the city's past while providing a strong sense of our future. Communities are constantly shifting in this part of the city — there is a cultural diversity barely matched elsewhere — and ten years from now it will have changed dramatically again. Asian-Montrealers are among the most recent to make this part of the city their own.

Côte-des-Neiges is one of the oldest settled areas on the island, established almost as long ago as Old Montreal itself. French and then English began living here in the late 17th century, creating a cluster of small villages with tanneries and summer estates for those downtown, market gardens and greenhouses. It was all linked to the Montreal by Chemin de la Côte-des-Neiges. Much of this land remained rural well into this century and, until the 1930s, there were still large tracts of farm land. Intensive development didn't begin until after WWII. The combination of ownership, privacy and spacious backyards attracted many Eastern Europeans in the late 1950s and newer immigrants in the last few years.

The area's first immigrants were Jews who left Europe after WWII. Some moved here as soon as they arrived in Montreal, others spent a few years in the older Jewish section along St-Laurent. Many of that first generation remain and the neighbourhood has the largest concentration of elderly Jewish people in the city. Recent arrivals, particularly Jews from Russia and Morocco, have settled throughout, from Decarie to Côte-des-Neiges.

The next major wave of immigrants came from the Caribbean beginning in the 1960s. Low incomes and discrimination forced them into the least desirable area, the streets closest to the CPR tracks. Almost all stores catering to the Caribbean community are north of Van Horne The most recent immigrant communities are from Latin America and South East Asia. Vietnamese, Laotians and Cambodians moved in during the late 1970s. They first lived in the older, cheaper, rundown apartment buildings on Barclay. The community has moved south as it has grown, marking progress with 11 blocks of shops along Victoria from Barclay to Édouard-Montpetit.

Many of the buildings on Barclay were unliveable until recently, infested with cockroaches and abandoned by their owners. Community groups working with the Société Habitation Development de Montréal are renovating over 600 apartments.

These buildings were constructed in the 1950s. They are more spacious than they look. The first tenants were post-war Jewish immigrants, followed by Blacks, Latin Americans and, most recently, Asians. WINNIE AND NELSON MANDELA PARK is one block north.

VICTORIA AVENUE has become the new "Main." This is where many people now first find a home when they arrive in Montreal. Then they often move to newer apartments near Queen Mary or Côte-des-Neiges, or to duplexes in Snowdon. Like Boulevard St-Laurent, Victoria Avenue leads to more prestigious communities: Westmount to the south and Town of Mount Royal and Ville Saint-Laurent to the north.

Take some time to walk a couple of blocks up and down Victoria. This is a street in transition. There are Jewish gift stores, butcher shops selling hallal (Moslem-approved) meat, Caribbean record stores, several Asian grocery stores, Philippino and Latin American corner stores, Vietnamese restaurants, Moroccan tearooms and Kosher pizza parlours.

TURN RIGHT ONTO VICTORIA. Plamondon was called 8th avenue until 1911. The street may honour the 19th century Québec artist Antoine Plamondon or the musician Rodolphe Plamondon.

The Vietnamese Community office is at 6338 Victoria. Project Genesis, an important community organization, is at 5940 Victoria. The Centre Sépharade Rabbinique, at 5850 Victoria, with a Mediterranean motif, is a converted Hydro-Québec station.

WALK INTO THE VAN HORNE SHOPPING CENTRE. The Brown Derby restaurant has been a communal meeting place for 40 years. The walls are decorated with murals depicting Jerusalem and customers babble in English, French, Yiddish, Russian and Hebrew. Many have breakfast here every day. On Sunday mornings there is often a crowd of men outside indulging in serious kibitzing as they solve the world's problems.

Cantor's Bakery started as a coffee and pastry shop near Moishes on St-Laurent and there has been a Cantor's in this area since the early 1950s. The Van Horne store was originally the chain's first factory store and it was located just up Van Horne Avenue, next to Clayman's pharmacy. It moved into this location in 1971 when Cantor's bought out the Richstone bakery chain. The store stocks dozens of kinds of breads. It also owns Maxi's, the other bakery in the Van Horne Shopping Centre. Max Cantor, the chain's owner, says Vietnamese in the area have developed a taste for bagels.

Shadd Academy, across from the shopping centre, is an English language high school for the Protestant School Board of Greater Montreal (PSBGM). It is named for Mary Ann Shadd, a prominent Black Canadian teacher, journalist and publisher who lived at the turn of this century. Shadd began in 1988, it's students are predominantly Black and Asian, and there is usually a display of African sculpture in the halls.

A generation ago, Shadd Academy was Van Horne Elementary School and the students where white and Jewish. Until only a few years ago, the PSBGM's local English language high school, Northmount, was on nearby Lavoie Street. Northmount is now Ecole Secondaire Van Horne, a French language PSBGM high school.

TURN EAST, ALONG VAN HORNE. Clayman's Pharmacy/

L'Escompte Clay has been on the corner of Van Horne and Victoria for more than 30 years. Until a few years ago, it was one of the last lunch counter pharmacies in the city. The lunch counter was taken out to make room for large postal counters to meet the needs of new Canadians mailing parcels to families "back home."

Congregation Zeirai Dath Vedaath is at 4730 Van Horne. There are dozens of these small synagogues, affectionately called "shtiblech" or small dwellings, throughout the city. Some are merely a room or two of a home, used for religious services.

Vietnamese New Year's celebration.
PHOTO BY LINDA RUTENBERG

Chua Tam Ba'o pagoda is at 4450 Van Horne. The building, which had been a vacant synagogue, became a pagoda in 1982. Tam Ba'o means "Three Treasures." These are Buddha, Dharma (learning the sacred texts) and Sangha (communal gatherings). Religious services are Sundays at 10:00 a.m. Soon after Tam Ba'o was founded, a group disenchanted with how it was run, formed another association, the Quan am Buddhist Society, which operates a few blocks away, at 3781 de Courtrai Street.

The Centre Merkhaz Sépharade, at 3917 Van Horne, is one of several synagogues used by Montreal's growing French speaking Sephardic community (Jews who have come here from North Africa and the Middle East).

Van Horne Avenue is named after Sir William Cornelius Van Horne who oversaw construction of the Canadian Pacific Railway. The railway was finished in 1884. Van Horne died in 1915 and this street was opened fifteen years later. Van Horne was also an amateur architect and helped plan Quebec City's Chateau Frontenac. Coincidentally, the houses from Lavoie to Côte-des-Neiges have some of the most unusual architectural detail in the city. Look at the roofs. The red tile has a Mediterranean flair. The towers and bay windows echo European chateaux. The rounded corners and windows near the edge of many buildings reflect the Art Moderne style popular during the 1930s and 1940s. The house at 4434 Van Horne is a bizarre combination. It's a Scottish castle with a Spanish arcade, a tiled roof, "pepperpot" towers, and bay windows near the back.

Many of these houses have a rude mixture of details. There may be a Spanish Mission effect in the roof tiles, 17th century Norman in the basic design, Tudor along the walls and Art Deco highlights. It's not uncommon to see all of these jumbled together, as in the buildings from 4081 to 4051 Van Horne.

3951 Van Horne has Tudor and Anglo-Norman design and is joined to a lovely segmented arch common to the Middle Ages —

"architectural details on a modern carcass," says urban historian François Rémillard.

3906-3890 Van Horne has a greystone terrace that could be in a 19th century British industrial town. These homes are also unusual for Montreal in that they are wider than they are deep.

3850 Van Horne is a lovely 17th century Norman-style house that's only 60 years old! It has an immense angular roof, tall chimney and protruding balcony. The style became very popular, particularly in the more established neighbouring community of Outremont.

3757 Van Horne is Qikiqtaalungmiut Iglungat, or Innuit for Baffin House. The building has just enough Spanish Mission detail above the balcony to give it a tropical air, which is a little ironic, since the home is used by the Baffin Island Regional Health Board for northern natives temporarily in Montreal for hospital care.

3737 Van Horne is a magnificent example of Art Moderne a style which emerged from Art Deco. There are lots of flowing lines alluding to aerodynamics and transportation; this 50 year old building suggests a cruise boat. It is also unusual because it's one of the few in the area with stucco on the walls, since most builders considered stone more natural. It was recently bought and reno-vated as Maison Pomerantz, a Jewish school affiliated with the Lubavitch Hassidic movement.

The Royal Bank building, across the street, used to be the Van Horne Theatre. Only a curved corner and molding near the roof remain of what was once an intricate Art Deco facade,

TURN LEFT ON CÔTE-DES-NEIGES. Look behind the Provisoir store at the corner of Côte-des-Neiges and Kent. This is Maison Roy, a charming Victorian farmhouse built in 1823. The original fieldstone walls were covered with stucco in 1940.

Ecole St-Pascal Baylon at the corner of Plamondon and Côte-des-Neiges, has students from more than 50 countries and is one of the most multi-ethnic schools in Montreal.

The church across the street is St-Pascal-Baylon and was built in 1917. There are weekday and Sunday morning services. On Sundays at 6:00 p.m., the mass is in Spanish.

Plaza Côte-des-Neiges is between Barclay and Mackenzie. This shopping centre was completed in 1968, with recent extensive renovations. It replaced a magnificent house and several large greenhouses owned by Camille Légaré, one of Montreal's first market gardeners and truck farmers. The greenhouses were built in 1884 and torn down in the 1950s.

On the Plaza's ground floor is Micin, a small store with an extensive selection of imported Chinese tablecloths, clothing and gifts; and Aliments importés — World Wide Imports with barrels of pickles, olives, and herrings, shelves of dried herbs and coffees, and stacks of rice, breads, and cheeses.

The "food court" downstairs has dishes from Breton-style crêpes to hamburgers, souvlaki, and Chinese food. It's cheap and bland — worth considering if the weather is horrid and the kids are cranky — but there is much better eating in most of the Chinese and Vietnamese restaurants outside the Plaza, along Côte-des-Neiges.

CONTINUE THROUGH THE PLAZA past the police station and back onto Côte-des-Neiges. Turn left and walk one short block down to de Courtrai street. Turn left again. The magnificent Vietnamese pagoda Hôi Phât Giào Quan is at 3781 de Courtrai (735-9425). Just behind it, but on the other side of the railroad tracks, at 7188 de Nancy street is another beautiful pagoda, run by the Buddhist Khmer Society (735-6901) and supported by the Cambodian community. Visitors are usually welcome at pagodas. When you enter, remove your shoes at the door.

The tour ends here. The Plamondon Métro is five blocks away; a bus goes to it down Barclay street. The Côte-des-Neiges Métro station is 10 blocks south; buses stop in front of the Plaza on Côte-des-Neiges.

SOME BOOKS AND ESSAYS

A Taste of India, Madhur Jaffrey, Pan Books, 1987. (Jaffrey covers Indian history and cultures through the foods of major cities and districts including Tamil Nadu, Delhi, Gujurat, Bengal, Kashmir and Hyderbad.)

Continuous Journey: A Social History of South Asians in Canada, N. Budrignani, D.M. Indira and R. Srivastira, McClelland and Stewart, 1985.

Days and Nights in Calcutta, Bharati Mukherjee, Penguin, 1988 (A Canadian writer's journey home).

Issei: Stories of Japanese Canadian Pioneers, Gordon G. Nakayama, NC Press, Toronto, 1984.

Obasan, Joy Kogawa, Penguin, 1983 (The story of wartime internment by one of Canada's best writers) and the sequel, *Itsuka*, Viking Canada, 1992.

Stone Voices: Wartime Writing of Japanese Canadian Issei, Keibo Oiwa, ed., Véhicule Press, Montreal, 1992 (Poignant diaries and letters by Japanese-Canadians interned in Canada during WWII.)

The South Asian Diaspora in Canada: Six Essays, Milton Israel, ed., The Multicultural History Society of Ontario, Toronto, 1986.

BLACK MONTREAL

POPULATION: 70,000

COMMUNITIES: Côte-des-Neiges, Park Extension, Ville St-Michel, Dollard des Ormeaux, Brossard, Montreal Nord, Little Burgundy.

SHOPPING: Boulevard Saint-Laurent, Victoria north of Van Horne, Sherbrooke St. W. in Notre Dame-de Grâce (NDG).

Black Montreal is diverse and growing; in fact, the current population may be almost double the official figure of 70,000 from the 1986 census. Broadly speaking, there are two prominent groups with little mixing between them: the older segment of the community has roots in Canada, the United States and the English-speaking West Indies while more recent Black Montrealers likely originate in Haiti or French-speaking African countries.

Canadian Black history started long ago. Some historians believe that Libyans may have visited Canada in 500 A.D. and that Africans landed here in the 14th century. The first recorded Black visitor was Matthew da Costa, in 1606, who is listed as Champlain's translator, having learned a native North American native language, Mic Mac, on a previous voyage. It would be a long time between this visit and the beginnings of a real Black community since slavery, of both Blacks and natives, was legal in Canada until 1834.

Blacks began settling in this country during the American revolution following British promises of freedom and land. They could be considered Canada's first refugees and were followed by many who escaped during the American Civil War. They first settled in Nova Scotia or Ontario, with some then moving to Montreal. In 1897 Blacks from Barbados sailed to Gaspé to work in fish plants. They mixed easily with white French Canadians, intermarriage was common, and many changed their names; for example, Woods became Dubois and Flowers, Lafleur.

Compared to European immigration, however, few Blacks entered the country because Canada's Immigration Act of 1910 specifically restricted non-white immigration. Ignoring the generations of Blacks already here, government officials argued that they "do not assimilate readily, cannot adapt themselves to our climatic conditions" and were culturally unable to adjust to capitalism! Those who did enter confronted other restrictions. They could be legally refused service in restaurants and had few choices as to where they might live.

The poorest Blacks lived near St-Laurent boulevard below Pine Avenue (av. des Pins) where rooms rented for $4 a week and flats went for $20 a month. A few who had done well built homes on the South Shore where a hundred foot square lot cost $50. Many successful Blacks were members of The 400 Club, for "blacks and lights, not blacks and whites."

However, nine out of ten families lived in the Saint-Antoine district, near the railway stations and yards. Whites called the area the West End or the Montreal Negro District (younger Blacks simply called it downtown).

The choice jobs were on the railroads. The American-owned Pullman Palace Car Company, which built and managed the railway sleeping cars, only hired Blacks to serve the predominantly white passengers. Whites couldn't work as porters, but Blacks weren't hired as engineers or conductors.

If you were black in this city when I grew up, you could be a dancer or a pimp — or you could work for the railways. I swore I'd never work for the railways, and I ended up spending my life doing it.

    — a train porter quoted in *Oscar Peterson* by Gene Lee.

Even well-educated Blacks worked the railways since most were barred from the professions. McGill wouldn't accept Blacks to study law or medicine so the brightest in the community furthered their studies in the United States — few came home.

The community's population fluctuated dramatically during summer when single men came from the United States to work on the railways or at one of Montreal's four race tracks. From 1919 to 1933 the United States imposed prohibition which restricted the manufacture and sale of alcoholic drinks. Many of these "summer Americans" began staying in Montreal throughout the year rather than returning home. They were soon running nightclubs, gambling joints and prostitution rings in St-Antoine street area which became notorious as the "Sporting District."

Stability came to the area with the arrival of West Indian families. The women got jobs as domestics and in factories while the men worked on the railways. Most of the early organizations, such as the Union Congregational Church, the United Negro Improvement Association and the Coloured Woman's Club, were started by the West Indian community. In the 1920s and 1940s, community leaders formed two unusual cooperatives. The Eureka Association bought property in Saint-Antoine and the Spathodia Association did the same in Ville Emard. Blacks could then buy the property at market rates, but without the prohibitive down payment (usually twice the amount) which they had to pay when they bought from whites.

During the 1930s, the Depression hit Montreal hard and the Saint-Antoine community worst of all. The population declined and many American Blacks left when their jobs ended. Conditions improved in the 1940s. The war brought work to the area; although the government initially decided that West Indians were not really British subjects and could not serve in the armed forces. They were only accepted after the community protested under the leadership of the Union Church's Reverend Charles Este.

The war did more than provide jobs, it began reducing disparities between Blacks and whites. New federal social assistance programs covered Black families and Black veterans received government help for training and education. They received loans to buy land and homes and many moved to the new Benny farm project in NDG and to other projects in Ville Saint-Laurent and Montreal North. Unions, which had grown during the war, made it harder to discriminate in the factory. They also forced the railway companies to end racist hiring policies, increase wages, and promote Blacks. However, when railways began hiring whites for porter jobs, fewer Blacks were needed.

Perhaps the best symbol of these post-war changes was the arrival of Jackie Robinson, the first Black to play major league baseball. An American, he signed with the Brooklyn Dodgers in 1945 and came north to their triple A team — the Montreal Royals. Today, Robinson's statue stands by the Olympic Stadium.

Montreal changed a lot after WWII. In 1955, Ottawa set up the Domestic Immigration Program to serve affluent whites looking for maids and housekeepers.

The program gave immigrants the right to apply as permanent residents after one year of work, essentially indentured service. Thousands of West Indian women left their families and jobs as teachers, clerks, and nurses to come here as domestic servants. Black men, however, still found it difficult to immigrate and those sponsored by West Indian girl-friends already here were told they had to marry them within 30 days of entering the country.

In 1962, racial quotas were removed from the immigration process and the number of West Indian newcomers doubled. Many were well educated and found jobs as skilled workers, managers and professionals accelerating the community's move out of Saint-Antoine in the 1960s and 1970s. At the same time, much of the area was being razed for the Ville Marie expressway (highway 720) and urban development. The plans may have been well-intentioned but the disruption to the community was catastrophic. Rebuilding took decades and when it was over the area had a new name — Little Burgundy — but only a few hundred of the pre-development community of 5,000 was still there. A new coalition of about 30 community groups recently started working together to improve the quality of life in this part of town.

People moved throughout the city. They went to newer buildings in Côte-des-Neiges, Rosemont, Côte St. Paul, Cartierville and Lasalle; to Crawford Park in Verdun and the Norgate Project in Ville Saint-Laurent. Côte des Neiges was particularly popular but as Blacks moved into larger apartment blocks the owners moved out. Services deteriorated and landlords' agreements ensured that many buildings were sold or rented only to whites. Although about a third of Montreal's English-speaking Black community still lives in the Côte-des-Neiges area, the Black middle class has moved to English-speaking areas of NDG, La Salle, the West Island and the South Shore.

HAITIAN

Almost all Haitians are of African descent. The original inhabitants of this Caribbean country were killed after Columbus landed in 1492 and Europeans transported slaves from neighbouring islands and Africa to work on their Haitian plantations.

In 1804 Haitians became the first Black people to win independence from a European power after a slave rebellion defeated Napoleon's army. However, periods of political violence enabled the United States to enter and govern the country as a colony from 1915 to 1934. In 1957, Dr. Francois "Papa Doc" Duvalier became president and was succeeded, in 1971, by his son Jean-Claude, "Baby Doc" who was driven from power in 1986. By then, Haiti which had been rich in corn, bananas, coffee, and minerals was the poorest nation in the western hemisphere, and one-fifth of its population had fled the country.

December of 1990 brought a civilian government to power; many of the new leadership, including president Father Jean-

Bertrand Aristide, spent years of exile in Montreal. In 1991, a military coup forced President Aristide to flee Haiti. The current leaders are recognised by few countries and there is an international effort to restore democratic government.

■■ VOODOO

Things You Should Know

While most Haitians are Roman Catholic, voodoo is also widely practised and combines ancestor worship, animism, and Catholicism.

Voodoo originated on the West Coast of Africa and came to Haiti when the French brought over West Africans as slaves; however, the French then outlawed voodoo because slaves used the religious gatherings to plan their revolt.

Voodoo may be used for good or evil. Ceremonies can be long and trances encourage the subject to return to African roots. The practice of sticking pins in dolls to place a curse on an enemy originated with the French in Brittany.

Professor Lucien Smarth of Université du Québec à Montréal estimates that 90-95% of those in Haiti practice Voodoo and says it is discreetly practised in Montreal.

Montreal and Haiti have had strong links for over 50 years. Quebec missionaries arrived in the 1940s and were followed by businessmen and tourists who painted a picture of Canada as an idyllic refuge.

The few Haitians in Québec before 1960 integrated fairly easily into a society of French speaking professionals. It was a good match. Quebec needed French-speaking doctors, teachers and professionals. These Haitians were the first immigrants to choose Quebec for its language and culture and many saw themselves as exiles who understood Quebec nationalism.

The next, much larger wave of Haitians began in the 1970s, most of whom were unskilled refugees more comfortable with Creole than French. They followed the more common immigrant route: up the St-Laurent corridor; through the Plateau Mont Royal area and Park Extension, to Montreal North, St. Michel, St. Leonard, Rosemont, Laval and Rivière-des-Prairies.

Almost half of Montreal's Black community is Haitian and Haitian youth has a tremendous impact on French language schools. Teachers are trying to involve them in Quebec society while parents fear schools remove their children from Haitian language (Creole) and culture.

MIKE'S MUSIC RAP

(with Michael Mark of Mike's Discount Record Centre)

When I was growing up in Trinidad in the 1950s the churches always had great music. **Gospel** had wonderful vocals and positive messages. **Calypso** and **Soca** reflected the social changes happening throughout the Caribbean.

Soca fuses soul, Latin and East Indian music. Shorty, Maestro, Lord Kitchener (an old Calypsonian) are famous Soca musicians. **Calypso** is 'domestic music.' If you go to a Caribbean country and listen to Calypso you can find out the news, the kind of government in power and so on. Check out records by The Mighty Gabby to find out what's happening back in Barbados.

Soul is the music of harmony, you can see its church roots. It promotes love, peace and unity. People dressed up to see a soul concert. Famous artists include Diana Ross, Marvin Gaye, James Brown and The Spinners. **Funk** steps away from Gospel and Soul, it is sort of the pop music of the black tradition. **Reggae**'s trademark is its beat. Reggae performers sing for their people. The Studio One label in Jamaica was one of the major reggae recording labels in the late 1960s.

Rap started in the late 1960s in the U.S. with groups like the Last Poets who combined drumming and speech. This was the same era as Malcolm X and Martin Luther King. Their speeches were recorded and became part of rap. People like James Brown rapped, but nobody called it that back then. Much of the new stuff on the market is too commercial, it's lost its original edge or it's too profane. Public Enemy is staying closer to the original. Queen Latifah is something else again. She has a great voice and she has political message without the violence of other rappers. If you want to find out who's hot or up and coming in the world of rap/funk pick up magazines like *Rap Master* or *Billboard*.

Montreal has a lot of great bands who are now starting to hit international levels of Rap, Reggae, and World-Beat. Check out Salahouden, an excellent local panist (steel drums). MCJ and Cool are rap artists who got a CBS recording contract in 1990. Catch local groups Kali & Dub, Jab Jab, Africa 1, The Images, Portfolio and dub poet Michael Pintard. Dixie Band is a local Haitian group with super compa beat and 15 records.

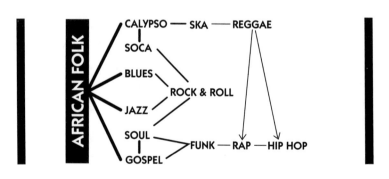

Upfront Magazine — ***N'oji Mzilikazi*** (367-0707) is a locally published music magazine for Canadian rappers.

EVENTS AND FESTIVALS

JANUARY 15 — *Martin Luther King Day* honours the assassinated Black American clergyman and civil rights leader who received the 1984 *Nobel Peace Prize* for working for racial equality.

FEBRUARY — *Black History Month* activities throughout the city: schools, clubs, community centres. Call the **Black Community Council of Quebec** (BCCQ) at 482-8802 or the **McGill Black Student's Network** at 398-6815.

JUNE — *Carifest*. Floats from all over the Caribbean, bands, rappers, reggae, soca, dancing and costumes in a big downtown Parade. Call the BCCQ at 482-8802.

SUMMER — *Afro-Fest*. Starts at the end of June with Carifest and runs through the summer with local authors, theatre, art exhibits, picnics and great music. For information call 932-1104.

Vues d'Afrique, 417 St-Pierre, Suite 412 (845-6218) presents 10 days of films with an African theme. This festival suffers from poor organization, but is usually held in the spring or summer.

Mont-Royal Jam Session is a percussive free-for-all on the slopes of the mountain. Bring drums and bongos on sunny summer Sundays, near the monument to Georges-Étienne Cartier on Park Avenue.

ORGANIZATIONS

People are always making it into a black / white thing. It's not enough to say love your neighbour, structural changes need to be made. You will never be in control of anything as long as you wait for someone else to act.

— Jean-Claude Icart, Haitian community leader

Early Black organizations were initiated as Blacks found themselves excluded from many white groups. In 1902 the newly-formed

Coloured Woman's Club helped the predominantly Protestant Black community cope with city-wide epidemics of typhoid, diphtheria, scarlet fever and smallpox since non-Catholics were responsible for their own health and welfare. The Union Congregational Church was formed in 1907 after Blacks were told to sit in the back of local Protestant churches and a Negro Chapter of the Red Cross was organized in 1915. Later groups formed either to respond to political pressures or as community associations. Today several organizations play important roles.

Barbados House (331-7231, 488-1571). Bajan activities for seniors, a drama group and sports program, and cultural programs with youth from other ethnic groups.

Black Arts Production / Black Studies Centre, 1968 de Maisonneuve W. (989-7373). Black Arts Production is a publicity and promotion company which works with art and cultural events like Afro-Fest. The Studies Centre engages in research and public education on issues involving Blacks.

Black Community Council of Quebec (BCCQ), 2121 Old Orchard (482-8802) is the largest community group, bringing together 11 English-speaking Black organizations.

Black Historical Society (656-5021) is an archive for Black history in Quebec run from the home of Bud Jones, a former Canadian boxing champion. His great-grandparents were freed slaves who came to Montreal in 1851.

Black Theatre Workshop, 1968 de Maisonneuve W. (932-1104) presents plays exploring Black culture and holds a Memorial Service on Martin Luther King Day each January. The workshop currently has no theatre of its own and stages productions in various English-language theatres throughout the city.

Centre Haïtien Regroupement et d'Intégration à la Société Canadienne et Québécoise, 8170 Boul. Gouin E. (648-6990) helps Haitians understand Quebec and Canadian society through workshops, videos and films on racism, crime, immigration, work, and housing.

Centre international de documentation et d'information Haitienne, Caribienne et Afro-Canadienne, 417 St-Pierre (845-0880) is a Haitian, Caribbean and African documentation centre used by students, organizations, governments, and visitors to these countries.

Communauté chrétienne des Haïtiens de Montréal, 6970 Marquette (725-9508) provides counselling for Haitians on legal rights, immigration procedures, language regulations, social services, education, employment and racism. When Haitian drivers couldn't get work with some local taxi companies, this group helped them form a cooperative called Métro-Taxi.

Concordia University Archives, 1455 de Maisonneuve W. (848-7775) has extensive documentation of Montreal's jazz history and nightlife, including photographs, musicians' scrapbooks, tapes, sheet music and arrangements.

Eglise Évangelique Emmaüs, 2379 Rosemont (486-3875) is a small community church with French gospel services Sundays at 10:00 a.m.

Garvey Institute, 2515 Delisle (684-7491) based on the philosophies of Marcus Garvey, offers courses in Black history, employment programs, math, French and English.

Jamaica Association of Montreal, 4065 Jean-Talon W. (737-8229) assists immigrants with housing, social services, French classes, and acts as a community centre when there are disasters or floods in Jamaica. It has become an unofficial consulate with passport forms and information from the Jamaican government. During the last week-end in July the association holds a Jamaica Day in Kent Park in Côte-des-Neiges.

Minority Business and Professional Network Forum, run by Faustina France-Carbonneau (923-3437) organizes conferences to bring business people together.

Montreal Association of Black Business Persons and Professionals, 2425 Grand, Suite 2 (486-8030) publishes a directory of Black business people and professionals, holds bi-monthly seminars on business-related topics and provides information and referral services for budding entrepreneurs.

National Congress of Black Women, 2035 Coursol (932-1107) is part of a national organization which supports programs in child development, civil liberties issues and education. The group has brought together leaders from the English and French-speaking Black communities and recently helped create a coalition of Chinese and Black organizations to combat racism.

Negro Community Centre (NCC), 2035 Coursol (932-1107) formed in 1927, by community leaders and the Union United Church. For a long time, it was at the core of a dynamic community and the NCC still provides day-care facilities, information and referral services. However, as Blacks moved out of the area, other groups, such as the Black Community Council of Québec, have taken up the political leadership.

Nigerian Canadian Association (481-0880) is one of the more active African groups with regular social events and political forums. It tries to bridge the English and French-speaking Black communities.

The Quebec Board of Black Educators (489-3721) consists of parents and teachers concerned with Black children in the school system.

MEDIA

The Afro Canadian (684-7491) is based on the philosophy of Marcus Garvey, who stressed independence, solidarity, and pride in African roots. The newspaper is mostly a continuing analysis of government policy and municipal affairs interspersed with poetry by local Black writers.

Canada Weekend Post, 958 Girouard (482-6401) is a monthly paper with a community focus.

Contrast is a general interest paper, available locally but published in Toronto. It has a few pages on Montreal.

CIBL 101.5 (526-2581) with the reggae show "Basses Frequences," African discs on "Rhythmes d'Afrique," and island dance music on "Punch Tropical."

CINQ 102.3-FM (495-2597) has several Creole and African shows.

CKUT 90.3-FM (398-6787) has several shows such as "Friends" (Black community news), "Amandla," (news about South Africa), "Présence Haitienne" (news and local events in Creole and French), "Skin Busy" (Reggae, ragamuffin, hip hop and soul music), and "Basabasa Soukou Soundz" (a solid African beat).

CJFM 96 (989-2536) plays Caribbean, latin, and African music on "Rhythms International."

RESTAURANTS AND CLUBS

$ indicates that a lunch or dinner should cost under $10 (without taxes, tips, or wine). $$ is under $25 and $$$ above that. Credit cards accepted are listed. "BYOB" means you can bring your own wine. Hours often vary with the seasons so please call ahead.

BAIT TUL MAL $ MC VISA

2459 Notre Dame W. (937-9339)

■ Bait Tul Mal means House of Refuge in Arabic. The name comes from the Prophet Mohammed's Treasure House where people went for help. The small menu includes meat and vegetable curries, cookies and pastries, and strawberry and mango drinks.

CARIBBEAN CURRY HOUSE $ BYOB

6892 Victoria (733-0828)

■ The kind of friendly place you'd want to stumble across in the islands. 12 kinds of rotis include beef, vegetarian, and shrimp. Roti wrappers, called dhal pouri, are freshly rolled out and cooked behind the counter. Daily specials such as cow's foot soup, oxtail stew, or flying fish are a tasty introduction to Caribbean cooking.

CARIBEC $$ VISA MC AMEX EN-ROUTE
5942 Sherbrooke W. (482-7493)

■ Excellent West Indian cooking, both the restaurant and chef are a cut above most Caribbean places. The buffet is inexpensive and a decent introduction to a few island dishes but consider regular menu specials such as flying fish (when available), curried goat roti, or delicious fried chicken. Delicious non-alcoholic island drinks and superb desserts like freshly grated coconut pie.

CHEZ FLORA $$ MC VISA
3615 St-Laurent (849-7270)

■ Good West Indian dishes in a very attractive restaurant on the Main. Guadeloupe dishes are a specialty and the bar has a potent selection of island rum drinks.

CLUB BALATTOU
4732 St-Laurent (845-5447)

■ African dance troupes and world-beat music groups perform at this bar and dance club, usually packed with a diverse crowd.

CLUB JUNGLE
6287 St-Hubert (272-8712)

■ Reggae, soca, dance music and hip hop with a DJ from Jamaica.

KEUR SAMBA
5408 Parc (278-5409)

■ Fabulous African music with lots of Yassou NaDou, American rap and a good-sized dance floor. Gets a good mixed crowd for dancing and more.

LA MER ROUGE $$ MC
254 Roy (843-0873)
■ Unusual and good. Doro Wot (chicken in hot berbère sauce), Tibs (an Ethiopian specialty made with beef cubes), and Atekelt Wot (vegetable curry with lots of garlic and ginger). Dishes are served together on a round platter with a spongy flat bread used for scooping. Forget knives and forks, this is African party food great for a group eating.

RAINBOW-ITES $
5345 de Maisonneuve W. (486-9465)
■ Half-a-dozen tables in a mini-Rastafarian shrine. Great music with room to dance. There's an auto-body shop downstairs and a karate class next door; but forget the ambience. Enjoy the food. Rainbow-ites has all that good West Indian stuff: sorrel, sea moss, Stone's Ginger Beer, Red Stripe Beer, fish, chicken, ox-tail, goat, cow's foot, yams, ackee and saltfish, Nu-pak pepper sauce on the table, and maybe the best rice and beans in town. In doubt? Ask for a combination plate and leave it up to whoever's cooking.

FOOD SOURCES

BOUCHERIE INTERNATIONALE, 5780 Sherbrooke W. (488-5600). A favourite of Montreal's Caribbean restaurants; it carries fresh rabbit, veal, oxtail, goat, cow's foot, grain chicken, pork, beef, hot island sauces, and sacks of rice and beans.

CARIBE BAKERY, 5716 Sherbrooke St. W. (481-5343). Twenty-five years ago a Laura Secord candy store was turned into a small patty and roti bakery, the first indication that NDG was evolving into a multi-ethnic neighborhood. Windsor Bell has been behind the counter all that time.

DE FRANCE, 1659 Bélanger E. (728-4024). Rice, beans, hot sauces, plantains, and other Caribbean vegetables. The shelves look a little bare at times, perhaps because there isn't much local competition; worth wandering through if you're in the area.

EPICERIE NDG, 5345 Sherbrooke W. (481-3034). The store is small, but the variety is large with several kinds of fresh herbs and hot peppers. There's a good spice selection and lots of island specialties such as sugar cane and plantain. The butcher counter usually has oxtail and pig's feet.

EXOTIC GROCER, 6495 Victoria (738-9775). Twenty years old with a wide variety of spices, salted meat, Asian and Caribbean foods. Also, tabloids from the Caribbean.

MARCHE MAKOSSA, 5895A Victoria (343-9584). A small grocery, new to the area, specializing in Caribbean foods — patties, dried and salted fish and meats, yams and plantain.

MELI-MELO, 640 Jarry E. (277-6409). A Caribbean grocery store with gifts and records from Haiti.

MOM'S CARIBBEAN HAVEN, 5791 Sherbrooke St. W. (481-3453). Honest cooking. Freshly baked patties, rotis, island-style thick cakes and cookies. There is a Mom and this is her place.

MR. SPICEE, 6889A Victoria (739-9714). Antilles bakery making bread for Caribbean restaurants throughout Montreal. The patties (wedges of flaky pastry with a spicy meat mixture) are hot from the oven. The rotis (flat bread) are freshly made and stuffed with beef, goat, chicken, chick peas, vegetables and potatoes.

NDG LICENSED GROCERY, 5345 Sherbrooke W. (481-3034). Fresh hot peppers and basics like dasheen, yam, plantain, goat meat, ox tail, and salt mackerel.

STEVE-ANNA, 3302 Bélanger (725-3776). A brother and sister run this grocery store with Haitian patties and Creole foods.

TROPICAL FOODS, 6841 Victoria (733-2332). West Indian and Indian food and Halal (prepared to Moslem standards) meat. Plantain chips, tasting a bit like banana and potato, are great with imported island-brewed ginger beer.

SHOPS AND SERVICES

BAIT TUL MAL, 2455 Notre Dame W. (939-1576). Co-owner Abdul Ali has the story behind every piece of African art in the store, particularly ceremonial masks and fetishes which are statues with religious significance. The masks, mostly from West and Central Africa, cost from $15 to over $1,000. Also objets d'art, musical instruments, jewellery and clothes.

BOUTIQUE SUKUMA, 4418 St-Denis (845-2112). Clothes, fabrics, and jewellery from Tanzania, Kenya, Uganda, Swaziland and Cameroon.

GIRAFFE, 2160 Crescent (499-8436). African crafts and objets d'art. Custom African bead jewellery.

MAHOMEY — BOUTIQUE AFRICAINE, Métro Peel station, Stanley St. entrance. (526-1748). This is one of those small shops that makes some Métro corridors feel like an underground bazaar. Mahomey imports clothing, chéchia (colourful leather and cloth pillbox hats) cosmetics, jewellery, bags, and small sculptures from the Cameroons, the Ivory Coast and Senegal.

MIKE'S DISCOUNT RECORD CENTRE, 6470 Victoria (733-5579). Funk-Dance-Reggae-Soca-Rap-House-Gospel on vinyl, tape and CD. Lots imported from New York city; also, Kangol hats like all the rappers wear.

◆ ◆ ◆

LITTLE BURGUNDY TOUR

Starts at Windsor Station
   near the Bonaventure Métro station
   Ends at Atwater Market
   near the Lionel-Groulx Métro station

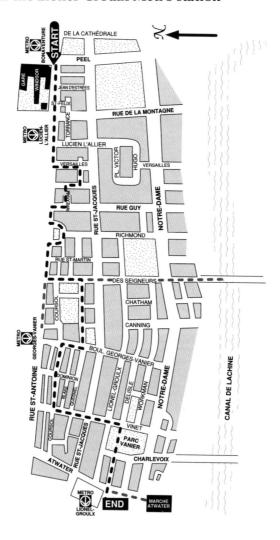

I didn't mind being here, I minded being classified as poor.
— Bud Jones, local historian

This tour takes us through two levels of history at the same time. A vivid story of French and English history, of landowners and entrepreneurs, emerges through the names of the streets. However there are no street signs for the other dimension of this tour, it is the buildings and vacant lots that alone can echo what was Black Montreal's most vibrant neighbourhood.

WE START FROM WINDSOR STATION on the north-west corner of Peel and St-Antoine. At the end of the 19th century, this was the eastern terminus and head office of the Canadian Pacific Railway (CPR). The station was designed by Bruce Price, architect of many hotels in the Canadian Pacific chain including Quebec City's Chateau Frontenac, and Ottawa's Chateau Laurier.

From this station, Europeans went west to start new lives on the prairies, Chinese went south to work in the U.S.A. or the Caribbean; and, later, Canadian soldiers went east on their way to two world wars. Today, the station is an impressive terminus for suburban commuters and the site for a new arena, which will replace the Forum, for the Montreal Canadiens Hockey Club.

The Alberta Lounge was across the street, on Peel Street, where the Château Champlain hotel now stands. It was a popular spot for passengers before boarding trains to Toronto, Halifax, Philadelphia, New York or Chicago. In the late forties, Oscar Peterson's jazz trio played here. Peterson, one of the world's best known jazz pianists, grew up nearby; his father, Daniel, was a porter on the trains.

WALK WEST ALONG ST-ANTOINE. The first important landowner in this area was Pierre Guy, for whom the nearby Guy street is named. He was an 18th century military officer and merchant whose family had served the court of Louis XIV. Guy lead the transition from the old seigneury land owning system of the French regime to the post-conquest British era and helped bring the

English and French bourgeoisie together into the colony's first governing assembly. Guy's land holdings included much of the land around us, known as "La Terre de la Bourgogne" as the gentle slope of the land, the fields, woods, and streams reminded the first French settlers of their former Burgundian countryside. During the early 1800s St-Antoine street had stately homes for doctors, lawyers and businessmen. 1320 St-Antoine W. was the home of John Torrance who lived from 1786-1870. He was born into a Scottish family which arrived in Montreal around 1800. He made his fortune as a tea importer and grocery merchant and invested successfully in railroads which connected Montreal to the United States. In 1833, Montreal was incorporated as a city and he was one of the original municipal councillors.

Originally, St-Antoine curved past the house, up beyond the railroad tracks and the Torrance home was far back from the road. It was described as "an elegant home with 42 rooms . . . on land that is renowned for its vast gardens and greenhouses." The estate disappeared after it passed out of the family. During the 1920s the building was a "porters' quarters," where men could rest between trips on the trains and in the 1940s and 1950s it housed an evangelical church and a small restaurant. Only part of the original building remains.

TORRANCE STREET, behind the house, marked the end of the estate and the front of the old St-Antoine hay market. Houses on the north side of St-Antoine were demolished when the railroad came through. The estates disappeared as the Canadian Pacific railway line split the area from downtown. Middle-level managers and artisans moved in and developers subdivided many of the homes, renting flats and rooms to immigrants and working-class families. The Lachine Canal opened up the district to factories and the railways carved up the last of the farm land.

The area was boxed in by the railroads. The Grand Trunk Railway, now the Canadian National Railway (CNR), was the southern boundary and ran between Notre Dame and St-Jacques streets. Stations were on Windsor and Peel Streets to the east. A couple of miles west was Glen Road and the rail yards. Blacks moved to Montreal to work on the railways and by 1900, there were two main areas in which they lived. The "old quarter" was between Windsor and Mountain Streets. The newer section, just to the west, had barbershops, restaurants, tailors and clubs catering to porters and "Red Cap" baggage handlers. By the 1920s, 90% of all Blacks in Montreal lived here although most in the area were white. However, whites could move out of the area fairly easily while Blacks seldom found housing elsewhere.

For more than forty years the corner of MOUNTAIN (rue de la Montagne) and ST-ANTOINE was the gateway to Montreal's famous "Sporting District." Porters came home from two weeks on the rails to jazz, gambling and whatever joys there were for tired men with pockets full of pay. The area had dozens of clubs and "blind pigs" — unlicensed rooms with cheap drinks and live music. Initially, the clubs were for private members and offered gambling, beer and billiards. The first ones started in the late 1800s around St-Laurent and St-Antoine. The best known places were the Recreation Key Club which was renamed the Utopia Club, the Standard Club at St-Antoine and Desrivières, and the Nemderoloc (*read it backwards!*) Club.

In 1928, Wilfred Israel, gave the area this description in a McGill Master's thesis on Montreal's Negro Community. "After 11:00 p.m. patrons are observed drifting in from their homes and from the auxiliary social centres in the sporting district. The jazz band of piano, violin and two saxophones grinds out the sensuous blue harmonies with a syncopation that sets the body in ready motion with sympathetic vibrations . . . . (one neighbour) claimed learning the piano version of 'Girl of my Dreams,' while asleep."

So tune out the traffic, pick a jazz tune, and tap your feet. It's nighttime; the clubs are opening and you've got you're pick.

There's the Beacon Grill at 1112 St. Antoine. The Terminal is next door. Just down Mountain Street are the Black Bottom, Café St-Michel, The Snake Pit, Harlem Paradise and Soul City. Further down was "the birthplace of the Canadian recording industry," a record factory started in 1899 by Emile Berliner on Aqueduct Street, now Rue Lucien-Allier.

Ahh, when it came to jazz, Montreal never had it so good. The most famous club was in that now vacant lot on the corner — Rockhead's Paradise at 1258 St-Antoine W. Rufus Rockhead quit the railroads in 1928 and opened the first nightclub actually owned by a Black. He cut quite a figure at the door and always had a fresh carnation or rose for the women. There was a long bar at ground level and a two-story nightclub above with a brass rail wrapped around the bandstand.

Rockhead's was closed twice by Quebec's Union Nationale government. The second time, for nine years, because Rufus backed the Liberals during a provincial election. Rufus suffered a stroke in 1975 and the club was sold two years later. A street has recently been named after him. It is further west, by the Lachine canal near Charlevoix street.

WALK WEST AND TURN LEFT ON VERSAILLES. Businessmen and merchant families first lived here. They left when the railway cut off the area from downtown and their homes became rooming houses for Irish, Italian, and Black workers. The Saint-Antoine district therefore retained a sizeable Black community for decades and a walking tour even as late as the 1950s, would have included schools, stores, and many residential streets lined with Victorian houses and old shade trees.

Bud Jones, head of the Black Historical Association, grew up here. "You used to be able to walk down this street during a warm summer evening and hear music coming from every house. Everyone had a job and played piano or trumpet or something. It was a wonderful feeling." In the last ten years or so, those Black families

Dancer at Rockhead's Paradise.
PHOTO BY EMILE OF MONTREAL. JOHN GILMORE
FONDS, CONCORDIA UNIVERSITY ARCHIVES.

who held onto their homes have been joined by young white professionals.

CONTINUE DOWN VERSAILLES, ALMOST TO ST-JACQUES. In the 1960s, the city of Montreal acquired three-quarters of the land between Atwater and Guy. The city controlled development. The Ville-Marie expressway was built over the top of St-Antoine street and much of row-housing between St-Antoine and St-Jacques was replaced by townhouses and condominiums. Families were uprooted and most eventually left the area. As development progressed, municipal officials gave it back its old name of Little Burgundy to encourage people to move in.

In the 1970s, the CNR moved its freight handling division a few miles west to the town of Lachine. Montreal re-zoned the land west of Mountain street as residential but the land east of Mountain is still vacant and is the last large piece of unbuilt land near downtown. Until 1980, sheds and a freight yard stood where there are now new apartment complexes.

WALK THROUGH THE ALLEY ON YOUR RIGHT. This path goes through to Lusignan Street, and meanders between the houses. Called "Place au Soleil," it is part of a city program to integrate alleys into the neighbourhoods.

TURN RIGHT ON LUSIGNAN. This street was once full of rooming houses for Blacks who wanted to be near Windsor station. In 1910, a family could rent a flat for about $12 a month. There is an unusual mix of residential and commercial buildings: a garment factory is in former ice house at 740 Lusignan and a paint factory is on the corner. Paul Lefebvre's furniture restoration shop is at 750 Lusignan and there is a lovely carriage house in the courtyard behind 764 Lusignan. The Coloured Canadian Legion was at the corner of St. Antoine and Lusignan streets. Times have changed, the site is a vacant lot and the Legion doesn't have separate halls for Black veterans.

TAKE A LEFT ONTO WREXHAM. This lovely row of houses is about 100 years old and was built for white business professionals. TURN RIGHT ON GUY. Some of the older buildings here were built in the 1850s.

TURN LEFT ON ST-ANTOINE. In the early 1800s, the land sloped gently from the mountain to the river. In the 1900s Richmond Park stretched up the hill with skating rinks and sport fields and Richmond Square was home to several waves of immigrants:

first English and Scots, then Irish, Germans, and Finns. Several of the original houses still stand. In the far corner is the wrought iron arch, the last legacy of the Richmond Apartments. The buildings were razed in the 1950s and became part of the St-Antoine district's first public housing project. The developers, who must have read a little local history, called it the Little Burgundy project and the name was used for all of the area between Guy and Atwater streets.

The modern looking building at 865 Richmond Square was, for a long time, the site of the Montreal Day Nursery which was founded in 1887 to assist single working mothers. The Nursery is now located in the downtown YMCA and this building houses Le Portage, a nationally known addiction rehabilitation and residence program.

Tyndale–St. Georges, at 876 Richmond Square, has run neighbourhood programs since almost the beginning of this century. The building also houses a pre-school, programs for refugees, a housing rights group, language classes, a Spanish mission, and a food program. There is a 'Community on the wall' mural inside.

CONTINUE WEST ON ST-ANTOINE. The houses along the west side of ST-MARTIN STREET have been renovated and restored by the City of Montreal so that their red brick and metal roofs complement older housing nearby. In the sixties, government officials believed they could create a better place to live by tearing down blocks of dilapidated Victorian row houses, replacing them with contemporary townhouses, community housing and apartment blocks. Planners assumed that everyone would have a car or use the Métro (there are three stations in the area) and that people would prefer to shop downtown. Consequently, there are few services, no schools, and hardly any shops or restaurants.

The building on the south-east corner of ST-ANTOINE AND DES SEIGNEURS was the Canadian Buttons factory. In 1970, the government expropriated the land; the factory moved to Lasalle and many employees went with it.

THE WALK CONTINUES DOWN DES SEIGNEURS but consider

walking a few blocks further along St-Antoine and then coming back. The observant passerby may note that the bricks at 1880 St-Antoine W. are larger than those in other, slightly older buildings. This is because the newer bricks are in a metric format.

St. Anthony of Padua at 1950 St-Antoine W. (932-7597) was on the north side of the street until the expressway was built. The church was founded in 1884 by the local Irish community, today the parish is multi-racial and extends from Sherbrooke street to the Lachine Canal and from Atwater to Mountain. The altar was taken from the original church and is hand-carved. Mass is celebrated in English on Tuesday and Thursday at 7:00 p.m. and Sunday morning at 10.

There are two small grocery stores, at 1984 and 2052 St-Antoine W., with snacks, imported produce and drinks from the islands. They are the only commercial stores in what was the city's main West Indian neighbourhood.

The J.P. Feron funeral parlour at 2252 St-Antoine W. was started by an Irishman. Local legend claims that because Mr. Feron needed money at one time and one of the Black community leaders helped him out, today any indigent Black person is cared for without charge.

The Good Shepherd Centre and residence is at 2338 St. Antoine W. This building is over a hundred years old and has served as a private residence, an army barracks, and a girls' residence. Most of Good Shepherd's programs serve English-speaking adults in the neighbourhood. There are several community groups sharing the building. The Social Justice Committee deals with Central American and Third World development. *Dans la rue* brings food and hot drinks to Montreal's street kids. *Terre des hommes* is concerned with health and education for Central American children.

RETURN TO DES SEIGNEURS AND WALK DOWN THE STREET. The building of the Lachine Canal transformed Montreal. The first seven miles of the canal opened in 1824 and linked Lachine, above the rapids, with the port of Montreal. Most of the

1500 men who built the canal were Irish fleeing famine in their country. Towards the end of the 19th century, the canal was widened, this time with the help of new immigrants from Italy. The canal's completion ended Quebec City's dominance as a trading centre and brought Montreal into the industrial era. Larger boats could now pass the Lachine rapids, go to Toronto and sail as far as Chicago. Factories were built alongside the canal and housing for workers and managers north of St-Jacques. Notre-Dame was the community's major commercial avenue.

AN INTERESTING SIDE TRIP leads to one of the main locks for the canal, about a kilometre (two-thirds of a mile) away, at the foot of des Seigneurs street. The Hushien Public Bath at Quesnel and Seigneurs (known locally as the Seigneurs Street bath) was built at the turn of the century. It is closed and may be demolished if the city builds a large sports centre near here.

It was on this part of des Seigneurs that Georges Vanier, the first French-Canadian Governor General, grew up. His family were local property owners and the neighbourhood has a Georges-Vanier street, library and Métro station. In 1984, the entire area was officially renamed Quartier Georges Vanier although most people still call it Little Burgundy — La Petite Bourgogne.

TURN RIGHT AND WALK THROUGH CAMPBELL PARK OR ALONG QUESNEL. This used to be Chatham Park and ended at Chatham Street. Redevelopment extended it to des Seigneurs, removing houses on Chatham and des Seigneurs.

Rue Quesnel used to be called Kamouraska, now the name for the housing cooperative which owns the row of hundred year old greystones on the street. Kamouraska is the rural Quebec village where a grisly 19th century murder took place and is also the title of Anne Hébert's novel about the event.

Frédéric-August Quesnel was a local 19th century lawyer, businessman and politician who made his fortune in the fur-trade. He was a classmate of (and later opposed) Louis Joseph Papineau who lead the Lower Canada Rebellion of 1837. Quesnel sold much of his land to Alexandre-Maurice Delisle and William Workman. Workman, born in Ireland, made a fortune in local land speculation by the time he was 40 and was mayor of Montreal from 1868–70.

TURN RIGHT ON GEORGES-VANIER AND LEFT ON COURSOL. Coursol strongly suggests what the district looked like through the first half of this century. The street may have remained intact because homes were owned by local families.

Charles-Joseph Coursol was a lawyer, politician and businessman who died in 1888. During his lifetime he was famous as the magistrate who released a group of 20 Confederate soldiers who fled to Canada after raiding St. Alban's Vermont during the American civil war. This was the war's most northern battle and the Americans were furious with Canada when Coursol set them free. Coursol later became a popular Conservative member of parliament who broke with his party over the hanging of Louis Riel but was reelected unopposed as an independent.

The Negro Community Centre (NCC) is at 2035 Coursol. It was built in 1890 as the West End Methodist Church and enlarged in 1928. In 1957 a gymnasium was added on the top floor. Through most of its history, the NCC thronged with children, adults and community groups. This area had a vibrant community and everyone knew each other. There was strong family support and people comfortably walked home at two or three in the morning, sure of seeing a neighbour wave from a stoop.

The Bible Way Pentecostal Church is at the corner of Coursol and Vinet. Services are at 11:00 a.m. and 6:30 p.m. Sundays. A prayer meeting is held Tuesdays at 7:30 p.m. This was originally the church of Saint Jude, built in 1878 when a white Anglican congregation moved out of another building a half-dozen blocks south. Blacks were tolerated here, but not really welcome, and most left upon forming the Union United Church, now on Atwater. The architecture on Coursol changes after Dominion Street.

The larger greystone houses were used by railway managers and more prosperous city merchants.

TURN LEFT ON VINET. One of the more innovative housing projects is on the north side of Quesnel, behind the Bible Way Church. These homes, built with pre-fabricated units, were designed by local architect Dan Hanganu as part of a citywide program called "Operation 20,000 homes" to keep the middle-class from leaving Montreal for the suburbs.

VINET AND ST-JACQUES was the centre of the old town of Ste-Cunégonde. Ste-Cunégonde Church, on the corner, was built in 1906. It has a magnificent dome with no interior supporting columns. The church was closed when the congregation could no longer afford to maintain it but a Latin mass is celebrated Sunday mornings at 10:30.

A statue of Pierre Le Moyne d'Iberville et d'Ardillières, is in the park across the street. D'Iberville was born in the 17th century, when this district was the town called Ville Marie. He was an adventurer famed for daring military zeal and massive pillaging.

CONTINUE SOUTH ON VINET. Parc Vinet is fairly new. The main recreation building is modeled on the early architecture of New France. The old, ornate building at Workman and Vinet is now the Georges-Vanier library. In the 19th century, the building was St. Jude Anglican Church. The town of Ste-Cunégonde bought it in 1877 and remodelled it as a city hall, post office, fire and police station. In 1882, Louis Cyr, Québec's famous strongman, was a policeman here. There is a life-size statue of Cyr about a mile to the west, on St. Jacques.

TURN RIGHT AT DELISLE AND WALK ACROSS TO CHARLE-VOIX. Deslisle, west of Charlevoix, has public housing on the left and private row housing on the right which dates from the 1880s.

The largest and oldest Black church in the area is the Union United at the corner of Delisle and Atwater. The church was formed in 1907 because Blacks often found they had to sit in the back or in segregated pews of white churches. It had a profound effect on community development, acting at various times as a local immigration office, community centre and employment bureau. In 1923, the congregation joined the United Church of Canada. Sunday services are at 11:00 a.m.; Montreal's famed Jubilation Gospel Choir frequently performs here. Oscar Peterson was born in the limestone building, now part of the Church at 3007 Deslisle.

Across the street is St-Irénée Catholic Church. Masses are held daily at 4:00 p.m. The Catholic Sri Lankan community holds a mass in Tamil, Sundays at 5:00 p.m.

The ATWATER MARKET, just to the south, was built in the 1930s to replace the old St-Antoine market on Torrance street. The market was recently renovated and has 60 stands for butchers, flower sellers and farmers. There is also a bakery and a miniature trout pond. A footbridge leads from the market to the Lachine Canal where there are picnic tables, walking, and cycling and cross country ski trails.

NOTRE-DAME STREET was built in the 1660s, it ran from Montreal to Lachine (a day's journey then) and was part of the Chemin de Roi — the King's Highway which stretched to Quebec City. The greystones built on Notre-Dame's south side are some of the last remnants of 19th century settlement. Several of the city's best antique stores are on this street, a few blocks east of Atwater.

THE LIONEL-GROULX MÉTRO STATION is on Atwater and Lionel-Groulx. Groulx, who died in 1967, was an historian, priest, and Québec nationalist. He has been called the spiritual father of modern Québec.

BOOKS, MUSIC AND FILMS

Everyone is coloured; for the white man, white is a neutral colour and it's normal for him to call a black man "coloured." But a Black man also thinks his colour his neutral, believe me, he looks at the white as "coloured."

— Foday M. Tounkara, *Un Africain à Montréal*
(La Pensée Universelle, Paris, 1980)

Blacks in Montreal, 1628-1986: An Urban Demography, D. W. Williams, Commission des droits de la personne du Québec Les Éditions Yvon Blais Inc., 1988

How to Make Love to a Negro, Dany Laferrière, David Homel, trans., Coach House Press, Toronto, 1987 — The ribald journey of a Haitian expatriate in Montreal.

Les Haitians au Québec, P. Denjean, U. de Q. Press, 1979.

Mother Solitude, Emile Olivier, David Lobdell, trans., Oberon Press, Toronto, 1989 — Haitian history with the pain and perception of an exile.

KOLA — *Black Literary Magazine* is published irregularly in Montreal.

Oscar Peterson, (Gene Lees, Lester & Orpen Dennys, Toronto, 1988) a biography of the famous Jazz pianist with much detail about his youth in Montreal's Little Burgundy district.

Swinging in Paradise (John Gilmore, Véhicule Press, 1988) is the definitive study of the jazz age in Montreal.

Films include *Bam Pay A!* — *Rends-moi mon pays!* (NFB), a film about a Haitian who goes back after 20 years in Montreal; *Taxi sans detour* (Vidéographe), is about discrimination against Haitian Taxi drivers; *Oliver Jones en Afrique* (NFB), chronicles the celebrated jazz pianists tours through Africa; *How to Make Love to a Negro Without Getting Tired* (Films Stock International), is a feature length version of Dany Laferrière's book; *Force de vivre* (Atelier Inter-Cultures), a father and daughter caught between Quebec and Haitian cultures.

Two musical works that relate to local Black history: Oscar Peterson's *Canadian Suite* makes musical stops from east to west, just like the train on which Peterson's father worked. *Lights of Little Burgundy* is pianist Oliver Jones' homage to his hometown.

CHINESE MONTREAL

POPULATION: 25,000

MAJOR COMMUNITIES: Chinatown, Brossard, Ville de Saint-Laurent, Saint-Louis du Parc, Isles des Soeurs, West Island, LaSalle

SHOPPING: Chinatown, Van Horne and Victoria, Taschereau Boulevard in Brossard.

Chinese history reaches back thousands of years. Confucius and Lao-Tse (the founder of Taoism) preached hundreds of years before Jesus Christ. The Qin dynasty, which ended in 206 B.C., built the Great Wall and gave the land its name of China ("Q" is pronounced "ch"). China means "Middle Kingdom" because the Chinese believed that they were the centre of the world. The Quing, China's last dynasty, ended when China became a republic in 1912.

In the 19th century, China's population was over half a billion and the country was in a state of political and economic stagnation. Russia, Japan and Europe were carving out parts of the Middle Kingdom for themselves. Britain was bringing opium into the southern part of the country and the "opium war" of 1842 forced China to open itself to the West. It was no accident that Chinese immigration to North America began around this time.

In 1858 the first Chinese workers entered British Columbia, a land they optimistically called "The Golden Mountain." White workers weren't receptive to the "orientals" who were paid less. Chinese coal miners received a dollar a day while whites were paid $2.50. Skilled Chinese workers on the Canadian Pacific Railway were paid the same wages as unskilled whites.

In 1885, with Canada's transcontinental railway finished, new Chinese immigrants had to pay a tax of $50 to enter Canada, while Europeans were given free farmland on the prairies. This infamous

Head Tax eventually was increased to $500 but still only applied to Chinese immigrants. When Canada removed the Head Tax in 1923, it imposed severe restrictions on who could enter the country, virtually ending any growth to the community. The law came into effect on July 1, Canada's birthday, known for generations of Chinese Canadians as "Humiliation Day." (Redress for the Head Tax is a significant issue. The Canadian government collected about $23 million from Chinese immigrants, many of whom are still alive in Montreal. The community is asking that the money be returned and feels that an apology, by itself, is insufficient.)

Once the transcontinental railway was finished many Chinese travelled east to work in the cities. They had few choices and little money to buy land. Most did not speak English or French. They worked on construction projects, in mines and forests, and as male domestics replacing white European women.

In 1900, Montreal was Canada's largest city. It had more than 328,000 people, most of whom could trace their ancestry back to France or Britain. Aliens were uncommon and usually feared. The *Montreal Gazette* editorialized: "John Chinaman is too much with us . . . He displaces Christian labour, and is in no sense a welcome or desirable addition to our population."

Chinese were stereotyped as passive, docile workers, perfectly suitable for some jobs. An advertisement in La Presse extolled the virtues of employing a Chinese houseboy: "Quelle joie dans ma famille . . . C'est que j'ai trouvé le secret de plaire à tous. Mon repassage est au parfait. Grâce à l'usage de l'emploi chinois . . . ."

Most Chinese teenagers who came to Montreal were nephews of railroad workers who had sent for them. A youth would work in a laundry, restaurant or grocery store. He might go back to China in his early twenties to marry but leave to live in Canada. His bride remained in China and he would return occasionally to father children. He would send money back, but few families made it over as there was never quite enough to pay for the passage and head tax. Often those who had saved enough money remained alone, not wanting their families to witness their poverty and humilation.

The few who prospered were still in a bind since, after the Head Tax ended, only Chinese who were Canadian citizens could bring over their families. Being a Canadian meant, under Chinese laws, that they would lose their Chinese citizenship. This might have been tolerable except that their new country had proved far from welcoming. Chinese were told they should not have the vote because they didn't understand democracy, that they were a threat to the moral well-being of the country, and that they hurt the economy by sending money back to China. Quebec forbade white women to work in Chinese businesses and marriage to a Canadian woman was unlikely since the woman would lose her citizenship by marrying a foreigner.

In 1901, there were 1,033 Chinese men and four Chinese women in Montreal; even by 1951, the ratio was still three to one. Despite the hardships, Montreal's Chinese community slowly evolved. Men from the same clan would combine financial resources and advance it, as a loan, to the clan-member who promised to pay the highest rate of interest. In this way, several men acquired enough capital to start a laundry, restaurant, or other small business.

Chinatown was ideally situated near the financial district and the city administration of Old Montreal. Other Chinese opened shops near St-Laurent boulevard: barbers, tailors and corner stores and restaurants that attracted both a Chinese and a white clientele.

The Chinese community remained ghettoized and mistrusted until WWII. The war changed that. When Japan attacked Pearl Harbour, Canada suddenly had a new ally in China. Overnight, Chinese Canadians were no longer aliens, they were on *our* side. Japanese-Canadians were banished to internment camps and local Chinese joined the armed forces. After the war, Canada's racist immigration policy began to change. In 1962 the government

■■ EMMA QUON'S STORY

I was born in Chinatown in 1916. Our home was on St. Urbain at la Gauchetière, around where the Lung Fung restaurant is now. There were hundreds of single men but only about 25 families. A group of us call ourselves "the pioneers." We used to meet twice a year, around Easter and Thanksgiving, but now there aren't many of us left.

Our community was very close. If any Chinese stranger came into town, you knew it. When Chinese travelers were held in immigration quarters at Windsor Station, someone would bring them Chinese food.

My father was a merchant. He arrived in the early 1900s and saved enough money to send for a wife. He couldn't afford to go back himself, so he asked his brother in China to pick one out and she came here and they were married. Now, no one would do that; but those arranged marriages were often happier than the ones today. My father had to pay a head tax of $500 to bring her over. That would be at least $20,000 today, maybe more.

We had non-Chinese friends at school but they never came to our house. Partly, this was because we did not have time. Right after our English school we had Chinese afternoon classes. We also felt they might be uncomfortable in a Chinese household. We were laughed at as kids. White parents would tell their children "if you don't behave, I'm going down to Chinatown and sell you to the Chinaman."

Our neighbourhood was small. Chinese stores and restaurants were on La Gauchetière and Clark; Saint-Lawrence developed later. We had a happy childhood. We didn't know we lived in slums.

... EMMA QUON'S STORY ...

There were youth groups and the church. There was a Chinese Y. Some people never left Chinatown because they didn't have to.

I went to school around the corner at Dufferin School. There were Jewish, Chinese and English kids. The Guy Favreau office complex now covers that area. That complex destroyed the community, it was a real social centre. Sundays were always social days as well as shopping days. Then, suddenly, there was no place to go.

Many people worked in laundries because they didn't speak French or English. You were fed by the people you worked for. Sometimes you slept in a small room in the back. Sometimes there wasn't even a room. These places were dark and dingy and small. The irons were heated on pot-bellied Quebec stoves all year round.

For many of us, Chinatown is an unknown factor today. Even as late as the 1970s you knew people. Now, with the influx of new Asians, their numbers have become so great that we have been snowed under. Those people, who came at the beginning of this century, were real heroes. The new arrivals don't appreciate what they went through.

removed racist criteria from its immigration policies, giving Chinese immigrants the same access to Canada they had known in 1884!

The Chinese community divides itself into distinct generations, depending upon when they arrived in Canada. The first are the old timers who came here before WWII. The next group are their children, born here — the first generation of Canadian Chinese. Then there are students who came from Hong Kong in the 1950s and decided to stay. They were followed by mainland Chinese who remained here as their country became more repressive. In June 1989, when China's leaders sent in the army to end demonstrations in Tiananmen Square, more than 500 Chinese visiting Montreal requested asylum.

The largest post-war influx of ethnic Chinese came from Vietnam as Quebec welcomed thousands of boat-people after Saigon fell to the Communists in 1975. The Chinese community is still changing as South Asian refugees arrive from Vietnam, Hong Kong, Laos and Cambodia. As well, in the last few years, thousands of relatively wealthy Chinese have immigrated to Montreal from Hong Kong and Taiwan. About half of them do stay here and Quebec hopes to attract more people before Hong Kong is returned to China in 1997.

RELIGION

People tend to view religions differently in the East than in the West. Gods must be appeased, so if one religion is good, why not three? Early missionaries were pleasantly surprised at how willingly the Chinese converted but never understood why they continued to practise other religions as well. Older French Canadians may remember helping the missionaries with donations to "acheter les petits Chinois."

Most of the first generations of Montreal Chinese are Catholics or Protestants. Many converted to Catholicism after the influenza epidemic of 1918 devastated the community. There was little medical help until the Sisters of Immaculate Conception opened a small hospital in Chinatown. Their work had an impact long after the epidemic ended. The Chinese Catholic Mission, Saint-Esprit Church, and a Catholic seniors' home remain important in Chinatown.

In Montreal, the role of the churches went beyond religion. Church leaders linked the Chinese community and non-Chinese authorities. Church workers tried to stop opium smoking and gambling among young Chinese men. Protestant missionaries preached on the streets, organized youth, gave language lessons and provided dormitory space. Most of all, the work done by the churches ensured that Chinese children would have the skills to succeed in western society.

Several churches still serve the community in Chinatown. **St. Esprit**, the **Chinese Catholic Mission**, is at 979 Coté St. (843-3339), and the **Montreal Chinese Pentecostal Church** is at 100 La Gauchetière E. (861-8097).

The **Montreal Chinese Presbyterian Church**, formerly in Chinatown, is now in Outremont at 5560 Hutchison (270-4782).

Many newcomers have kept Buddhism as their main religion, often augmented by Confucianism, Taoism and Christianity. Confucianism and Taoism are philosophies, or approaches to life, rather than religions. They stress moral behaviour, order, humanity and wisdom with Taoism (Daoism) emphasizing meditation and contemplation.

Buddhism developed from Hinduism about 2,600 years ago. It is based on the Four Noble Truths: life involves suffering, suffering comes from desire, eliminating desire ends suffering, and practising Buddhism eliminates desire. One of the larger and newer Buddhist temples (called pagodas) is **Chua Lie Hoa** at 715 Boulevard Provencher in Brossard.

It is not unusual to walk into a restaurant or store, smell the sweet perfume of burning incense and see an alcove with a small statue venerating Buddhas or Taoist immortals identified with Luck, Longevity, and Prosperity. Popular statues include Tam Gong, who is consulted before marriages, business plans and travel and Guan Gong, the God of War, who is supposed to stop evil and restore goodness.

Chinese Laundries

The Chinese hand laundry met two needs: work for the Chinese immigrant and clean clothes for the downtown professional. Hand laundries gave the Chinese a business which could be housed where they lived, cost little to set up, and didn't require workers to speak much English or French. Furthermore, Chinatown was in a perfect location to take advantage of the growing number of managers, clerks and bureaucrats working in the civic administration in Old Montreal, in the better department stores on Saint Lawrence (now St-Laurent) boulevard and in the financial and newspaper enterprises which had sprung up around St-James (now St-Jacques) street.

The first Chinese hand laundry was opened in 1877 by Jos Song Long. Most laundries were run by one or two people who worked from 7:00 a.m. until midnight. By 1920, there were almost 300 hand laundries throughout the city and suburbs. Practically all were owned by Chinese while whites worked at one of the 20 large steam-laundry companies. These steam laundries had started in the 1890s cleaning linen for hospitals and hotels. As the hand laundry business grew, they encouraged the provincial government to tax all laundries the same amount. In 1915, this was $50, not too much for large companies, but a month's worth of work for a hand laundry owner. The community formed the Chinese Benevolent Association in protest, supported without success, by the Archbishop of Montreal.

The tax stayed on the books until 1984, but even by the early 1940s hand laundries were going out of business. The Depression wiped many of them out and immigration laws made it difficult to bring young workers into the country. Even successful owners had closed down their shops, preferring to start more lucrative businesses such as restaurants and grocery stores. In the suburbs, non-Chinese owned companies began using "dry cleaning" and offered to pickup and deliver. The final blow arrived after wwii as a growing white middle-class became more affluent and began to put washing machines and driers right in the house!

FESTIVALS

WINTER — CHINESE NEW YEAR. Many local groups participate with demonstrations of traditional dance, music, recitations and karate. There is usually a lineup for the free Chinese meal at the Chinese Community Centre on St-Dominique near de La Gauchetière.

WINTER FEST. Traditionally, three days before Christmas, Chinese families gathered to celebrate the harvest.These days, it's a time for family reunions with a large meal, songs, dances and parties. Sweet rice flour dumplings are eaten. Their round shape symbolizes perfection and completeness. A free buffet meal and dance are held at the Chinese United Centre building, 1001 St-Dominique. For more information call the **Chinese United Centre** (861-4541).

SPRING — THE INTERNATIONAL CHINESE FILM FESTIVAL (521-1984) is organised each spring by InterCinéArt, a non-profit organization. There are art exhibitions, forums and several dozen screenings of traditional and modern films by Chinese filmmakers.

CONFUCIUS FESTIVAL, June 8th to 17th, begins with a Confucian ceremony and includes an exhibition of calligraphy at Complèxe Guy-Favreau. Chinese opera, Kung Fu sessions and a Lion & Dragon Dance take place in Sun-Yat-sen park and in the streets of Chinatown.

DRAGON BOAT FESTIVAL / DUAN WU. On the 5th day of the 5th month, (usually near Mother's Day) Dragon Boat teams race against each other in remembrance of Qu Yuan, a favourite Chinese poet who lived nearly 2000 years ago. The Dragon Boats are quite spectacular; they can cost $20,000 each and have up to 50 rowers. The race takes place at the Olympic Basin.

AUTUMN MOON FESTIVAL. This annual late-summer celebration is one of the most popular festivals in Chinatown. Activities include a Lion & Dragon dance, Chinese folk music and demonstrations of Chinese chess, calligraphy and painting.

COWHERDER AND WEAVING MAID. On the 7th night of the 7th moon the legendary Cowherder and Weaving Maid meet each other for their annual tryst at a bridge formed by magpies. At least, that's the way the story goes. This festival is a big one for unmarried women. They pray to the moon and contemplate relationships between men and women. There are often celebrations of this festival at community halls. Check with Chinese Family Services or the United Centre.

ORGANIZATIONS

Clans are the most enduring Chinese organizations. Those with same surname are linked paternally to a common clan. The Wong, Hum, Lee and other clans still have social clubs on the upper floors of buildings on La Gauchetière Street. Newcomers with the same surname know that they can come for advice and help in finding jobs and a place to live. (In Chinese, the family name is written first. For example, Mao Zedong's surname was Mao.)

District associations began as burial societies for overseas Chinese. Members hailed from specific provinces in China and associations sent money back to China and also helped residents in Canada.

Fraternal-political associations were concerned with the welfare of members and represented political factions in China, until the Communists came to power in 1949. The Associations were funded in several ways: selling shares in the group, membership dues, exit fees from those who returned to China, building rents and gambling. Gambling and illegal immigration proved vulnerable areas, ripe for street battles and informants who might want to see an opponent jailed or deported.

As the community grew older, many groups became irrelevant. Some became mutual-aid societies while others vainly held on, hoping that the nationalists in Taiwan would eventually overturn China's Communist government. Canada's diplomatic recognition of the People's Republic of China in 1970 was a political defeat for many Chinese organizations in Montreal.

The Chinese Benevolent Associations (CBAs) brought together the smaller, diverse associations that formed in Chinese communities. Montreal's CBA was called the Chinese Association of Montreal. It was set up in the early 1900s to protect Chinese hand laundry owners against the encroachments of larger white-owned mechanized laundry owners. It strove for local unity, represented the community to government and fought discrimination.

L'Association Culturelle Chinoise de l'Institut Kaï Leung, 680 rue Ste-Catherine W. (866-6140) was started in 1977 as a Kung Fu and Tai Chi school under Master Kaï Leung who came from China. The Association, which has many non-Chinese members, gives courses in Chinese calligraphy, painting, literature and philosophy and has workshops for people planning to travel in China. Each summer it organizes a Confucius street festival in Chinatown.

Canada Chinese Cultural Society of Montreal, 1117 Ste-Catherine W. (849-3526) shares cultures without political or religious barriers. It is one of the few groups with members from several Chinese communities as well as many occidentals. There are lots of social activities: sugaring off, trips to Atlantic City, regular Chinese feasts, cooking demonstrations, music and dance shows.

Chinese Family Services, 987 Coté (861-5244) was established in 1976, to provide services for the Chinese community and help it adapt to Quebec society. It has emerged as a leading community group helping children and parents cope with changes in the educational systems, working with battered women, and most recently helping Chinese scholars, who can no longer return to China, become residents of Canada.

Chinese Neighbourhood Society, 5615A Parc (273-9088) is a grassroots social-service group for several thousand poor Chinese, most of whom have little education and work in manual jobs. Many need help with government forms, local notices and taxes. It has recently started community groups for the elderly and for immigrant women. It occasionally offers walking tours of Chinatown and has courses in art, music and Chinese. A separate group assists women over 18 years of age to find jobs, get into language courses, cultural programs, and has courses in sewing, pattern making, hairdressing and other vocations.

Chinese United Centre, 211 la Gauchetière (861-4541) has built a seniors' residence and rental housing for those with low incomes. It has a library and lends videos in Mandarin and Cantonese and books in Chinese languages, English and French. Gradually, the Centre has replaced other groups, providing the community with a common front for negotiating with the city and other levels of government about future development.

La Société de Tai Chi Taoïste de Montréal, 4510 St-Denis (845-4376). Tai Chi is one the fastest growing martial arts in Montreal. At its basic level, it is an excellent form of isometric exercise based on repetitive movement, stretching and breathing and is particularly good for older people. More advanced study may include meditation, greater physical contact and weapons. This organization has clubs throughout the world and is headed by Master Moy Lin-Shin, a Taoist Monk, who moved to Canada from China. (N.B.: One of the authors, Barry Lazar, claims Tai Chi has been fantastic for his back during the writing of *The Guide to Ethnic Montreal*.)

■■ CONFESSIONS OF A CHINESE PALMIST

Mr. C. Ku-Yan specializes in Oriental Palmistry at 3424 Hôtel de Ville. His card reads "Health, Love, Business, Money . . . . Past, Present and Future in English, Chinese or Spanish at $50.00 per session."

My interest started when I was teenager visiting Hong Kong. A man, claiming to be a fortune teller, took my money and promised to teach me; but it was a scam and I lost my money. A couple of years later, a monk in Macao told my fortune for $4. He warned me that disaster would happen before I turned 21. On December 30th, one day before the end of the year and the time limit on the prediction, fire broke loose in my home. I was in hospital for a month. This incident was the real beginning of my study of palmistry, Chinese astrology and face reading.

I do this strictly as a hobby, as an art, not for the money; but I charge money because otherwise people do not respect you in this world. People who are in it as a business are cheating themselves and their customers. Their minds are busy thinking of dollars instead of concentrating on the job of fortune telling.

Each session can last from 10 minutes to an hour. The better the fortune, the shorter the session. A hard hand, one full of misfortune and problems, takes much longer to analyze. A good hand reader is someone who doesn't look at your face while studying your hand.

MEDIA

None of Montreal's Chinese newspapers publish in English or French. Most publish weekly and have a mixture of national and international news translated from other media; and one or two reporters who cover events in the community.

Worldwide Chinese Journal, 4970 Queen Mary (738-7801) A fortnightly publication in Chinese for recent immigrants; news from China, Hongkong, and Taiwan.

Les Nouvelles chinoises / The Chinese News, 1051 St-Laurent (954-0214) tries to have a lively design with a focus on international and community events.

Le Mondial, Journal Chinois de Montréal, 15 la Gauchetière E. (875-6746) has community events and news from China.

Da Chung Bao News, 170 Réne-Lévesque W. (397-1104) has a circulation of 15,000. The company also publishes *Chinada* featuring Canadian news.

Ruth Lam (861-8142) is the dynamo of Chinese media. She works on a newspaper, produces the cable television program *La Voix de Chine* and hosts Chinese talk programs in French, English, Cantonese and Mandarin on CFMB 1410. Radio Centre-ville CINQ 102.3-FM also has programs in Chinese.

RESTAURANTS AND CLUBS

$ indicates that a lunch or dinner should cost under $10 (without taxes, tips, or wine). $$ is under $25 and $$$ above that. Many Chinese restaurants offer a small discount for customers who pay in cash. Credit cards accepted are listed. "BYOB" means that you can bring your own wine. Hours often vary with the seasons so please call.

Food is so central to Chinese life that the polite way of greeting someone is to ask "Have you eaten enough yet?" The polite answer is always "yes," even if you are starving. Any other answer compels the speaker to invite you in for a meal. Noodles are traditionally eaten at Chinese birthdays to encourage longevity.

HOW TO GET A GOOD CHINESE MEAL

We've noticed that there is a lot of occidental frustration out there; so here are a few suggestions to take you beyond "Meal no. 3 with almond cookie."

Avoid Monday meals. *That's when most chefs in Chinatown take the day off.*

Dim sum is not Chinese for "fast food." *Dim sum is a series of small dishes, literally "little snacks." These are bite-sized morsels common to southern Chinese cooking and frequently served for lunch — great way to sample several kinds of Chinese appetizers. Many restaurants in Chinatown feature dim sum and draw large crowds, so get to the restaurant by noon or chance a long wait. Ask for a table near the kitchen so you can get food when it's hot. The best dishes disappear quickly and very late lunchers may find only a few carts of sodden dumplings being trundled down the aisles. Traditionally, dim sum is an accompaniment to good talk. A meal should last quite a while, with new dishes coming to the table sporadically.*

Go with a group. *Chinese food is almost impossible to enjoy eating on your own; with more people, there is a better chance of stumbling across a great dish.*

Order more than you'll eat. *Again, that increases your chances of getting a dish you'll remember. Besides, most places in Chinatown are relatively inexpensive. What you don't eat goes home. Microwaves were invented for reheating Chinese food.*

Forget the menu. *The person who seats you is often the manager or owner. Tell him or her how many are in your group and what you want to spend per person. Warn him about specifics (no MSG, shellfish or whatever) and leave the rest to him. This seems a little brash but a Chinese friend who* *was raised in Chinatown says that's what she does. It's a wonderful method for the adventurous. We've tried it and left the table quite satisfied.*

◆

BON BLE RIZ　$$ AMEX MC VISA
1437 boul St-Laurent (844-1447)
3474 Ave du Parc (845-9149)

■ Bon Blé has lots of local fans for its well-prepared but sometimes uninspired dishes. The noodle dishes are its strength. BBR, as it likes to call itself, is famed for dinner-time demonstrations of arm-length noodle making. Call to ensure which nights the shows go on.

CAFE CHINE　$$ AMEX EN-ROUTE MC VISA
Holiday Inn, Chinatown 99 Viger W. (878-9888)

■ Formal Hong Kong style dining under a pagoda or beside a flowing stream. Excellent soups such as shredded duck with Enoki mushrooms. Most dishes are cooked in a tasty but un-spicy Cantonese style. Luncheon dim sum are ordered individually and brought to the table. Look for steamed shrimp and scallop dumplings. Ask for "Laser dumplings" — sweet peanut covered mounds stuffed with warm black sesame seed paste. Cafe Chine is great for groups of 10 or more who want to enjoy a banquet style menu — sumptuous pre-arranged multi-course meals start under $20 a person.

By the way, notice the phone number. Lots of "8"s. Homonyms are important in Chinese and the word for "8" is similar to the word for "prosperous." Similarly there is no "fourth" floor in the elevator since the number "4" sounds like the word for "death." Notice the address, too. "9" is another popular number — it sounds like the word for "long" as in "long life."

CHEZ FLAMINGO　$$ AMEX EN-ROUTE MC VISA
1809 Ste-Catherine W. (937-7418)

PARADISE DE CHINE $$ AMEX EN-ROUTE MC VISA
619 Decarie (747-8998)
LE GOURMET DE SECHUAN $$ AMEX EN-ROUTE MC VISA
862 Mont-Royal E. (527-8888)
■ Three restaurants under the same management serving an attractive, uncomplicated selection of Cantonese and mildly spicy Szechuan dishes. The staff training and preparation of more difficult dishes (like Peking duck) is done at the Flamingo. Vegetables are varied and well prepared. Signature dishes from southern and northern cooking styles include an unusual crispy spinach with pepper shrimp, thick Pekinese spareribs in a robust honey-sauce, and tasty, gelatinous tientsing bean paste strips. The Flamingo is usually crowded on weekend evenings when the chef demonstrates making yard-long Shanghai noodles.

JOZ $$ MC VISA
5717 Monkland (481-4406)
■ A smart little Beijing-style restaurant in NDG. Not an extensive menu, but there is good Ma Po tofu, dumplings (Joz are dumplings in Mandarin) and good stuffed eggplant. The service is attentive; the setting is almost elegant and the open, back courtyard is very pleasant on warm summer evenings. It doesn't have the verve of some of the better places downtown or in Chinatown, but if you're in the area it's hard to do better.

KEUNG KEE $$ VISA MC
70 La Gauchetière W., 2nd floor (393-1668)
■ Unusually good Cantonese cooking. (The chef is a partner). Comfortable yet classy for Chinatown, great for adventuresome eaters. Look for "Tip-Tripe" of pork's stomach, a delicate steamed chicken "Tung kong style," fried squid with curry, stewed goat with bean cake, Fish head pot, health soups like ginseng and chicken and warm or cool sweet Chinese soups for dessert.

■■ CHINESE TABLE MANNERS

Chinese banquets are wonderful feasts. Community organizations, such as the Chinese Family Services, often use banquets as fundraisers and sell tickets to the public. When you go, consider the dining etiquette of Gabrielle Boudreau of the Kai Leung Institute.

Eat the food in front of you. *Several Chinese dishes are often served on a round, swivel platter. Do not be tempted to reach for something on the other side of the platter. This is considered very impolite since it appears that you are only taking what you want, the best stuff, and leaving the rest for the others.*

Invert chopsticks. *Use the thick ends for serving, the narrower ends bring food to the mouth.*

Eat small portions. *Chinese banquets can have a dozen courses.*

Eat only after the most important guest at the table has started. *If that's you, then eat and stop holding everyone up.*

Serve others before filling your cup. *The same goes for sauces. If you want the teapot refilled, leave the lid up.*

When the food is gone, dinner is over. *Usually, Chinese meals are so elaborate and lengthy that there is plenty of time to talk during dinner without hanging around for coffees and liqueurs.*

LOTTE $$ MC VISA AMEX
Furama Hotel, 215 René-Lévesque E. (393-3838)
■ Reviews from average to superb but certainly worth trying (there's dancing to a combo on Thursday, Friday and Sunday

evenings) Good dim sum until 2:30 p.m. Unusual dinner dishes include vegetables such as mong choy in preserved peanut cake, baby squid with salt and pepper, scallops with Chinese broccoli (Guy Lan), Yee Mien noodle (hot then cold winter melon sautéed with mushrooms, vegetables, soy sauce and oyster sauce), and sweet hot green bean soup for dessert.

LOON SHING $ MC VISA
4745 Grande Allée, Brossard (445-2276, 3913)
■ A small South Shore Cantonese restaurant catering to the growing Chinese community in Greenfield Park, Brossard and Saint-Lambert. It's packed on weekends. Ingredients are fresh (the owner gets them in Chinatown each morning). The Special Wonton soup has a tasty chicken broth and plump wonton filled with a mixture of pork and shrimp. This is a good place to trust the Chinese menu, particularly if you're with four or more. There's a standard 10% discount for cash and takeout orders.

LUONG-HUU $
84 la Gauchetière W. (397-9410)
■ It looks like a good pastry shop with a dairy stand but there is much more including nightly singalongs with Chinese videos. The menu leans to Cantonese-Vietnamese food. Actually there are two menus, one just with pictures of a dozen or so popular dishes (for those who like to point and order) and a longer one, in English, French, Vietnamese, and Chinese. The seafood noodle dishes are particularly good. The shrimp with pepper and salt (number 41) are superb. This is one of the few Chinese restaurants where you should save room for dessert. Try a green bean or melon cake with one of the fruit shakes such as apple, melon, lychee, loganberry or jackfruit. The durian drink is, be warned, extremely pungent.

MANBO $
81 La Gauchetière W. (392-7778)
■ Chinese Buddhist vegetarian restaurant unfortunately a long

way from its Hong Kong counterparts. Interesting attempts at replicating barbecued pork, spareribs, and similar dishes with wheat gluten and tofu. They don't use MSG.

MAYALINE $$ AMEX MC VISA
970 St-Laurent (866-2276)
■ Hearty, almost peasant style cooking but the staff seems to discourage Westerners from trying dishes that are tasty but a little different — like boiled chicken with greens or fried cuttle fish. Service can be slow.

MON NAN $$ AMEX MC VISA
1098 Clark (866-7123)
■ This small Cantonese restaurant serves an excellent seafood fondue weekday evenings when the weather gets cool. Bubbling pots of spicy and savory broths are brought to your table and you can select as much as you like from a buffet of vegetables, mushrooms, fish, thinly-sliced meat, noodles and sauces.

SHAN TUNG $ AMEX MC VISA BYOB
1050 Clark (866-6693)
■ Good Szechuan cooking, but the big draw here is Peking duck. No need to reserve, it's always ready and is served in three courses: first the crisp duck skin which you roll in thin pancakes with a dollop of hoisin sauce and some slivered green onions, then a platter of stir fried duck meat and vegetables, and finally a sumptuous soup made with the bones and smaller pieces of duck meat. Parking's a problem in the area and there's a steep flight of stairs to the restaurant. There's a $3.00 corkage fee if you bring your own bottle of wine.

TAI PING $$ AMEX MC VISA
1115 Clark (397-1108; Fax: 397-6894)
■ This is the latest addition to David Wong's growing Clark St. conglomerate. His Chinese bookstore is across the street and the

restaurant corridors lead to his Oriental Cinema on St-Laurent. Tai Ping is big and bustling — Chinese power lunch territory — note the fax line. Luncheon dim sum is very good here; at night, the menu leans towards fish, seafood, and Cantonese dishes which are very fresh although the preparation can be bland. Noodle dishes are superb. The staff is unusually adept at explaining the intricacies of the separate Chinese language menu which has special dinners that are very good value for larger groups. There are two flights of stairs; but a large elevator is in the corridor.

TONG NAM $ MC VISA
1019 St-Laurent (875-8242)
■ The jar of miniature hot peppers on the table and the unusual use of mint and other herbs in the cooking hints that this is a different Chinatown restaurant. But the broad range of Chinese and Thai dishes are undifferentiated on the menu. The soups are particularly good, especially the hot and sour with chicken and tofu. The shrimp roll is ample for two and the thin strips of marinated and cooked Thai beef are mild but tasty.

TONG POR $ MC VISA
43 la Gauchetière E. (393-9975)
■ Excellent daily dim sum with some unusual Thai dishes (such as cold, spicy chicken feet). Call around 10:30 in the morning if you want to reserve a table for a large group; even then, you can wait a good half hour before a table is available. Dim sum prices are reduced between 2:00 p.m. and 3:00 p.m.

TUNG AH $$$ (through the back door) AMEX MC VISA
1172 Bishop (397-5555)
■ Delicious Cantonese food in a luxurious setting. The chef was trained in Tung Ah's ten-year-old Hong Kong restaurant. Superb seafood egg rolls served with home-made plum sauce; good Singapore noodles and fresh seafood. BBQ pork and duck are prepared

in-house and brought to the table at room temperature (as they should); the delectable soya chicken is served with a mild, flavourful shallot sauce. A few interesting deserts like rice mud balls (peanut covered balls of sweet rice with a dollop of peanut butter inside). Dinner can be pricey but luncheon dim sum and business specials are less expensive. There's two hours of free parking in the lot across the street.

M.K. WONG $$ AMEX MC VISA
1180 Decarie (337-2262), Ville Saint-Laurent
■ Don't be fooled by the generic fast-food exterior. There's surprisingly good, freshly-prepared Chinese food inside and an inexpensive buffet. Ask about unusual dishes like dumplings with peanut sauce, vegetarian specials with a variety of vegetables, chili and salt baked shrimp, or oysters with ginger and green onions.

YANGTZE $$ MC VISA
4645 Van Horne (733-7171)
■ For over 36 years, this has been the definitive Chinese-Canadian restaurant. The staff is friendly, the menu unintimidating. There's nothing out-of-the ordinary here; but once in a while owner Norman Lum has something special in the back like Chinese-style marinated salmon bones. Otherwise, stick to the basics: honeyed dry garlic shrimp, noodle dishes and perhaps the best egg rolls and plum sauce in the city.

ZEN $$$ VISA MC AMEX EN-ROUTE
Four Season's Hotel 1050 Sherbrooke W. (499-0801)
■ Outstanding service and setting with a wide array of Cantonese and Szechuan dishes. Vegetable dishes can be bland but most meat and fish dishes are superb and attractively presented. Several dishes are hard to find elsewhere such as salt and pepper soft shell crab or sweet red bean soup with taro. The crispy duck is a showstopper with two waiters carving and preparing this dish, Peking style, at the table.

FOOD SOURCES

See additional listings in the chapter on ASIAN MONTREAL

CHONG WAH NOODLE MFG CO. 1665 Sanguinet (844-2847). Several kinds of freshly-made wheat noodles sell for well under a dollar a pound (usually a 5 lb. minimum). Take them home, put them into one pound packs if you want. They freeze well. Use them like any noodle (but defrost them at room temperature before cooking them in boiling water).

DRAGON'S BEARD CANDY, 992 St-Laurent Stall #2 (528-1309). Johnny Chin hand pulls thousands of delicate strands of this rarely made Chinese candy. Its a tasty snack and a great show.

KIEN VINH CORP., 1062 Saint-Laurent (393-1030). A large grocery store with all the staples and a few extras like imported Chinese soft drinks. By the way, when you're low on cash, but would like to give a Chinese friend a present, buy a dozen or so oranges. They show your friends that you are thinking about their health and citrus is a traditional gift for the Chinese New Year.

PATISSERIE DE BONNE FORTUNE, 1110B boul. St-Laurent (878-9988). Interesting savory and sweet pastries. Glazed buns with pork, beef, chicken. French-style almond pastries. Cookies, fruit and egg rolls.

PATISSERIE C.J. REGENT, 68 la Gauchetière W. (866-1628). There are tables in the back of the bakery for a quick bite to eat. Some of the baked goods are Chinese style and some are a combination of the East and the West. There are many interesting combinations like a hot dog sandwiched in a glazed bun or a curry-filled bun. This patisserie also caters and bakes cakes for weddings and anniversaries.

SUN SING LUNG, 72A La Gauchetière W. (861-0815) has been here for two generations. It has a growing take-out section with home-made egg rolls, cooked and barbecued meats and steamed buns; it's also a good store for those who enjoy preparing Chinese dishes and want suggestions for using ingredients like red dates, liver sausage and mustard greens.

SHOPS AND SERVICES

Chinatown is an official tourist area so all the shops are open throughout the weekend. Sunday is the traditional day for eating, shopping and socializing in the Chinese community. Many stores close on Monday.

BOUTIQUE MELA, 1014 Clark (879-1114) has traditional Chinese embroidered blouses and dresses, silk jackets and scarves; also intricate mahjongg sets starting at $60.

THE CHINESE GARDEN at the Montreal Botanical Gardens 4101 Sherbrooke E. (872-1400). The City of Montreal is formally "twinned" with Shanghai. This magnificent garden, the largest classical southern Chinese garden ever built outside China, was built over a two-year period by hundreds of Shanghai gardeners. There are courtyards, bamboo, lotus and chrysanthemum, pavilions, pagodas, lanterns, bridges, an ice statue festival in the winter, and a pond with a two-storey stone boat reminiscent of the one built for the dowager empress of China at the turn of the century.

CHINA PAGODA, 384 St-Catherine W. (871-3870). Oriental imports include lanterns and lace table cloths from mainland China.

DISTRIBUTIONS DR. SUN LTEE., 1000 Clark (393-9567). Chinese newspapers from Asia and Canada and Chinese comic books.

GALERIE DE CHINE — CHINA GALLERY 94 La Gauchetière W. (878-2116). This small second floor gallery is as much a place to buy the works of contemporary Chinese artists as to learn about calligraphy and Chinese art. There is also a small selection of gifts and artist supplies.

LAM IMPORTERS, 2030 St-Laurent (843-5874, 7060). Large volume and sometimes low prices. Look for Chinese dishes and crafts, watches, electronic guitars, and calculators.

LA LIBRAIRIE CHINOISE, Sun Ko Wah 1106 Clark (866-3108). A wonderful store for browsing with traditional red and gold good luck envelopes, English and Chinese fiction from China, newspapers and magazines from major Chinese communities in North America, imported music and videos, and, on occasion, Beijing's version of the world in English, the *China Daily*.

GEORGE WONG CHINESE LAUNDRY, 322 Victoria, West-mount (484-2379). It's not anywhere near Chinatown but there are no more laundries there anyway. This place is cluttered, more like a living room stacked with ironing and dozens of small parcels wrapped with brown paper. Shirts, pants and suits cost a little less than at the dry-cleaners nearby.

A NOTE ON NON-WESTERN MEDICINE

Much of oriental medicine is preventive. Traditionally, the Chinese doctor was paid when you were well and might owe you money if you got sick.

If you're serious about going to a herbalist or acupuncturist, discuss this with your own doctor and consult several who practice oriental medicine before making a decision. Remember that those practising oriental techniques do not need a special license here; prospective patients should be wary of their expertise. Make sure the person is aware of your medical history and has a degree from a recognized teaching institution. Speak with a few people who are patients.

Acupuncture appears to be good for relieving back pain or aches in the joints. Sessions cost between $40 and $60 an hour. There are different approaches including Chinese, Japanese and Korean. Many practitioners prescribe herbs and ointments as well. Most professionals will spend at least *an hour with a prospective patient before deciding on what combinations of remedies to use.*

AUX HERBES D'ORIENT, Place du Quartier Chinois 990 Saint-Urbain (861-8037).

The herb doctor next door keeps this shop busy by sending clients in to fill their prescriptions.

CHI LIANG LO, 55 rue de La Gauchetière W. (954-0132). Herbalist and member of the Chinese Medicine and Acupuncture Association of Canada.

THE CLINIC OF NATURAL LIFE MEDICINE, 2425 Grand (481-4028) is run by David Goldman who studied Japanese acupuncture and herbal medicine. (In the interest of investigative reporting, *Ethnic Guide* co-author Barry Lazar went through a half-dozen sessions and spent a lot of time taking naps while stuck with pins. He says his arthritic pain has disappeared. Now he'd like to see if it works on high cholesterol!)

CLINIQUE D'ACUPUNCTURE ORIENTALE KWANG KIM, 765 Mont-Royal E. (597-1777). Kwang Oh Kim came here from Korea 10 years ago and is an accomplished herbalist and acupuncturist. Occidentals will feel comfortable talking about oriental treatments and remedies that may seem unusual. There is no pressure to buy anything. In fact, if you are now mystified by the Ginseng capsules you spontaneously bought in Chinatown, bring them here for a quick consultation.

HUI TACK WING HERBES DE CHINE, 1112 St-Laurent (878-9933). The staff of this small shop is helpful with queries about herbs for health and to combat illness, how dried seahorses improve vision, and why birds' nests are good for the skin.

MAGASIN DES HERBES DE L'ASIE QUOC TE, 1024 St-Laurent (875-8156) is one of the larger herb stores in Chinatown with a huge variety of ginseng products and a friendly staff.

WALKING TOUR OF CHINATOWN

Start at Métro Champ-de-Mars
End at Métro Place-d'Armes

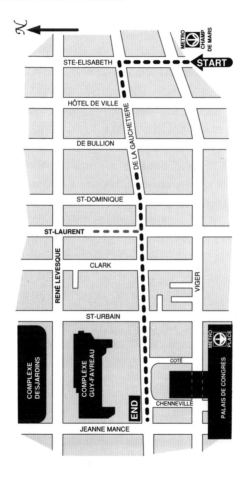

This has been Montreal's Chinatown as long as most of us can remember. During the late 1950s and early 1960s, speculators purchased old buildings and demolished them and vacant land became parking lots waiting for an attractive offer. Inexpensive rental housing disappeared.

The community's plan to redevelop the area, never got off the ground because of feuding among competing Chinese organizations. Government plans prevailed and land for several blocks of homes and businesses was turned into provincial and federal office buildings. The expropriation almost killed the community. It demolished the Chinese Presbyterian Church, the Chinese Pentecostal Church, a Chinese food factory, several Chinese grocery stores and homes. By the mid-1970s, only a couple of hundred senior citizens were still living there.

Revival of Montreal's Chinatown started in the 1980s with the installation of a pedestrian mall on la Gauchetière and construction of the Catholic Community Centre and a senior citizens' home. Chinese Montrealers live throughout the city and suburbs; Chinatown, centred at la Gauchetière and St-Laurent, remains the heart of the community and has attracted a newer generation of Asian developers.

Today French, English, Cantonese, Mandarin, and Vietnamese are commonly heard in stores in Chinatown as well as Chinese provincial dialects like Fu-chian and Chao-chun. It's not unusual to see Canadian festivals celebrated in the area, with green fortune cookies on St-Patrick's Day or pink bean-curd hearts on Valentine's Day.

START AT THE CHAMP-DE-MARS MÉTRO STATION. The Champ-de-Mars refers to the Roman god of war and is a common French name for militia marching grounds. This land was acquired by the Jesuits at the end of the 17th century and was used by the militia for drills. To the south is Old Montreal and the Saint-Lawrence river. The large building with the green copper roof is the back of the City Hall of Montreal, 275 Notre Dame East. Built in 1878, a fire destroyed most of it in 1922. It was rebuilt in the Beaux-Arts style popular at the time. The front is quite elaborate.

To the west is the City's convention centre, the Palais des Congrès, and the Place-d'Armes Métro where the tour ends.

WALK NORTH, UP STE-ELISABETH. This is the eastern fringe of Chinatown. The west side of this street is completely taken up by a Chinese senior citizens home and its new extension. For the last decade, Chinatown has increasingly become a community of the elderly. The city wants to maintain the residential character of the area and will not permit new shops and businesses to open on la Gauchetière east of St-Laurent.

TURN LEFT AND WALK WEST ALONG LA GAUCHETIÈRE. There is a small alley between Ste-Elisabeth and l'Hôtel-de-Ville with a garage blocking the way. The house's previous owners were Chinese, which may account for the oriental design. As the name states, AVENUE DE L'HÔTEL-DE-VILLE once led directly to City Hall. Most of the houses on the east side of the street, below La Gauchetière, were built in the early part of this century. They housed single families and gradually became rooming houses. In the last 15 years many have been remodelled by young professionals. The row houses on the east side of Hôtel-de-Ville may be designated by the province as architecturally important buildings; this would prevent new construction on the block.

THE CORNER OF DE BULLION AND LA GAUCHETIÈRE is the site of one of the area's few commercial buildings — the Sincere Real Estate brokerage company. It is owned by Kenneth Cheung who once ran for mayor; he's been trying for several years to get the area east of St-Laurent rezoned for more commercial development.

CENTRE HOSPITALIER SAINT-CHARLES BORROMÉE is on the north side of La Gauchetière between de Bullion and St-Dominique. This was originally, the Montreal General Hospital and the oldest part of the building dates from 1821. (In 1949, land was acquired north of the downtown area on the slopes of Mount Royal where a new Montreal General Hospital was built.) In 1956, this building reopened as a seniors' home; in 1968 it became a hospital for long term care and adult rehabilitation.

The Montreal Chinese Pentecostal Church is at 100 la Gauchetière E. The Chinese United Centre Building is at 1001 St-Dominique. It was built in 1984, primarily as a seniors' housing project and has an auditorium for local events.

At the end of the 19th century, the area around LA GAUCHETIÈRE AND ST-LAURENT was populated by English, Irish, French Canadians, and some Jews. St-Laurent was called Saint Lawrence the Main and was a major commercial street in Montreal. There were several department and hardware stores and rents were higher, so Chinese merchants set up their stores on la Gauchetière. Almost all immigrant groups spent some time in this area. Only the Chinese have remained.

During the 1940s, this was the seamiest side of the city. One columnist wrote "whether you're looking for a gal or a gun, a haircut or a hustler, a hock shop or a hamburger — you'll find it on St. Lawrence boulevard."

The area stagnated for decades. However, there have been many positive changes in the past few years. Vietnamese and new immigrants from Hong Kong have taken over much of St-Laurent between Viger and René-Lévesque. On Sundays, the area has a marvellous bazaar-like atmosphere. Grocers extend their stores onto the sidewalk with fresh fruits, imported canned goods and crates of thousand-year-old-eggs (actually, eggs which have been potted for about a month). On festival days, such as the August Moon, there are dragon dances, martial-art demonstrations, games of Chinese chess and firecrackers.

The Dart Coon Club is upstairs at 1072 Saint-Laurent. This organization is now a social club but was once part of the military arm of a now defunct political group, based in China, known as the Free Mason Society. The Chinese Free Masons were not linked to the international fraternal movement of Free Masons.

Herb Johnson's Band at the Chinese Paradise Grill,
57 La Gauchetière, in the late 1930s.
JOHN GILMORE FONDS, CONCORDIA UNIVERSITY ARCHIVES.

CONTINUE ALONG LA GAUCHETIÈRE These few blocks have been the heart of Chinatown since the early 1900s and are now a pedestrian mall between St-Laurent and Jeanne Mance. The arches and lamp standards were erected in 1982. The work was done by artists and architects within the community under the direction of the City of Montreal. Works on Saint-Urbain are based on Chinese mythology. A plaque to the Monkey King is taken from a Buddhist legend in which the monkey cunningly becomes king of the animals. A sculpted mural shows musicians marching toward paradise. Several engraved bronze paving stones solicit fortune, health and happiness.

THE PARK AT THE CORNER OF CLARK AND LA GAUCHE-
TIÈRE was named after China's modern-day founder, Dr. Sun Yat Sen — the only person the Chinese community could agree on.

There is a tiny courtyard fronted by Chinese style wrought-iron gates between 64 and 70 La Gauchetière. The oldest grocery store in the area is Sun Ling Lung at 72A La Gauchetière W. Several of the Chinese clans or family associations have social rooms on the second and third floors of the older buildings. One of the largest is the Lee Association at 90 La Gauchetière.

112 La Gauchetière was originally the Chevra Shaas synagogue, built in 1905. From 1940 to 1962 it was the site of the Montreal Chinese Hospital. The hospital moved quite far north to 7500 St-Denis; the community was relatively poor then and the land was cheap. Current plans foresee bringing the hospital, which is primarily for the elderly, back to Chinatown. It will probably take over most of the block on Viger Street, between du Bullion and l'Hôtel-de-Ville.

CLARK STREET is the only north-south block which still gives a sense of the old community with its many rooming houses, shops and private residences. Almost all of that first generation of stores and restaurants are gone. Two of the oldest, Leong Jung Produce and the Sun Sun restaurant closed recently, unable to compete with the new generation of Asian entrepreneurs.

An older building houses the Sun Ko Wah bookstore, 1001 Clark is the office of the practically moribund Chinese Nationalist League of Canada, a final whisper of the hope that Taiwan's government would eventually rule in Beijing. It is now a men's social club. The Chinese United Centre on La Gauchetière hopes to build a seven-storey Cultural Centre at 1086 Clark.

COMPLÈXE GUY-FAVREAU fills the block from St-Urbain to Jeanne-Mance along la Gauchetière. It's named for a former federal justice minister. In the early 1970s, the construction for this and the Palais des Congrès slightly farther west on La Gauchetière forced out hundreds of people. Guy-Favreau is the federal government's political counterpoint to the province's COMPLÈXE DESJARDINS, built on the other side of boulevard René-Lévesque.

The National Film Board has a lending library, theatre and regular presentations in Guy-Favreau. The YMCA also has a branch with an indoor jogging track, a swimming pool, and meeting rooms for community organizations. An interesting sidetrip takes you underground from Guy-Favreau to Complèxe Desjardins and into the cultural centre of Place des Arts.

The Guy-Favreau apartments overlooking La Gauchetière were built in the early 1980s. This is not public housing. Two-bedroom apartments can cost over $1000. Most of the tenants are young and single. Few are Chinese.

The Wing Building at the corner of La Gauchetière and Côté may be the oldest building in Chinatown. It was built in 1826 by James O'Donnel, the architect of the Notre Dame Basilica in Old Montreal. The Wing Building has been a military school, a paperbox factory and warehouse. Wing Hing Lung is a Chinese expression for "a long life" and Wing's is known for its fortune cookies and noodles. The company was founded by Arthur Lee who was born in Chinatown about 70 years ago. As a young man, he worked on Canadian Pacific's steamships and during one long trip arrived in Hong Kong. The first building he came to was a restaurant named Wing. He vowed that if he ever got back to Montreal and opened a business, it would also be called Wing's. To demonstrate his pride in Canada, Mr. Lee gave all his children names which include "Ga" — the first syllable in Canada as it is pronounced in Chinese.

The Free Presbyterian Church Building was at 985 Coté. Most of the building was constructed, as a church, in 1848 and arched windows are still visible from the south side. The building now houses several community organizations including the Chinese Family Services and a small bonsai store, on the fourth floor, which is open weekdays from 9:00 to 5:00 and Saturdays from 9:00 to 1:00. The elevator is slow, but it works. The Chinese Catholic Community Centre is at 979 Coté.

The Palais des Congrès and its large outdoor plaza abut la Gauchetière. The Palais was supposed to link Old Montreal with Chinatown. Instead it has been an effective barrier to further growth. On the other side of the plaza is RUE CHENNEVILLE. In the mid-19th century, this area was known as Little Dublin with enough Irish to support the construction of St. Patrick's Cathedral, a few blocks away on St-Alexandre.

The Chinese Catholic Mission of Saint-Esprit at 205 la Gauchetière W. was built in 1835 as the Secessionist Church of Scotland. From 1896 to 1936 it was known as the Chapelle Notre-Dame-des-Anges and from 1936 to 1944 as Saint-Cyrille and Saint Méthode. The original bell tower was built in 1872 and had two levels of columns. The one now on the Church was erected in 1957. The Church was classified as an historic site in 1977. The tableau of Christ and the apostles, behind the altar, was painted recently by Mrs. Zhang, a local artist. In 1990, her son painted the Stations of the Cross, displayed on the interior walls. Those accustomed to white, muscular, Renaissance-style saints may be pleasantly surprised at this simpler, more austere, Oriental interpretation.

Several community groups have offices in the Centre Uni de la Communauté Chinoise de Montréal / Montreal Chinese Community United Centre, at 211 La Gauchetière W. Several hundred seniors live here and there is also a room for showing videos and films from China.

The end of this tour is also near the historic beginning of Chinatown. In 1877 Jos Song Long opened Montreal's first Chinese hand laundry at 633 Craig St. West (now St-Antoine) at the corner of Saint-Georges (now Jeanne-Mance).

THE PLACE-D'ARMES MÉTRO STATION can be reached through the Palais des Congrès. While waiting for the Métro, notice the small but interesting exhibit on archaeological excavations in Old Montreal.

BOOKS AND FILMS

Beyond the Golden Mountain: Chinese Cultural Traditions in Canada, Ban Seng Hoe; Canadian Museum of Civilization, 1989.

The Chinese in Canada, Peter S. Li; Oxford University Press, Toronto, 1988.

Les Chinois à Montréal, 1877-1951, Denise Helly; Institut québécois de recherche sur la culture, 1987. A detailed study on the first Chinese Montrealers.

Foxspirit: A Woman in Mao's China, Zhimei Zhang, Véhicule Press, Montreal, 1992. A story, by a Chinese Montrealer, of life in China before and during the revolution.

Voices from Tiananmen Square, Mok Chui Yu, J.F. Harrison editors; Black Rose Books, Montreal, 1990. A powerful collection of writings by those who led student demonstrations in China.

Films about Chinese Montrealers include *My Name is Susan Yee* (NFB) Montreal as seen through the eyes of a ten-year-old Chinese-Canadian girl and *Silence into silence: Chinese Neighbourhood Society* (Vidéographe) about the role of women in Chinese Canadian family life. There are many short films based on Chinese folktales such as *Bamboo, Lions and Dragons* (NFB).

EUROPEAN MONTREAL

POPULATION: 510,000

MAJOR COMMUNITIES: Throughout Montreal.

SHOPPING: Boulevard St-Laurent (between Sherbrooke and Mount-Royal, also known as "the Main"), Monkland in NDG, Centre in Pointe Saint-Charles, Beaubien in Rosemont, West Island.

Study my dear brethren,
Think and read;
Learn what is foreign
But forget not your own.
　　　— From "Heroes" by Taras Shevchenko

In 1535, Jacques Cartier sailed into the Saint Lawrence on the saint's feast day and named the river after him. He became Montreal's first European visitor when he landed on a large island in the Saint Lawrence river. Cartier was looking for gold or at least a passage to the Orient and found an Indian settlement called Hochelaga, "the place of the beaver dam." Guided by natives, he climbed to the top of the island's small mountain, planted a cross, and called the land Mont Royal for the King of France. Thus, Montreal's history began as a strategically-located French outpost where settlers vied with Iroquois for control of the fur trade.

The first group of settlers arrived 350 years ago and the community grew slowly. Quebec City remained the administrative capital and main port for quite some time while Montreal was a fur trading centre. By the mid-1700s Montreal's population was about 5,000, almost all of whom lived in the area we now know as Old Montreal.

The British conquest of New France in 1760 was the beginning of the city's transformation to a major urban centre. By the 1830s it was home to 30,000 traders, merchants, and their families, most of whom had roots in England, Scotland or Ireland.

A few Germans had arrived with French forces in the late 1600s, but most Central and Eastern Europeans were attracted to Britain's North American colonies for two reasons: religious freedom and the availability of land. By the 1800s, there were German-speaking Protestant communities in the Maritimes and Upper and Lower Canada and German-speaking Mennonites were moving to the Prairies.

At the end of the 19th century, the new country of Canada was actively soliciting Europeans to settle the prairies. A list of favoured nationalities was created with British and American farmers at the top, followed by French, Belgian, Dutch, Scandinavians, Swiss, Finns, Russians, Austro-Hungarians, Germans, Ukrainians, and Poles. At the bottom of the list were Southern Europeans, those from the Middle East, Jews, Asians, Gypsies, and Blacks. Although the federal government wanted Europeans to farm in the West, after weeks of travelling Montreal was the first large city they came to; for many, this was their first and only stop.

In 1900, the Montreal's population was well over 300,000. The neighbourhood around St-Antoine and St-Laurent had gone from "Little Dublin" in the 1840s to "Little Italy" and was becoming more than a little Eastern Europe. By the 1930s, it was a culturally-rich but desperately-poor part of town. Most immigrants knew little about the country they had come to. Canada and the United States were simply part of a larger entity called North America. Newcomers to Montreal were surprised to find that they had stepped onto the stage of an ongoing drama.

Then as now, the subject was nationalism. The Roman Catholic church was waging a battle against modern liberalism. The image of Quebec, fostered by the Church, was of a pre-Conquest French

Canada: pastoral villages and homogeneous neighbourhoods with common values, shared traditions and no room for immigrants. The Irish, who arrived during the early 19th century, were barely acceptable because they were white *and* Catholic; although, being British, the Church felt they were potentially subversive.

Then there were others such as German Lutherans, Eastern Orthodox Ukrainians, and Hungarian socialists with different customs, religions and languages. The Church did little to make them feel at home. One Ukrainian immigrant said, "How could we make confession when the priest couldn't understand our language? We would cross ourselves three times and everybody else would just do it once." Priests were telling their parishioners not to rent houses to foreigners even as they sat beside them in church. Instead, new parishes were set up for ethnic communities and by 1928, one could receive communion in Italian, Ukrainian, Polish, Syrian, Hungarian, and Chinese.

Education posed a different problem. At first there was some accommodation and the largely French-speaking Catholic School Commission of Montreal (CÉCM) held classes in language, history and geography for Italians, Poles and Ukrainians. Soon, more than half of all immigrant children attended Catholic run schools; but by 1930 Quebec's political leaders were worried. Montreal's Mayor Camillien Houde described the schools as a "Tower of Babel where our own are losing their language and their faith." Immigrants who were not Roman Catholic began sending their children to the more welcoming but overwhelmingly English-speaking Protestant school system. In the 1960s, the pendulum began swinging the other way. Immigrants were faulted for not speaking French and for anglicizing their children. Freedom of choice ended and today almost all immigrant children attend French-language schools.

Immigration increased markedly after WWII as the Soviet Union, England and the United States redrew Europe's political map. All of a sudden there was, in Churchill's words, "an iron curtain" dividing Europe into an East and a West. Many did leave Western European countries like Germany and Holland and came to Canada because Europe was facing years of post-war economic hardship. Migration dwindled in the 1960s as their economies recovered, however Eastern European countries have not seen the same recovery. Recent years have been particularly difficult and more than ten thousand Europeans, mostly from Eastern Europe, have come to Montreal since 1986.

About one in four Montrealers has some European ancestry apart from British or French. However, this chapter, of *The Guide to Ethnic Montreal* is concerned with the substantial group of communities that have roots in Central and Eastern Europe.

Films about Montreal's European character include *Our Street was Paved with Gold*, (NFB) a history of immigrant Montreal from the docks through the Main; *Ukrainians in Quebec* (Les Courts Metrages) is a documentary with interviews from early immigrants; and *In Praise of Older Women*, (Astral Films) based on the book of the same name by Stephen Vizinczey. Tom Berenger (in an early role) plays a Hungarian refugee learning about life and love in Canada.

BALTIC (ESTONIAN, LATVIAN & LITHUANIAN)

These three neighbouring countries on the Baltic Sea were distinct nations between WWI and WWII. During WWII, Germany allowed the Soviet Union to occupy them and it was only in 1991 that they again achieved independence.

Most Baltic immigrants were WWII displaced persons ("DPS") who were brought to Canada as contract labourers for mines, logging camps and as domestic servants. They would work for a year and then be eligible for permanent residency and Canadian citizenship.

Lithuanians form most of Montreal's 5,000-member Baltic community. Many chose this city because they had previously lived in France; others felt Montreal comfortably combined elements of American and European life.

Estonian belongs to an ancient group of languages that include Finnish and Hungarian. Latvian (also known as Lettish) and Lithuanian have common roots as the last remnants of true Baltic languages. Here's how to say "thank-you" in each: *Tänan* (Estonian), *Paldies* (Latvian), *Aciu* — sounds like "achoo" (Lithuanian).

The Baltic Federation of Montreal, 550 33rd ave. (637-4348) coordinates activities among the three groups, works with government on behalf of Baltic countries and commemorates events such as the August 23, 1939 pact between Hitler and Stalin, which placed the Baltic States within the Soviet domain.

The radio program "Émission lituanienne" is broadcast on CFMB 1410 (483-2362). Locally published Latvian newspapers include **Journal letton MLB Zinotojas** (457-9832) which has published Canadian news in Latvian for 44 years, and the fortnightly **Lithuanian Independent** (366-6220) with news from the Baltics and a page or so of information in French and English.

BULGARIAN

Almost half of Montreal's 2,000 Bulgarians are recently-arrived refugees. Although it is trying to assist these newcomers, the established Bulgarian community, which came after WWII, has found it difficult understanding a younger generation reared under Communism.

The **Bulgarian-Canadian Cultural Organization** (733-2350) organizes social activities for the community.

Société culturelle Québec-Bulgarie (273-6095) brings Bulgarian culture to Quebecers and familiarizes new arrivals with life in Quebec. This is a diverse group of about 200 people, most of whom, while not Bulgarian, have lived in the Balkans, studied there or married Bulgarians. The Society organizes language classes and informal events such as dinners and wine tastings.

CZECHOSLOVAKIAN

Czechoslovakia is largely made up of the Czech and Slovak peoples and this linguistic and ethnic division is reflected in Montreal where about half identify themselves with one group or the other.

The community was much larger shortly after WWII, when many Germans and Russians preferred to be identified as Czechs. Today, most of the 6,000 or so Czechs live in western Montreal.

The **Czech Association of Canada**, 4605 West Broadway, Montreal West (489-7712) assisted newcomers to Canada at the turn of this century. Then, women found jobs as domestics while men travelled further west looking for work as farmhands. Today, with little immigration, the community's main concern is for its elderly. In November, the Association holds a fund-raising bazaar in Westmount's Victoria Hall.

DUTCH

The Kingdom of the Netherlands, commonly known as Holland, is one of the most densely populated countries in the world. For centuries, the Dutch migrated to territories in the East Indies which ended as their colonies became independent after WWII. Many may immigrated to Canada because Queen Juliana and her family found a haven here during WWII and because Canadian troops helped liberate the Netherlands.

There are about 12,000 Dutch in Montreal; the community seems to pride itself on assimilating as quickly as possible. Few Dutch Montrealers belong to any Dutch organization and most are married to partners who aren't Dutch. The community's biggest concern is its aging population for whom it has recently opened a home on the West Island.

Dutch business people stay in touch with each other through the **Canada-Netherlands Chamber of Commerce**, 300 St-Sacrement (288-4466). Important Dutch-based companies in Montreal include KLM Airline, Phillips Electronics, and DeKuyper distillers. A group of local Dutch businessmen, affiliated with the chamber, run Club Borrel Bitterballen which keeps up the Dutch tradition of jenevar and bitterballen: get-togethers with Holland-style gin and fried snacks.

Club Borrel Bitterballen is private, but it's easy to get your own group going. All it takes is the right kind of gin and snacks from Dutch specialty stores listed in the Food Sources section of this chapter. Jenever has a stronger flavour than English gin. De Kuypers makes it locally as Geneva gin; some local jenever experts claim that De Kuypers' version is stronger and has a more traditonal taste than what is now commonly available in Holland.

Each year, on April 30, the Netherland Consul-General holds a community event in honour of the birthday of the Queen of Holland. There is a Dutch tradition that on the evening of December 5, Sinterklas (Santa Claus) and his helper sail from Spain to the Netherlands. Dutch children leave shoes outside their doors hoping to wake up and find them filled with toys. In Montreal, there's no boat from Spain but the community throws a big party anyway. For information on where it's held, call the Jansens at 694-4728.

◆ ◆ ◆

GERMAN

After the English and French, German Canadians form the largest ethnic community in Canada. Most of Montreal's 45,000 Germans are "Auslandsdeutscher"; their families did not come from Germany but from other European countries and the United States.

The community had its official start in Montreal with the founding of the German Society in 1835. Although there were less than a hundred members, it was an exceptionally diverse group: doctors, clerks, a sheriff, a bailiff, a constable, butchers, merchants, tailors, grocers, a bookbinder, a painter, and several members who described their occupations simply as "gentlemen." They settled, as did the British, with businessmen residing between Notre Dame and Dorchester (René-Lévesque), skilled artisans living further south near the port and factories, and others moving to immigrant areas, principally along St-Laurent. Some moved up to Prince Arthur and Jeanne Mance where there was a Lutheran Church and also around Pine avenue and Hôtel de Ville where St. Barnabas, a German Catholic Church, was built. German organizations included the Teutonia which started as a glee club in the 1880s, and by the 1930s, was a social club where English, Scottish, Finnish and Scandinavian girls could meet German men.

The community remained fairly small until Germany's economic depression of the 1920s. Canada had placed Germans on its preferred list of immigrants and tens of thousands came here. They were skilled, urban and fairly well-educated and, rather than staying in the immigrant core of the Main, most went to Verdun, Notre Dame de Grace, Villeray, and particularly to the growing district of Rosemont where there were new, inexpensive two-storey flats.

While German immigration stopped during WWII, Canada became a sort of international prisoner depot with 26 internment camps of which the smallest held 300 men on Montreal's Saint

Helen's Island. At first, these camps were for Canadians of Japanese, Austrian, German and Italian origin who the government felt might be potential spies and traitors. The numbers grew dramatically when Britain, fearing a German invasion, sent over 37,000 prisoners including captured German soldiers, German Jews, and Nazi sympathizers!

At the end of wwii, Europe was awash with displaced persons, including millions of German refugees. 50,000 immediately came to Canada with another quarter-million immigrating after 1950. The flow only stopped when Germany's economy improved in the 1960s. Today, Montreal's German speaking community is elderly, highly assimilated, and has a low profile.

École allemande Alexander Von Humboldt, 216 promenade Victoria, Baie d'Urfé (457-2886). Alexander Von Humboldt was a German explorer and writer and German schools are often named after him. This private school, founded in 1980, has about 200 children who are fluent in German. The curriculum follows the German system and is popular with German speaking Montrealers as well as Swiss, Germans and Austrians who have been transferred to Quebec for a short time.

German Benevolent Society (486-1863) was formed over 150 years ago. It is a large volunteer network that has some German-speaking cultural events and assists local members of the community as well as German-speaking nationals who might have difficulties in Montreal. The Society holds a charity ball every year in February.

Goëthe Institute of Montreal, 418 Sherbrooke E. (499-0159) Goëthe Institutes, common in many countries, were originally set up by the German government as cultural centres for those who do not speak German. Montreal's institute shows films from Germany and has exhibitions and concerts as well as German language courses and a library with books, records, videos and tapes in German, French and English.

Librarie Allemand (845-7489) is a German-language bookstore at the same address.

HUNGARIAN

Hungarians arrived in Canada in several distinct waves with the first group settling on the prairies where they called their new homes 'Beke Var' — Fortresses of Peace. In the Depression of the 1930s, Hungarian labourers migrated to the cities seeking work, after WWII an educated elite fled Communist Hungary. These newcomers spoke German but little English or French and were not well accepted because many French Canadians believed they were fascists while the Church was convinced they were socialists. However, English Montreal was more receptive and post-war Hungarian immigrants moved into the western parts of the city.

Those who came to Montreal during, and shortly after, the Hungarian revolt of 1956 had an easier time and many lived on boulevard St-Laurent — 'the Main' — below Pine avenue. In recent years, as with other European communities which have become anglicized, the young have left Montreal and their parents are now leaving to be with them. Today, community leaders estimate there may be less than 12,000 Hungarians in Montreal, about half the size it was in the late 1960s.

Traces of the old boulevard St-Laurent community remain with the **Csarda Restaurant** 3479 St-Laurent (843-7519), the **Slovenia Meat Market** at 3653 St-Laurent (842-3558), and the **St. Stephens Club** at 3463 St-Laurent (844-9686). St. Stephen, Hungary's patron saint, united the Magyars (Hungarians) under Christianity over a thousand years ago.

The community celebrates Hungary's 1848 independence from Austria on March 15 and the 1956 Hungarian Revolt on October 23. St. Stephen's Ball is an important social event and debutante

ball which raises money for a university scholarship fund, Hungarian language courses at McGill University, and Foyer Hongrois —
a seniors' home.

The **Comité hongrois de Montreal**, 2580 St-Jacques W.
(934-1777) brings together 22 different Hungarian cultural
groups.

POLISH

For hundreds of years other nations have claimed parts of Poland
as their own. When North America opened up in the late 1800s,
most of Poland was under Austrian or Russian rule and hundreds
of thousands of Poles eagerly emigrated to Canada. As Roman
Catholics, those who came to Montreal were more easily accepted
than other Eastern Europeans.

Another hundred thousand Poles came in two waves following
WWII. The first group were a mixed group of intellectuals, concentration camp survivors, refugees, and Polish soldiers who were
in Western Europe at the end of the war. Another wave fled
Communist Poland in the 1950s, 60s, and 70s. In the last few years
well-educated workers and students have left Poland for political
and economic reasons. There are about 28,000 Poles in Montreal.
While Canada has changed its policy and no longer accepts people
from Poland as refugees, there are still over a thousand Poles in
Montreal (the largest number, by far, of any European group)
waiting for the government to decide their status.

Each immigrant group has established its own community in a
different part of the city, usually where there was good inexpensive
housing when it arrived. Pointe St-Charles still has Polish stores
dating from the 1920s and east end Montreal was home to many
Poles such as the noted poet and critic Louis Dudek. After WWII,

the Main and Mile End areas (between St-Laurent and Park avenue) attracted Poles and other European immigrants. The Roman Catholic church of St. Michael the Archangel at the corner of St-Urbain and St-Viateur has been a Polish church for 25 years. In recent years, more Polish newcomers have settled in Lachine, Notre-Dame-de-Grâce and Rosemont. May 3 is celebrated as Solidarity Day, honouring the labour union Solidarnosc and commemorating the start of democratic reform in Poland.

A Statue of Copernicus stands in front of the Dow Planetarium, Peel and St-Antoine. Niklas Koppernigk, or Nicolaus Copernicus, was the 16th century Polish astronomer who demonstrated that the Earth revolved around the sun. The statue was erected in 1967 by the Polish community to commemorate three anniversaries: Canada's centennial year, Montreal's 325th anniversary and 1000 years of Christianity in Poland.

Polish Canadian Congress of Quebec, 5175 Cote-Saint-Luc, (486-6595) started in 1942 and now represents about 30 Polish groups. It provides assistance to seniors and families and is now chiefly concerned with assisting recently-arrived Poles still waiting for their claims as refugees to be processed. Recently, the Congress has been sending Polish-Canadian urban planners and business people to Poland to assist in the reconstruction of the Polish economy.

Polish Library, 3479 Peel (398-6978) Open Monday — 10:00 a.m. to 8:00 p.m., Thursday — 4:00 to 8:00 p.m., and Saturday — 2:00 to 6:00 p.m. This 50 year-old-library is open to everyone and has over 35,000 books in Polish, English and French on Polish history, language and culture. It also stocks newspapers from Poland and has a large selection of Polish books on audio-tape.

Polish Society of the White Eagle, 1956 Frontenac (524-3116). Established in 1902, this is one of the oldest, active European organizations in Montreal. It started as a social group and has been in the same building, near Notre-Dame-de-Czestochowa

Catholic Parish, since 1929. Today, most of its members are seniors.

ROMANIAN

In 1903, about a hundred Romanians were living near St-Laurent and Iberville; today there are about 5,000 people in the community which is organized through its parishes. The first, Saint-Trinité, was created in 1912 and soon after that the Church of Sainte-Marie de l'Annonciation was built at the corner of Chapleau and Rachel. In 1972 this church was rebuilt on the corner of Christophe Colombe and Jarry, but the community became divided and created another parish, St-Jean Baptiste, with a church on the corner of Masson and Papineau.

In 1982 a $1,000,000 community centre opened at 8060 Christophe-Colombe next to the Romanian Orthodox Church. In recent years over a thousand newcomers have arrived from Romania. Local events are broadcast on weekly Romanian language radio program on CFMB 1410. The **Fédération des Associations Rumaines du Canada**, 3500 Fullum (521-1777) acts as an umbrella organization for Romanian cultural groups.

A large part of the Jewish community also has roots in Romania and for several years there was a Montreal Romanian-Jewish Organization. Until WWII, **Moishe's Steak House**, 3961 St-Laurent (845-3509) was called Moishe's Romanian Paradise.

UKRAINIAN

The Ukrainian homeland, north of the Black Sea, was part of the Soviet Union for most of this century and is now an independent republic within the Commonwealth of Independent States. The

Ukraine has always been a rich farming area with few natural borders. The Soviets were only the most recent rulers and, except for a few years following WWI, the Ukraine had not been independent since the 13th century.

In the 1800s, most Ukrainians were serfs (impoverished tenant farmers) and Ukrainian leaders decided they had to settle their people elsewhere. First they tried Brazil and tens of thousands migrated there in 1890 where, unused to the tropics, they barely survived. In 1891, a couple of peasants settled in Canada and wrote back that land here was cheap and plentiful. Soon Ukrainians were arriving by the boatload, encouraged by agents who travelled through Eastern Europe giving $5 to men and $2 to women and children to assist their move to Canada.

Most Ukrainians settled, as they had planned, on the Prairies; others arrived broke and Montreal became their new home. The Ukrainian Society for the Protection of Immigrants existed from 1904-1906. When Ukrainian immigrants arrived in Montreal, this group would seek them out and persuade many to stay here rather than continuing west to a farm.

By the 1930s, almost 4,000 Ukrainians lived in Pointe Saint-Charles in the south-west part of the city. Other popular areas were Frontenac in the east-end, Lachine and Côte-St-Paul in the south-west and Rosemont, Ahuntsic, and St-Michel north of the downtown core. Many Ukrainians anglicized their names. Yuriy became George, Iwan was John and Andruch changed to Andrew. Some kept Ukrainian names at home and used Canadian names outside. Family names changed as well. Holodiwski might become Holden and Krushelniski, Krush.

Most were unskilled workers. One man started a window cleaning company and brought in others who learned the trade and in turn set up their own operations. By the mid-1930s, almost half of all window cleaning companies in the city were Ukrainian owned and staffed.

In 1917, a Ukrainian church was built on Iberville street, but not until 1930 did the Orthodox Church receive a charter from the Quebec Government. Until then, the priest had no authority to perform marriages, christenings or burial rites. To get the charter, the community had to prove to the provincial government that Ukrainians weren't Communist. This wasn't an easy task since the community had split into several ideological groups such as the Ukrainian Farm Labour Temple Association which declared that the Ukraine's future lay within the U.S.S.R.

The federal government was particularly suspicious of Ukrainians. If they came from the Soviet Union they were considered Communists. During WWI Austria held much of the Ukraine and Ukrainians who were not Canadian citizens became enemy aliens. Several thousand were interned under the War Measures Act and some were arrested when they tried to enlist in the Canadian army. On the other hand many Ukrainian Montrealers had fought in the brief Ukrainian revolt against the Russians at the end of WWI and, on Sundays, it was easy to find community halls holding "lectures, debates, dramas, musical banquets, protests against Polish government 'pacification' campaigns on Soviet persecution or the dangers of Communism."

While the opposing forces made for a stimulating brew, they prevented the community from presenting a united front to the federal government. With the outbreak of WWII, the Canadian government actually stepped in and, to ensure unity and a high enlistment in the armed forces, set up the Ukrainian National Committee which exists today as the **Ukrainian Congress of Canada** at 3244 Beaubien St. E. (593-1000).

After WWII, between 35,000 and 40,000 Ukrainian displaced persons were resettled in Canada. Most moved to cities in Ontario and Quebec and took a long time to integrate into the established Ukrainian community. These newcomers felt that they had been forced to come here and believed they would return to the Ukraine as soon as it was independent from the U.S.S.R.

In 1947 a Ukrainian church was built in Pointe Saint-Charles, at the corner of Grand Trunk and Shearer. The community gradually moved away and many people re-settled in Rosemont. In 1991 the Ukrainian community celebrated 100 years in Canada. With a strong community of about 20,000, it has retained its distinctiveness, more than other Eastern European groups, through adherence to the Eastern Orthodox Church, through its distinct language, and through its unwavering support for liberating the Ukrainian republic from the Soviet Union.

■■ UKRAINIAN EASTER EGGS

These are usually chicken eggs and, when properly painted, they can last for years. As the work begins, the artist traditionally makes the sign of the cross and prays "God help me!" so that the designs' religious meaning is passed on to those who see the eggs Easter morning. Complex artwork may take days to finish and if an egg breaks, the shell is usually buried at a cemetery or other holy ground. If left for too long in direct light, they may explode so store painted eggs carefully. Egg painting courses are taught at Montreal's Ukrainian Orthodox churches. For more information, call Ukrainian Adaptations (272-8050).

At Easter, paska (raisin loafs molded into fancy shapes) and decorated Easter eggs are displayed and blessed by the priest.

Ukrainian Folk Ensemble (334-1740) teaches traditional Ukrainian dances and performs at community events.

YUGOSLAV

Until recently Yugoslavia was made up of the republics of Serbia, Croatia, Bosnia and Herzegovina, Macedonia, Slovenia, and Montenegro each of which existed as Kingdoms for centuries. Yugoslavia itself was a modern state, formed as Europe redefined itself after WWI, and became a federal republic of six states under Tito's Communist government in 1945. Tito died in 1980; many feel he kept the country together. Simmering ethnic tensions boiled over as the Soviet Union retreated from Eastern Europe and there has been civil war since Croatia and Slovenia declared independence in 1991.

Most of the Montreal's 6,000 Yugoslavs are Croatian who immigrated to Montreal in the 1960s. In the last few years, several hundred Croatians have come to Montreal, many of them seeking refugee status.

The **Association catholique croate Saint-Nicolas-Tavelic** 4990 Place de la Savane (739-7497) helps newcomers translate information, provides social services and aids in meetings with government officials. The association houses a community school teaching the language, culture, history, music and dance of Croatia. Community events include April 10th Independence Day, May 12th Mother's and Father's Day and in November a religious feast honouring the patron saint of the church, St-Nicolas, who was martyred in Jerusalem four centuries ago. In August, Croatia day is marked with a picnic and activities in the park behind the Church.

The Serbian community has a community centre next to the **Serbian Orthodox Church** at 349 Melville in Westmount (932-8529). The folklore dance group, Avala operates out of the community centre.

◆ ◆ ◆

RESTAURANTS AND CLUBS

$ indicates that a lunch or dinner should cost under $ 1 0 (without taxes, tips, or wine). $$ is under $25 and $$$ above that. Credit cards accepted are listed. Hours often vary with the seasons so please call ahead.

ALPENHAUS $$ VISA MC AMEX DINERS EN-ROUTE
1279 St-Marc (935-2285)

■ A downtown landmark for 25 years. Nothing fancy, just solid Swiss staples like fondues, schnitzels, and excellent desserts. In the winter Alpenhaus holds a "festival" with specials on beef, cheese, chocolate, and Chinese-style fondues.

BERLIN $$ EN-ROUTE MC VISA
101 Fairmont W. (270-7398)

■ Local Germans came here to celebrate the dismantling of the Berlin wall. The restaurant gets a youngish crowd and the big draw is the beer: two dozen imported from Germany, Holland, Denmark, and even New Zealand. The menu is hearty, home-style Hamburgian cooking (the owner's mother, who is from northern Germany, cooks in the back): fresh cakes and strudels, kasespatzle (noodles with cheese), vegetable gulasch, currywurst (two thick sausages with a curry sauce); the Wurstplatte has three different spicy sausages, sauerkraut and fried potatoes, apple schnapps and a fresh house dressing. There are salads, chicken and fish dishes like fried or steamed trout and a marinated herring appetizer; but most of the fare is fairly heavy, so Berlin tends to be packed in the winter and not too busy when the weather is warm.

CAFE TOMAN $
1421 Mackay (844-1605)

■ A lovely second-floor Old World café with sumptuous marzipan, chocolate, pastries and other desserts (to eat here or take out). The orange chocolate mousse is dense and delicious. The creamy hazelnut cake is superb and the hot chocolate and coffee are excellent. The virtuous can start with tasty but simple luncheon fare like home-made vegetable soup and a liverwurst sandwich; but, oh my, those desserts!

CHESA $$ MC VISA AMEX EN-ROUTE
5136 Decarie (486-1723)
■ Nice if you are in the area or returning to the city after a day of skiing. Unpretentious, comfortable Swiss-style restaurant with posters of the Alps and good fondues, locally made air dried beef, and an excellent smoked ham. The desserts are not made on the premises and can be passed.

CRACOVIE $ AMEX MC VISA
1246 Stanley (866-2195)
■ First cousin to the Mazurka with good stick-to-the-ribs Polish food at pre-perestroika prices. Bigos (a rich cabbage and meat stew), smoked sausage, and perogy dumplings. Daily specials are filling. The "Polish plate" has a sampling of several dishes.

CSARDA $$ VISA MC
3479 St-Laurent (843-7519)
■ For more than 30 years Csarda has served good, solid Hungarian cooking: Matzoh bouillon, cauliflower soup, beef goulash served with little dumplings of nockerli, spiced braised beef with mushrooms in a paprika sauce, and heavily paprikaed cabbage rolls stuffed with pork and rice. Excellent desserts include walnut cake, apple squares and palanchinka (crepes) filled with sweetened cheese, poppy seeds and walnuts.

MAZURKA $ AMEX EN-ROUTE MC VISA
64 Prince Arthur E. (844-3539)
■ For 35 years, Montrealers have enjoyed inexpensive, hearty Polish cooking here. The menu is extensive but almost everyone seems to be eating perogy — wonderful stuffed dumplings

(cheese, meat or potato) or latkes (potato pancakes). The soups and schnitzel are also superb.

OLD MUNICH $$ (open from 4:00 p.m. Thursday to Sunday)
1170 St-Denis (288-8011)
■ A huge German beer hall, lederhosen, Bavarian decor and an oompapa band. It's a polka lovers' paradise attracting all ages of people for a boisterous evening of dancing, singing and drinking. Sure, there's food (like bland wiener schnitzel and German sausages); but its the beer, the trolley of schnapps, and the next chorus of "Roll out the Barrel" that have kept crowds coming here for 25 years.

PLANICA $$ AMEX EN-ROUTE MC VISA
5325 Garland Place (737-1611)
■ A stuccoed country inn with Yugoslav cooking in the Snowdon district. Appetizers include grilled peppers, sausage, freshly smoked salmon, and crunchy krapki (minced mushroom and ham croquettes). Main dishes vary from good to excellent. Weiner schnitzel and the untranslated mixed grills (cvapcici, pcjeskavica, and raznjici) are superb as are thickly cut rounds of fried potatoes and a salad of thinly-sliced melt-in-the-mouth potato. Platters of palacinka (soft crepes) are stuffed with meat, cheese, or vegetables. Ask what the chef is concocting in the kitchen (dessert placinkas with melted dark chocolate and freshly whipped cream on one good night). Other desserts include apple strudel, walnut torte and gibanica (layers of poppy-seed, cottage cheese and raisin wrapped in strudel dough). Good coffee.

STASH'S RESTAURANT BAZAAR $$ VISA MC AMEX
461 St-Sulpice (861-2915)
■ An old Montreal favourite for over 20 years. Good, plentiful Polish cooking which includes a marvellous white borscht made with fermented rye flour, excellent perogy dumplings and several

main course dishes. The Polish Primer is a good three course introduction to a half dozen dishes. Save room for desserts, particularly the layered cakes and apple squares. Reopening this summer after a recent fire.

WILLIAM TELL $$ AMEX EN-ROUTE MC VISA
2055 Stanley (288-0139)
■ Charming downtown Swiss restaurant. Good veal dishes, excellent fondues and desserts. A good place to enjoy traditional raclette — scrapings from a half-wheel of melting cheese served with boiled potatoes and assorted condiments.

FOOD SOURCES

DUTCH MILL, 4890A Sources Blvd. (684-5823). Over 20 years old, and until recently on Côte-des-Neiges, this small family-run store has several kinds of gouda cheeses and other foods imported from Holland. A good place to get snacks of bitterballen (beef croquettes) and other Dutch specialties.

EURO-PLUS, 279B Bord-du-Lac, Point Claire Village Shopping Centre (694-4728). Netherlands-on-the-West-Island: Dutch mustards, superb chocolates, nine kinds of herring, smoked eel (from Quebec waters, but cured in Holland!), Indonesian foods, and, since Euro-plus' owners are cheese wholesalers, some of the best prices on the island for imported cheeses. The sharp-tasting Krimelkaas (crumbly-cheese) gouda is aged for four years.

BOUCHERIE HONGROISE, 3843 St-Laurent (844-6734). Slabs of pork ribs, bacon, and prosciutto (aged and dated) hang above the counter — all made on the premises by Angelol. The refrigeration unit holds freshly-made wursts (the smoked liverwurst is superb) and coldcuts made here which you won't find elsewhere. Munch lunch standing up from a steam-table of sausages, veal and pork cutlets, and smoked ham thinly-sliced for sandwiches.

CHARCUTERIE SYRENA, 788 Décarie Ville St-Laurent (748-9464). There are coldcuts and other delicatessen fare; but save the calories for dense rich Polish cakes stuffed with apples or baked with cheese and chocolate; imported jams, syrups and candies; and seasonal dishes like blueberry or sour cherry perogy.

KRAK, 5962 Monkland (481-9833). Krakovian (as from the city of Kracow in Poland) pastries are made downstairs and the hams, smoky Kielbasa sausage and salamis are culled from half a dozen local Polish butchers. The freshly-made doughnuts are worth the trip.

MARIANNE DELICATESSEN, 4355 St. Laurent (842-5778). A small Polish delicatessen filled with pirogies, Baltic sourdough bread, imported jams, cold cuts and sausages. Good one-stop shopping for a picnic on the mountain.

ROSEMONT-PATISSERIE POLONAISE, 2894 Rosemont (728-7711), open from Tuesday to Sunday. A small, friendly, Polish bakery — sourdough and wholewheat breads, cheese cakes, cake with thick layers of poppy seeds, donuts, and some Polish imports.

SLOVENIA MEAT MARKET, 3653 St-Laurent (842-3558). Old-fashioned delicatessen with imported foods from Yugoslavia and succulent, hot sausage sandwiches.

VIEILLE EUROPE, 3855 St-Laurent (842-5773). Browsers heaven, it's dangerous to walk through the doors on an empty stomach: smoked meats, racks of sausages, mountains of cheeses at very good prices, caviar, coffees roasted on the premises, pastas and patés.

WAYNE'S DELICATESSEN, 1766 Centre Pointe-Saint-Charles (931-9855), closed Mondays. The store is 60 years old (Wayne is

Slovenia Meat Market.
PHOTO BY NEAL DAVID HÉBERT

the latest owner) and has always catered to the area's Eastern European community. Excellent rolls and baked goods (the cheese cake is superb) and Wayne's own smoked kielbasa sausage is among the best in the city. Also in the area are **European Sausage**'s factory store, 1746 Richmond (932-4545) and **Quebec Smoked Meat Products**, 1889 Centre (935-5297).

ZAGREB, 3766 St-Laurent (844-3265). Central European delicatessen with a large variety of smoked meats and sausages.

◆ ◆ ◆

SHOPS AND SERVICES

ARKA, 3656 St. Laurent (842-3496). Clothing, Ukrainian books, fabric, china with unique Ukrainian designs in black and red, painted wooden eggs. 'Hocul' wood carvings, Ukrainian newspapers, tapes, books and videos.

B.C. PROMOTIONS, 7360 Terrebonne (481-2447). Hungarian book distributor with several titles in French and English.

UKRAINIAN ADAPTATIONS GIFT SHOP, 2306A Rosemont (272-8050). Imported giftware, table cloths, hand decorated eggs by the carton, postcards and paintings with vignettes of cossacks, birch trees and cabbages.

UKRAINIAN WALKING TOUR

Start at Beaubien and 12th avenue
(bus 67 from Métro Beaubien or bus 18 East from Métro St-Michel)
End at Parc de l'Ukraine

THIS WALK BEGINS ON THE CORNER OF 12TH AVENUE AND BEAUBIEN, a few blocks south of the St-Michel Métro station.

For many of us, Montreal is North America's European city and it is folly to suggest that there are only one or two areas where European communities have formed. As groups settled, most neighbourhoods gradually fused into larger cosmopolitan districts. Some, like the south-west working-class district of Pointe St-Charles, have a few older stores and churches — memories of when the area echoed with more Polish and Ukrainian than French or English; while other parts of the city, such as Rosemont and along boul. St-Laurent, maintain their identities.

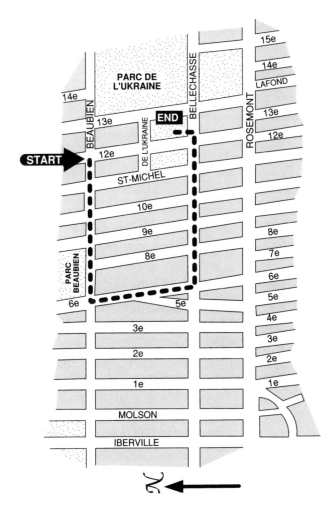

Throughout the late 19th and early 20th century, Eastern European communities were established wherever there was work and, in 1904, settlement began in the east end of the city when the Canadian Pacific Railway (CPR) opened up ten blocks of locomotive factories along Rosemont boulevard. Rosemont itself didn't last long. It was really a developer's dream, created in 1905 from two adjacent smaller villages and then incorporated into the city of Montreal a few years later. Much of the land was owned by a local businessman, Ucal-Henri Dandurand who named the town after his mother Rose. Dandurand made a fortune in real estate when the CPR set up its factory and shops in the area. His newspaper ads were not too subtle. "You want to make money?" they screamed "You can make barrels of money. Buy land in Rosemont!"

During the area's industrial peak, Rosemont stretched from the villages of St-Michel and St-Léonard in the north to CPR's Angus shopyards. Today the district's northern border is Rosemont boulevard with boulevard Saint-Michel to the east, Rachel street to the south and de Lorimier avenue to the west.

Since the 1930s, the Ukrainians have been the largest non-French ethnic group in Rosemont. They settled there after living for several years in other parts of the city, particularly Pointe Saint-Charles where heavy industry developed along the canal and in the lower boul. St-Laurent area. After WWI, many immigrants moved away from the Main to eastern Montreal where there was employment in new plants like Montreal Light, Heat and Power and the Montreal Locomotive Works.

By 1931, many of Montreal's 4,000 Ukrainians were moving into the eastern part of the city; but landlords, encouraged by the Catholic Church, were reluctant to rent to them. The Church was concerned that its authority would be undermined by a large concentration of immigrants adhering to a different religion and tried to keep the community small and diffuse. However, Ukrainians created a neighbourhood with churches, financial institutions, community halls, and shops; one that has existed for over 60 years.

EUROPEAN SAUSAGE IS ON THE CORNER OF 12TH AND BEAUBIEN. The company has been making sausages in Pointe Saint-Charles since 1929. There is a variety of hams and salamis, European breads, perogy (stuffed dumplings), pastries and Ukrainian and Polish magazines and newspapers.

WALK WEST ON BEAUBIEN. The Ukrainian Community Centre is at 3260 Beaubien E. Next door is the Caisse Populaire Ukrainienne which has served the community for over 40 years; and, across the street, the Caisse Économique Ukrainienne. The Caisse Populaire also sells books in Ukrainian and posts information on community events.

Paska Travel is next door. Travel agencies have traditionally been more than just a place to arrange travel plans; they helped newly-arrived immigrants with government forms, arranged for money to be sent back home, and advised on how to bring the rest of the family over. They were information and translation centres and 'middlemen' to government and municipal bureaucrats.

Further west, at 3186 Beaubien is Charcuterie Europe, another old style delicatessen with thick slabs of smoky bacon and a counter full of cured meats. Eastern Europeans brought with them many of the delicacies Montrealers now take for granted: bagels, hard spicy salamis, brined vegetables like sour pickles and sauerkraut and, of course, smoked meat.

The large complex under construction on 8th Avenue is a new addition to a seniors' residence recently completed by the Ukrainian community. In the foyer are notices of bazaars and community events. Sometimes, it is possible to walk through this centre, to the St-Marc seniors' residence on 6th Avenue. If not, return to Beaubien and walk down 6th.

TURN LEFT ON 6TH. The COFI Maurice Lefebvre is at 6361 6th Avenue. A COFI is an orientation and French language teaching centre for new immigrants. Recent arrivals study full time in a 30-week course, paid by the Quebec government. The COFI Maurice Lefebvre was opened in 1980 and is named to honour a Quebec priest who was killed in Bolivia while working for social justice.

Incidentally, the house at 6245 5th St., at the v-shaped intersection of 5th and 6th, may be the narrowest in Montreal.

TURN LEFT (EAST) ON BELLECHASSE. This is a lovely residential neighbourhood, yet within walking distance of the Canadian Pacific's huge shops in the Angus yards and the Frontenac yards, both several blocks south.

The Ukrainian Catholic Church of the Assumption of the Blessed Virgin Mary is near the corner of Bellechasse and boul. St-Michel. It was built in 1955. In front of the church is a large monument that was erected in 1988 to commemorate the millennium of Christian worship in the Ukraine.

The Ukrainian Orthodox Cathedral, St-Sophia, is across the way, at 6255 St-Michel. It was built in 1960 and named for both St. Sophia in Kiev and the 6th century mother church in Istanbul. It has the distinctive byzantine architecture of the onion dome and ornate, gilded interior. The acoustics are wonderful and if you happen to enter as the choir is singing, there is an almost ethereal quality to the sound which seems to emanate from everywhere. Equally marvellous is the smaller and more intimate service at the Orthodox Church of St-Mary the Protectress, a kilometre (about a ½ mile) further west at 2246 Rosemont.

Adjacent to the Church is Parc de l'Ukraine at the corner of Avenue de l'Ukraine and St-Michel Boulevard, a nice place for a picnic.

The walk ends here, but there is much to see in the area. Along Rosemont, a kilometre further east, is the massive recreational complex that includes Parc Maisonneuve, the Botanical Gardens and the Olympic Stadium.

To the west, along Rosemont, but past boulevard St-Michel, are shops and stores including an interesting, little Ukrainian store — Ukrainian Adaptations at 2306A Rosemont. It's a family enterprise specializing in the traditional Ukrainian hand-painted (by local artists) eggs known as 'pysanka'; and there are egg-painting kits for those who prefer to do it themselves. Every Easter the Leluch family, which owns the store, demonstrate the craft at the Queen

Elizabeth and Château Champlain hotels. The family also imports porcelain and decorates it with the traditional red and white cross-stitch of Ukrainian designs.

THE ROSEMONT MÉTRO STATION is best reached by the westward bound 197 bus.

GREEK MONTREAL

POPULATION: 51,000

MAJOR COMMUNITIES: Park Extension and Mile End, Laval,
West Island, South Shore

SHOPPING: Park Extension

Greeks have wandered the earth from the time of Ulysses. The first
to visit Canada was probably one of Samuel de Champlain's explorers, a man known to us only as "Le Grec." The first Greeks to really
settle in Montreal were also sailors. They left their ships, married
French-Canadians, and were subsumed into Quebec life. We know
little about the early Greek community in Montreal but by the
mid-19th century, several men from the Peloponnesus were living
near the port. More followed, some from the town of Kastoria,
known for its fur trade, found work here as furriers. A few
entrepreneurs discovered Quebec's sweet tooth and began selling
syrupy Greek pastries like baklava. The Great Eastern Greek
Confectionary Company set up on St-Paul street and was showing
its products at the Quebec exhibition of 1877.

Greece, which was under Turkish rule for over 350 years,
became an independent monarchy in 1829. Greeks who remained
in countries that were still part of the Ottoman Empire felt
persecuted but many who moved to North America were unprepared for life in a large city like Montreal. They didn't speak French
or English and found everything difficult: urban life, the climate,
and even the religion since Orthodox rites were unknown here. A
Greek community formed around Dorchester (now René-
Lévesque) and St. Lawrence Main Street (now boul. St-Laurent
but still called "The Main").

New immigrants often worked in Greek-owned restaurants
since it was easier to work for someone who understood the

culture and spoke the same language. After a few years and a little saving, the newcomer would open his own coffeeshop, ice cream parlour or lunch counter. By 1921, with a community of less than 2,000 people, Greeks operated over a third of the 150 restaurants owned by ethnics. In comparison, Italians, with 15,000 people, owned 14 restaurants.

During wwii, Greece was occupied by soldiers from Germany, Italy and Bulgaria. Montreal's Greek community rallied to support the resistance and organized its own Red Cross chapter to support the war effort. After the war, antagonism between those supporting the Greek monarchy and the Communists increased. Greece erupted in a civil war which lasted until 1949; it devastated the country and left a quarter of the adult population unemployed.

By 1955, as many as 3,000 Greek immigrants were arriving in Montreal each year, most were unskilled workers who dreamt of making money and returning home. Many attempted to do this but, like the family of Christos Sirros, Quebec's Minister for Native Affairs, they moved back and forth several times before finally returning here to stay.

The Greek community quickly outgrew the Main and moved to newer, affordable housing to the north. Greeks became dominant in Mile End, which stretches along Park Avenue, and further north in Park Extension — an area between Jean-Talon and the Metropolitain expressway.

It was during this post-war period that the Greek community began to identify with Anglo Montreal. This was a subtle process since most newcomers were sponsored by friends or relatives and, in the 1950s and 1960s, they did not have to know French or English to immigrate. Those who didn't work for Greeks, usually ended up in the garment trade working for English-speaking Jews. Public schools in Quebec fall under denominational boards and, not being Catholic, most Greek children went to Protestant schools, which were mostly taught in English. By 1980, over 20%

of students in PSBGM schools were from Greek families. This demographic shift sparked the provincial government to create language legislation requiring children of new immigrants to attend schools where instruction was in French.

During the 1970s, the profile of the Greek community began changing. Recently arrived immigrants had worked in European industrial cities, acquiring skills and organizational abilities, they understood urban living and many of them spoke English and French. The election of the Parti Québecois, in 1976, also slowed the community's growth as many Greek families joined the exodus of English-speaking Montrealers out of the province. At the same time, Greece was changing considerably. In 1967, "the colonels" had taken over the government in a junta under Col. George Papadopoulos. Democracy was restored in 1974 and by 1976 Greece had more stability than it had known in decades. Immigration to Quebec dropped to a few hundred a year and has remained at that level.

The community is still evolving. Greek-Montrealers born here now outnumber those who immigrated from Greece. The leaders of this new generation are trilingual professionals committed to life in Montreal and are less interested in maintaining the ties that bound their parents to Greece.

March 25 is Independence Day and commemorates the end of centuries of Turkish rule in 1821. Celebrations are usually held on the Sunday closest to this date with a mass and procession from Evangelismos church at 777 St-Roch in Park Extension and a parade through the area.

RELIGION

The Orthodox and Roman Catholic churches of Christianity became independent of each other in the 11th century. The Orthodox church is Eastern or Greek Orthodox and has its Patriarch in

Constantinople. Orthodox priests can marry and adherents reject papal claims such as infallibility, the immaculate conception and purgatory. Within orthodoxy, most follow the Gregorian calendar, introduced by Pope Gregory XIII in the 16th century and accepted by the Orthodox faith in 1923. A minority of churches adhere to the older Julian calendar, feeling that the Gregorian is a concession to Catholicism and the authority of the Pope in Rome.

In the 1960s and 1970s, the Orthodox Church tried to increase its hold in communities throughout North America. Montreal's Hellenic Community was the only community in North America to successfully challenge this authority. The bishop is based in Toronto and is committed to the spiritual growth of the church, but the Hellenic Community owns the land and directs non-religious affairs in all local new calendar churches. These are the Cathedral of Saint-Georges at 2455 Côte Ste-Catherine, Saint-Jean-Baptiste at 5220 Grande-Allé in Saint-Hubert, and Koimisis Tis Theotokou at 7700 de l'Épée and Évangelismos Tis Theotokou at 777 St-Roch. Each church has a choir, a women's welfare auxiliary, and youth groups.

In 1986, fire destroyed the 94 year-old Holy Trinity Greek Orthodox church at the corner of Sherbrooke and St-Laurent. Almost everything, including priceless religious artifacts, was lost. The Hellenic Community hopes to build a community centre on the property.

ORGANIZATIONS

The Greek community is one of the most extensively organized in Montreal. The pillars of Hellenism are history, culture, language, and religion; even at the turn of this century there was a Greek school, a community centre and a church.

After WWII, newcomers became exasperated with existing organizations. The Greek establishment controlled the Koinotita, the community's governing body. A community split widened after the colonels' coup in 1967 with older members of the community supporting the dictatorship while the newcomers, including many political exiles, created competing organizations.

In the early 1970s, the federal government intervened and, with the local branch of the YMCA, helped set up two new organizations: the Federation of Parents and Guardians, which organized afternoon school programs for Greek children; and the Greek Workers Association for those in service jobs, restaurants and the garment trade.

Association of Greek Workers, 5359 Parc (279-3526). The association was created in 1971 as part of the Mile End Project to help Greeks become part of the larger society and has remained a strong advocate of workers' rights. It publishes a monthly newsletter *Ergatika New* (Workers News) and has a weekly radio program on Radio Centre-Ville.

Centre d'études Grecques de Montréal, 5757 Wilderton (340-3576) offers adult education programs in Greek language, history, culture and religion. Recent courses have dealt with the role of women in Ancient Greece, Greek cooking, Byzantine civilization and Church architecture. A branch of the centre (with the same address and phone number) is the Montreal Institute of Hellenic Studies and Archaeology.

Le Cercle des écrivains grecs de Montréal, 5435 Parc (274-5856) was founded in 1979 for Montreal-area Greek writers.

The Cretans' Association of Montreal, 5220 Parc (270-2993). The Greek community prides itself on having scores of organizations, but most are social clubs for people from specific villages or regions within Greece. Those from Crete form one of the largest and oldest associations in Montreal. The "Cretan Shelter" on Park Avenue is a lively club for Greek culture in Montreal and supports public works projects in Crete.

The Greek Chronic Care Foundation, a new program within the

Hellenic Community, hopes to build a hospital for the Greek elderly. It may take over the Chinese hospital on St-Denis when a new Chinese Hospital is built in Chinatown.

Hellenic Community of Montreal, 5777 Wilderton (738-2421). This organization started over 80 years ago as the Koinotita (community) and has maintained leadership in the Greek community. The Hellenic Community has a sweeping presence matched by few other ethnic umbrella organizations. It runs all Greek Orthodox new calendar churches in the Montreal area and several Greek day schools including École Socrate (attached to the Catholic school commission), the Platon afternoon school, and Philothé, an arts school. It's location at the corner of Wilderton and Côte-Ste-Catherine includes an athletic centre, a seniors' residence, St. George's Greek Orthodox Cathedral, schools, libraries and the offices for a monthly newspaper and a Greek community radio program.

Hellenic Federation of Parents and Guardians of Greater Montreal, 451 Ogilvy (279-7216). Formed in 1970 as an afternoon school to teach Greek to children of Greek parents, the Federation runs classes throughout the week in both Protestant and Catholic schools for about 1,000 students taught by 35 teachers. The offices on Ogilvy also have a library with books donated by the Ministry of Culture in Greece; folk dance classes and Scout meetings are held in the gymnasium.

The Hellenic Restauranteurs Association, 263 Duluth E. (849-1911). About 1,000 Greek Montrealers manage or own many of the restaurants around Montreal. These include fine Greek, Chinese, Italian and French restaurants, as well as snackbars, souvlaki stands and Jewish-style delis.

This group started in 1984 because many Greek restaurant owners had difficulty with French and English government documents. They came together to help each other and ended up forming an association.

MEDIA

Most adults in the Greek community were born in Greece. They are interested in what is happening "back home" and avidly read the weekly shipment of newspapers and magazines flown in from Athens. Locally-published Greek newspapers have always found it difficult to compete. Those which survive often have local organizations behind them, such as *Koinotika Nea* (Our Community) put out by the Hellenic Community and *Drassis* (Action) published by the Association of Greek Workers.

To Ellinokanadidko Vima (La Tribue Helléno-Canadienne), 5316 Parc (272-6873) started in 1964 and focuses on community affairs and coverage of issues in Quebec and Canada.

Ellinikos Tachydromos (Le Courrier Grec), 3620 St-Laurent (849-9745) an older progressive weekly which opposed Greece's military dictatorship in the 1960s and 1970s.

Greek Canadian Reportaz (Reportage), 7438 Durocher (279-7772) which has a mix of local information and news from Greece.

Three stations have Greek language programs: CFMB 1410, Cable CHRC 89.9-FM and Radio Centreville CINQ 102.3-FM.

CFMB is a private multi-ethnic radio station that regularly features Greek programs, particularly in the evening. Programs are fairly apolitical compared with Radio Centreville's more activist stance.

CHCR, 5899 Parc (273-2481) the "Hellenic Voice of Canada" is an all-Greek station with music, news and public affairs programs; it also broadcasts Orthodox church services. It started in 1965 as a cable radio station for the Greek community. It's offices are in the heart of Park avenue's Greek commercial strip and the station is played in many Greek shops and restaurants.

On television, the half-hour-long *Hellenic Pulse* television program is on CFCF, Sunday mornings at 9:30 a.m. *Télé-Drassis*

(272-4000) and *Télévision hellenique de Montreal* (273-2481) are locally-produced cable television programs.

BOOKS AND FILMS

Books and films on Montreals' Greek community include the rather academic book *La communauté Grecque du Québec*, by Tina Ionannou (published by the Institut Québécois de recherche sur la culture, 1983); and the film *Cold Pizza*, (NFB) about two young boys who try to make money by delivering pizza, so they can visit Greece.

RESTAURANTS AND CLUBS

$ indicates that a lunch or dinner should cost under $10 (without taxes, tips, or wine). $$ is under $25 and $$$ above that. Hours often vary with the seasons so please call ahead.

HERMES RESTAURANT $$
1010 Jean-Talon (272-3880)
■ For close to 30 years Hermes has been serving traditional steam table food. Go straight to the back and check out the lamb and pasta, calf's brain, moussaka, deep-fried fish, chicory greens, and daily specials. There is always someone behind the counter to answer questions and entice tremulous gourmets to try something new. The food trades off spices for garlic and oil, lots of garlic and oil. Appetizers include squid, crab and other seafoods. The decor offers a classical education in antiqued masonry and columns, Grecian statues and vases, and handmade lampshades.

JARRY VARIETE & CAFE $
655 Jarry W. (272-2505)
■ Walk through the store any late afternoon or Sunday morning, go to the back, sit down, have a cup of coffee and listen. This is a

traditional "kafeneion" or Greek coffee bar that has always been a good place to go for local news and gossip.

MILOS $$$

5357 Parc, stairs to the restrooms (272-3522, 5242)

■ Once upon a time there were dozens of small Greek steam table restaurants, lots of coffee and pastry shops and only a few psarotaverna (fish taverns). Now its hard to find a lamb stew or a tray of moussaka and there are more fishnets in local restaurants than in the Greek islands. There are several Greek fish restaurants on Park Avenue and Duluth street. Most offer good, if expensive, fare. Milos has been around longer than most and even the head of the Greek Restaurant Association (who has his own place) says it's one of the best because they bring in their own fish and seafood. The fish is fresh and cooked to a quick but tender char; the squid is crisp and succulent; ask for soft shell crab. Mushrooms, mixed fried vegetables and zucchini are also superb.

SOUVLAKI ELATOS $

550 Jarry W. (273-5358, 273-6084)

■ Authentic and friendly and with great souvlaki, it's a nice local hang-out. The doner is stacked high with layers of pork, beef and lamb. The chicken brochettes have a zesty touch in the marinade and the souvlaki is fresh enough to still taste good when reheated the next day at home. Unfortunately, here, as in every other place, the souvlaki is made with pork instead of lamb, but that's Elatos' only fault. The pastries, brought in from local bakeries, are worth the calories. The custard filled galaktoboureko is a welcome alternative for those who find baklava a bit cloying.

FOOD SOURCES

ATHINA, 375 Bernard (279-4010). A Greek grocery store with bulk grains and beans, feta by the barrel, Kalamata olives from

Greece and several brands of Greek olive and cooking oils (many people like to take thicker, cheaper, Greek oil and cut it with a lighter olive or corn oil).

CAFE HELIOS, 5719 Parc (272-4646). A small family-run (two families actually) store that has been selling Greek-style coffees for more than a decade. The beans are minimally roasted and finely ground. Aficionados claim this gives coffee a taste which is less harsh than French or Italian roasts.

MIMOSA, 769 Jean-Talon W. (271-2432). Jean-Talon, from Park to l'Acadie, has several Greek grocery stores and excellent bakeries. This one has a wonderful selection including tiropitas (cheese filled pastries), hard crusty wholewheat bread dusted with flour, baklava soaked in a honey syrup, and almond cookies rolled in icing sugar.

MOURELATOS BROS., 881 Jean-Talon W. (277-0877) and at 4919 Notre Dame W. in Chomedey (681-4300). One of the oldest and more successful Greek groceries. The brothers opened their first store in Park Extension in 1956 at the height of Greek immigration and in the 1980s followed their clientele to Chomedey and opened up a bigger store. They have all the basics for Greek cooking including herbs, vine leaves, olive oils, and Greek cheeses.

MELISHINOS, 996 Jean-Talon W. (273-2200). Coffee lovers and those with an appreciation for fine machinery will enjoy the window display (it looks like it hasn't changed in many years). There are lots of coffee machines including Vesuna, a 30-year-old brand that brews great espresso.

NEW NAVARIO BAKERY & PASTRY SHOP, 5563 Park (279-7725). Long-established in what was once the heart of the Greek community. Great for Greek pastries, filo dough, and bread. Traditionally baked goods such as Vasilpota, a brioche that is honours Saint-Basil and is eaten at New Year's (January 8). At

Easter, there are loaves of bread with eggs painted red for the blood of Christ.

POISSONERIE NOUVEAU TRATA, 776 Jean-Talon W. (279-3312). Fresh fish and seafood including kalamaria (squid), crab, shrimp, cuttle fish and cod.

SUPER MARCHE DELTA, 690 Jean-Talon (273-6511). One of several good-sized Greek grocery stores on Jean-Talon between Durocher and l'Acadie. Lots of Greek staples here (gifts of olives and cheese indicate hospitality).

SHOPS AND SERVICES

APPOLLONIAN, 965 Jean-Talon W. (272-7098). The local Greek wedding gift store for more than 20 years. Everything is here, except the cake and dress: porcelain coffee sets, ornamental serving dishes, frilly lampshades and semi-erotic Greek statuary.

'CHRIST' HANDY STORE, 654 Ogilvy (270-4022). The name says it all: vivid portraits of Christ at the crucifixion and other religious articles, as well as Greek videos, papers, and books. There is also a nice display of Greek dolls.

VENUS VARIETES, 909 Jean-Talon W. (276-3364). Let's imagine that your grandparents are Greek and have never thrown anything out. This is their attic: ceramics with classical designs, Greek cassettes, records and videos, religious articles such as buttons of the Saints, key chains, and crosses, and Greek nougats and jellies.

GREEK WALKING TOUR

Start and end at Métro Parc

Park Extension is a roll-up-your-sleeves-and-get-down-to-work-kind-of-place, separated from the city on three sides. To the north is the Metropolitain expressway (highway 40), to the east the

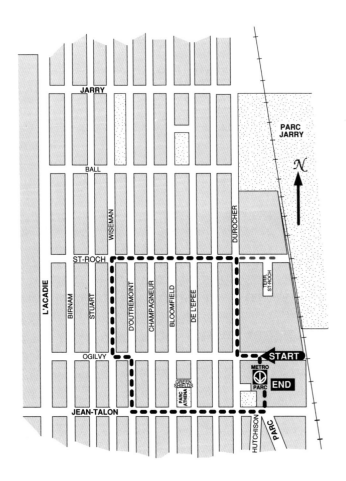

railway, and to the west, along boulevard l'Acadie, a 2 km-long fence cuts it off from the more luxurious homes and gardens of the Town of Mount Royal.

Park Extension lies above Jean-Talon. Park Avenue links the area with downtown; this polyglot neighbourhood is often the first home for newcomers to Montreal, whether they come from foreign countries or rural Québec. St-Laurent — The Main may have evolved into condos and chic boutiques but there is nothing precious about Park Ex.

During the 1960s tens of thousands of Greek immigrants moved here and made this an overwhelmingly Hellenic community. By the 1980s, many had moved to larger houses in Chomedey, Ville Saint-Laurent, the West Island and the South Shore, leaving poorer families and the elderly here. Today, Park Extension still has a Greek character but it is increasingly home for new Montrealers, notably Haitians, Sri Lankans, and Latin Americans.

START FROM THE STATION PARC MÉTRO. If you come by car, there is a large parking lot next to the station. Parc Métro is located in a Canadian Pacific Railway station built in 1931 as a passenger station with routes to the suburbs and ski hills around Montreal. In 1984 the station was closed and sold to the City of Montreal which hopes to reopen it as a multi-function community centre.

The station's designer, Colin Drewitt, used cool travertine walls, exterior columns and an expansive interior to create this neo-classic monument. The station itself is blocked off but large windows provide an opulent view from what was the Ladies Waiting Room. Art deco fixtures hang from the ceiling, a bronze fish gapes from a water fountain. Across the palatial concourse are signs for a barber shop and the offices of railway superintendents. A dark corridor, on the other side, leads to a passenger platform that was over a quarter-mile long. A sheen of dust and pigeon feathers covers the floor, perhaps waiting for the late night crew of cleaners which never shows up. If there are ghosts in the city, they must congregate here.

Across the street is the CFCF Television / Quatre Saisons media complex. Tours are given, but reservations are necessary. Call 273-6311 for more information.

WALK LEFT ON OGILVY and then right on Durocher. The Federation of Hellenic Parents and Guardians is at the corner of Ogilvy and Durocher, housed in the old Empire movie theatre. The

Concourse of Jean-Talon Railway Station, 1932.
CANADIAN PACIFIC ARCHIVES

Federation manages Greek afternoon and Saturday schools. It's offices are upstairs and the theatre is now a gym and stage for community events.

Durocher is one of the older streets in the area with housing ranging from turn of the century single family homes to small apartment buildings. Halfway up the block is a lovely smidgen of park with small trees and several picnic tables. It is used by the CFCF/Quatre Saisons staff and there is no access from this street.

A small daycare is at the corner of Durocher and St-Roch. It used to be the Hercules Donut Shop and inside is the restaurant's legacy, a wall-size mural of the Acropolis. The daycare centre has about 50 kids, mostly from local Asian, Haitian, Latin American and French-Canadian families; only a few Greek kids go here now.

FOR A SHORT SIDE TRIP TURN RIGHT (EAST) ON ST-ROCH. There is a superb view of Mount Royal from the top of the bridge over the railroad tracks. The squat building on the Park Extension side is the Quebec government's regional orientation centre for new immigrants. Jarry Park, on the other side, is the only large park and athletic complex in the area. The stadium, with its grass field, was the Montreal Expos' first home.

CONTINUE WEST ALONG ST-ROCH. This street has remained the same for years. There are butchers displaying whole undressed goats and lambs, fish markets, travel agencies, dentist offices, restaurants, coffee bars, and grocery stores — all with Greek signs and staff. Chaussures Astral, at 525 St-Roch, claims to serve customers in French, English, Spanish, Italian and Greek. Across the street is the Québec Doner Gyro souvlaki stand. Further along the street, just above the Afroditi Bakery, is the Pan Arcadian Brotherhood du Canada. Those who choose to live in Greek need never leave these few blocks.

But the neighbourhood is changing. Today, less than a quarter of the residents are Greek and most of them are elderly. A community newspaper, *Notre Quartier — Our Neighbourhood*, has articles in Greek, Spanish, and Creole. The corner store at de L'Épée and St-Roch serves coffee to the old Greek crowd at the snack bar in the back while selling curry powders, rose water, betelnuts and Hindi videos up front.

Koimisis Tis Theotokou is the church at the corner of de L'Épée and St-Roch. This lovely little building was purchased in 1968 and transformed into a Greek Orthodox Church. It has an ornate gilded interior and it's easy to get a good look at the detail. Across the street is Barthelemy-Vimont, a public school used as a Greek community school on Saturdays.

LOOK UP AS YOU WALK ALONG ST-ROCH. Several community associations have their names lettered across second storey windows. These are social clubs for people hailing from specific parts of Greece. Some groups have their own restaurants such as the Tirpolis at 679 St-Roch.

The Church of Evangelismos at 777 St-Roch was built as the community outgrew Koimisis Tis Theotokou. Formerly it housed a Catholic parish and became Orthodox in 1975. The annual parade celebrating Greece's independence from Turkey starts here. Evangelismos is named for the community's first church which first held services in 1910, when most Greeks lived in the lower boul. St-Laurent area.

TURN LEFT ON WISEMAN. The Greek Orthdox church is divided into sects based on the newer Gregorian or older Julian calendar. The building at the corner is the only old calendar church left and is maintained by a priest and a few members of a small congregation. Almost all Montreal Greeks are Greek Orthdox and members of the new calendar churches.

CONTINUE DOWN WISEMAN AND TURN LEFT ON OGILVY. Centre Ogilvy is at 821 Ogilvy, between Wiseman and Outre-mont. It's an old church that is now a community centre mostly used by the Hellenic Veterans Association. Only a few Greek Montrealers enlisted with Canadian forces during WWII but this place is packed, mostly with older men who were part of the Resistance in Greece.

Although Greece was controlled by the Axis powers, the Resistance was so strong that Stalin credited it with stalling Hitler's march into Russia. Not all of the men here fought with the Resistance, however, some may even have been on the other side; but as one member of the community says, "after all this time, what can you do?" The crowd is convivial, the backgammon and card games fierce, and the air filled with the pungent perfume of strong cigarettes and thick Greek coffee. Across the street is the more sedate Flanders Hall, home to the 63rd branch of the Royal Canadian Legion.

If you're with kids and want a short break, consider dropping into the PARK EXTENSION BRANCH OF THE MONTREAL CHILD-REN'S LIBRARY AT 7408 BLOOMFIELD, corner Ogilvy. There are lots of toys for toddlers and reading rooms with books for kids in more than a dozen languages including Arabic, Greek, Hindi,

Polish, Spanish and Vietnamese. The library is open Monday and Wednesday mornings and every afternoon except Sunday. Across the street from the library is the Armenian Evangelical Church, a reminder of when this area had a substantial Armenian population.

TURN RIGHT ON OUTREMONT AND WALK TO JEAN-TALON. Montreal has become one of the world's ten largest Greek cities and, from this corner, its easy to see why. To the right is the Banque Nationale de Grèce, the Kriti Greek Food Marché Restaurant and I. Reed Pharmacienne — FAPMAKO OIO. To the left are Draperies Theodenis, the Omega Travel Agency, and the Zappion Restaurant Grecque and Country and Western Bar. Further west, 4 Frères supermarket sells tzatziki sauce, table-size tins of vine leaves, wheels of hard Greek cheeses and blocks of imported feta.

PARC ATHENA, on Jean-Talon between Bloomfield and de l'Épee, was named by the City of Montreal in 1986. It honours the community and celebrates the Greek goddess of wisdom and the arts. Nouvelles Universelles, facing the park, is one of the few old-fashioned newsstands left in the city. Next door to it is the Livingstone Presbyterian Church (272-7330) with services in English, Hungarian and Greek; a testament to how the neighbourhood has changed since the church was founded in 1909. The English service is performed by the Hungarian minister to a congregation which includes a few older Scots and recently arrived Sri Lankans, Trinidadians and Guineans.

This part of Jean-Talon is great for browsing, and occasionally there are wonderful sidewalk sales. The PARC MÉTRO STATION is a couple of blocks away. Otherwise, take the 80 bus down Park avenue where, particularly between Bernard and Mont-Royal, there are several cafés and Greek restaurants, owned by Greek Montrealers who have long since moved to other parts of town. The bus continues through downtown Montreal to the Place-des-Arts Métro station and then Old Montreal.

ITALIAN MONTREAL

POPULATION: 186,000

MAJOR COMMUNITIES: Little Italy, Saint-Léonard and
Saint-Michel, Notre-Dame-de-Grâce, Ville-Émard,
Rivière-des-Prairies, Lasalle and Côte St-Luc.

SHOPPING AND FOOD: Boulevard St-Laurent (between
St-Zotique and Jean Talon); Upper Lachine Road west
of Girouard; Jean Talon in Ville Saint-Léonard

> *I get upset when people talk about us as ethnic. What do others know
> what it means to be Italian. There is no social value to the word
> "ethnic." If you know me, know me for my culture. That has a positive
> value.*
>
> — Vincenzo Galati, Vice-President,
> National Congress of Italian Canadians

Québec history is also Italian. At the corner of Ste-Catherine and
Atwater, in Cabot Square, is a statue of Giovanni Caboto — John
Cabot — Jean Cabot: the Italian who, in the service of England,
"discovered" Canada in 1497. Other Italians who are prominent
in our early history include John da Verrazzano, a 16th century
Florentine, who sailed the coast from the Carolinas to Nova Scotia
and Father Francesco Giuseppe Bressani who, in 1642, was the first
European to travel through the interior of Quebec and Ontario.

Serious immigration from Italy commenced in the 1880s. Montreal was a favourite destination since it was easy to get to from
Italy and offered opportunities for unskilled workers. Poor
immigrants from a land called "the most Catholic country in
Europe" thought Quebec might be more welcoming than other
parts of North America.

Southern Italians arrived first and almost all were men who left the depressed agricultural regions of Sicily, Napoli and Calabria. Others would follow from impoverished towns near Rome and the more northern regions of Tuscany, Friuli, and Piedmont.

The first groups passed through Montreal in the late 1800s. They were men who helped build the railways and canals or worked in forests and mines. Most returned to Italy in the winter but over the years more would stay through the winter, as they found full-time work in the cities. With settlement, immigration increased despite a ministerial directive that "No steps are to be taken to assist or encourage Italian immigration." But bureaucratic indifference in Canada was better than poverty in Italy, so they kept coming.

Ottawa was really looking for farmers from Northern Europe. The Italians, however, remembered the poverty and harsh village life they had left and had no intention of settling in rural areas. They moved to the cities and the jobs they found in the building trades became the foundation for an Italian-based construction industry in Montreal.

Most Italians lived in the parish of Mont-Carmel, in blocks clustered around Dorchester boulevard (now René-Lévesque) from Saint-Laurent to St-Denis. One reporter wrote that it was a "pure, unadulterated slum filled with crowded, unsanitary tenements." It wasn't an exaggeration. Many newcomers had been promised jobs while they were still in Italy. They were recruited by Italians who had come here earlier; men, called padrones, who were agents for the steamship companies, mines, and railroads. The most notorious padrone was Antonio Cordasco. His St. James (St-Jacques) street office, in the heart of Montreal's old financial district, was next to the Canadian Pacific Railway, probably the largest employer of immigrant labour in the country.

In 1904, almost 4,000 men passed through Cordasco's office. They paid him $10 each to find them work and the CPR gave

Cordasco up to another dollar per man. Those who worked got $1.50 a day at a time when lodging in a rooming house might cost $2.50 a week. Not content to act quietly, Cordasco had the workers set up a parade to honour him at which he was crowned "King of Labour." Neither Montreal's small Italian establishment, nor Ottawa, was amused; people were becoming worried about unemployed immigrant workers in downtown Montreal. By the end of 1904, the government had formed a Royal Commission into the Immigration of Italian Labourers to Montreal and the publicity drove out Cordasco and other padrones, but it would be decades before the lives of most Italian Montrealers would improve.

Italians were drawn to Montreal because it was a Catholic city, but they found they didn't fit in with the overwhelming French-Canadian Catholic establishment. Priests couldn't preach or give sacraments in Italian and the service was different.

By 1905, the Montreal Italian Catholic community was strong enough to demand its own parish on the corner of Dorchester and St-André. Molson's brewery owned the land and donated it to the community. According to Sam Capozzi, president of the community centre Casa d'Italia, "that's why Italians always drank Molson's." The church held a few hundred people but served thousands. It set a precedent since its territory was ethnic and was technically the largest parish in the city, serving Italians from Redpath Avenue (then at the western fringe of Montreal) to Delormier in the east, and ran from Mount Royal Avenue in the north to the St. Lawrence River. The parish, called Notre-Dame-du-Mont-Carmel, has since relocated to Saint-Léonard.

By 1911, there were 7,000 Italians in Montreal, mostly men who worked on construction projects, with the Grand Trunk or Canadian Pacific railways or with Montreal Tramways. Many were moving away from the core of the city to areas where they could buy land, build homes, grow fruit and vegetables, and write back home to say they had become landowners. The most popular areas were in Montcalm and Mile End in the north and Ville Émard and NDG in the west.

Mile-End was the largest of these communities. It sprang up between Saint-Laurent and St-Denis and its name came from the CPR station of Mile End at the corner of Bellechase and St. Lawrence. By 1930, half of Montreal's Italian community, lived in the Montcalm–Mile End area and 6,000 lived within a few blocks of Dante Street in Mile End's Little Italy.

In 1910, a second Italian parish was created with a church at the corner of Dante and Henri Julien. At that time, there was talk of extraordinary events taking place in the Italian region of Campobasso. Several people claimed to have seen the Virgin appear and ruins of an old church were found in the nearby district of La Difesa.

Since many of the new residents in Mile End came from Campobasso, they called the new church La Madonna Della Difesa — Our Lady of Protection. The parish was huge, 18 square miles, with a territory that covered 28 French Canadian and five Irish Catholic churches. This new parish had over 10,800 members. Montreal's Italian community had come a long way from the village parish ministering to individual religious needs.

Italian immigration to Canada slowed after 1930. This was partly because it was easier to get into Canada if you were British, American, or from Northern Europe. At the same time, Mussolini, Italy's dictator from 1924 to 1943, discouraged emigration; during the 1930s more people left Canada for Italy than immigrated here.

Enthusiasm for Mussolini reached a high point in Montreal in 1933. La Madonna Della Difesa unveiled a fresco of Mussolini and other major ecclesiastical and political figures in the church. Italo Balbo, a WWI hero and Italy's first air minister, flew an Italian air fleet over Montreal to St-Hubert Airport.

In 1939, Italy aligned with Germany and invaded France. Both the general public and the government turned against Italians in

Canada. Police sealed off bridges to Montreal and searched cars for Italians. The Canadian government claimed that those of "Italian racial origin who have become naturalized British subjects since September 1, 1929, are considered possible enemies." The curé of Mont-Carmel was arrested and Italian property was seized, including the Casa d'Italia — the Italian community centre on Jean-Talon E. After the war, some changed their names: Rossini became Ross, Riccioni changed to Richards and Giacomo was Anglicized to Jackman. In November, 1990 Prime Minister Mulroney offered the government's apology for interning over 700 Italian Canadians during the war.

After the war, Canada lifted the "enemy alien" designation for Italians and hundreds of thousands immigrated to Quebec. They came under government regulations which favoured keeping families together. On average, each Italian family brought over 15 people which soon made the Italian community the largest (after French and English) in Montreal.

Montreal Italians are likely to say that their families came from Calabria, Friuli or Sicily rather than Italy. Neighbourhoods reflect this. Ville Saint-Michel's southern part is strongly Sicilian. Those from the regions of Calabria, Campania and Molise tend to live a few blocks north and in neighbouring Saint-Léonard. Ville Emard and Notre-Dame-de-Grâce have many Italians from the area around Campobasso and the central region of Marche.

The north-eastern communities of Saint-Michel (now part of Montreal) and Saint-Léonard were particularly attractive to Italian developers. Italian builders such as Giuseppe Silvestri and Luigi Barone built hundreds of these mini-palazzos and advertised them as dream homes on Montreal's Italian cable television. They knew Italian workers wanted homes which reflected their success and new status in Canada so they made sure the homes were bright and airy with chandeliers, marble in the hall and a *cantina* (a wine cellar, a kitchen, and pantry) in the basement.

As new citizens, Italian Montrealers knew education was important and felt that while French was important, English was crucial to success in the new land. In Quebec, public schools follow Catholic or Protestant religious lines. Most of those in Saint-Léonard were under the French language Saint-Léonard Roman Catholic School Commission. In 1964, the Commission introduced bilingual classes in several local schools but in the fall of 1967, following a government report recommending that "Quebec be as French as Ontario is English," the Commission opted to phase out bilingual education.

Italians, who made up a quarter of St-Léonard, wanted the right to choose the language of education for their children. The English Catholic Parents Association was formed and set up secret English language classes for children. The Commission voted to maintain bilingual education for one year, but this decision was opposed by those who felt the delay would stop movement back to a French-only system.

On September 10, 1969 over 1500 French-only supporters marched up Jean-Talon through the business centre of Saint-Léonard. The group pushed through police barricades and rioted when they came up against hundreds of Italian residents on the other side.

The crisis had repercussions in Quebec's on-going language and education debates. A month after the riot the provincial government passed Bill 63 giving parents a choice in the language of education but that ended in 1974 when Bill 22 made French the official language of Québec. Under that legislation, students were tested for competency before going to an English language school. Families were furious as some children entered French-only classes while others went to English-language schools. The current legislation, Bill 101, demands that almost all new immigrants attend French language schools. Only those parents with six years of education in English in Canada can send their children to

English language public schools in Québec.

Today, 80% of Italian Montrealers speak French and over 60% speak French and English. Most also speak some Italian at home. The Italian community is highly integrated into all levels of city life and the province has trade offices in Milan and Rome.

Here are four useful words: *prego* is "please"; *grazie* is "thank you"; *capisci* means "understand!" as in, "I'm talking to you, capisci!" and *ciao!* which has no equivalent in English. Ciao! is friendlier than "see ya" but less formal than "Good-bye."

■■ SOCCER

Every four years Little Italy turns into a haven for soccer enthusiasts. The next World Cup series is in 1994. Fans fill local cafés and bars to watch their beloved Team Italia. The streets of Little Italy are lined with the red, green and white of the Italian flag. Shops carry World Cup key chains, posters, and T-shirts. Most espresso bars have a television blaring to the crowd. **Trattoria dai Baffoni**, *at 68 59 St-Laurent, is a good spot to watch it all. At least you'll probably find a seat there.*

While waiting for World Cup to come around, tap into the local soccer scene. There are about 125 teams, from kids to seniors, organized by the **Concordia Soccer Association** *(722-3578). The season runs from January to October.*

The pros play with SupraMontréal, in a 12 team national league. The season is from May to October at **Centre Claude-Robillard** *(389-2774). With 9000 seats, this stadium brings sports back to human scale. The field is grass and the $5 general admission is right, too.*

▪▪ BASIC BOCCI

Bocci means balls. It's also spelled bocce and no matter how you spell it, it's Italian lawn bowling. It's popular in Piedmont, Liguria, and most regions of Italy. There are several indoor and outdoor courts in Montreal.

Officially, Bocci is played on a clay court, or campo *about 75 feet long and 8 feet wide. Players are split into 2 teams. They throw four bocci underhanded towards a smaller ball, called the boccino or pallino . . . Getting your bocci closer to the boccino than your opponent's gets you a point. 12 points wins the game.*

ORGANIZATIONS

The first local Italian organization, set up in 1875, was a semi-secret nationalistic group called the Societa Nazionale, modeled on Quebec's Societé Saint-Jean Baptiste. In 1902, with Montreal suffering a major influenza epidemic, the Societa became more of a mutual-aid association, opened an employment office and set up housing for migrant and destitute workers.

Most early associations were based on a town or region in Italy. They paid illness and funeral benefits. As competition increased among them for members, some, such as the Order of Italo-Canadians introduced other services such as free nursing and dental care, and evening education classes.

By the 1930s, there were over 50 sport, political, labour, and mutual aid societies for Montreal's 24,000 Italians. The Institute of Italian Culture gave Montrealers concerts, Italian courses and held illustrated lectures on Italian art and history in the old Mount Royal

Hotel. An international workers' group — the Opera Nazionale Dopolavoro — had an Italian baseball team which played in a semi-pro league. The stadium was on the corner of Atwater and Ste-Catherine, now the site of Place Alexis-Nihon.

Before WWII, pride in Italy helped the community forge many local organizations. The largest group was the Ordine Figli d'Italia — the Sons of Italy. The Order, which started in the U.S.A. as a mutual aid society in 1905, began as a response to discrimination and made members proud of their culture. Montreal's first chapter started in 1919. Dues were $1 a month. This was at a time when factory workers made about $500 a year and those in construction $250. Although the Order ended up as a Fascist association, it initially was important as bereavement society, helping families when a member died.

In 1935, Italy attacked Ethiopia and Canadian public opinion turned against Italy and most local Italian associations soon ceased operating.

After WWII, the community started new organizations. The Canadian Italian Business and Professional Association was set up in 1949 and helped found La Fiducie Canadienne Italienne, a trust company which would finance local Italian business. The Mouvement Progressiste Italo-Québecois existed in the early 1970s. It was the first organization to identify itself with Québec. It was started by academics and workers, had several publications and linked up with left-wing, non-Italian groups in Montréal, such as FRAP, a municipal opposition party during the early 1970s. The Mouvement ended in 1974; but many of its members helped start other progressive community organizations such as the workers group and Centro Donne, the Italian women's centre.

Today there are about 200 groups and associations in the Italian community. Most bring together families from a specific region.

Casa d'Italia, 505 Jean-Talon E. (279-6357). Casa was built in the 1930s with some funding from the Italian government and was

Casa d'Italia community centre.
NEREO LORENZI, COURTESY CASA D'ITALIA

confiscated during WWII. It was restructured after the war and now is an important community centre with several organizations, social services and an Italian library.

Centro Donne / Centre des femmes, 2348 Jean-Talon E. (727-7430) helps women adapt to life in Québec and has brought wider attention to violence against women in the Italian community. It also has a youth group dealing with the pressures children of Italian immigrants face in Montreal. The Centre frequently takes political stands on issues.

There are lots of groups promoting Italian culture. **Club Recreatif Italo Canadien di** NDG (484-2481, 488-9796) is different since its members have roots in all regions of Italy. There is a carnival and dance in February and an Italian Summer Festival in Loyola Park honouring Ste. Catherine de Sienne. It's on the weekend before Father's Day and activities include greased pole climbing, spaghetti eating contests, music, dancing, and fireworks.

Congresso Nazionale degli Italo Canadesi / National Congress of Italian-Canadians, 505 Jean-Talon E. (279-6357). Local prominent Italians formed the Congresso after WWII to unite the many Italian associations, to promote and safeguard Italian culture, and to represent the community at various levels of government. It was also formed to counter community leaders linked to the Order of the Sons of Italy who claimed to speak for the Italian community. Quebec's Congresso is part of the national umbrella organization.

Consiglio Regionale degli Anziani Italo-Canadesi (273-6588) assists seniors with pensions, social services, hospitals and bureaucracy.

Fogolar Furlan (721-6364). Furlanis come from northern Italy and have their own language. Montreal's club has 100 members and lots of action, including an indoor bocci court. Feasts include New Year's and St. Valentines. While there are many Italian regional associations, this one insists you don't have to be Italian to join!

Istituto Italiano di Cultura, 1200 Dr. Penfield (849-3473), has concerts, exhibitions, films and lectures on Italian culture several times a month. The lectures are usually in Italian. Membership is $20 a year

Patronato Italo-Canadese di Asssistenza agli Immigranti (PICAI), 6865 Christophe-Colombe (271-5590). 6,000 youth are enrolled in Saturday morning Italian culture and language classes throughout Montreal.

Fiduce Canadienne Italienne, 6999 St-Laurent (270-4124) was started in 1975 by Italian business leaders for workers in the area and to promote joint business ventures. There is a great deal of community pride in this Montreal-based trust company which has five branches through the city.

Italian festivals include October 12 which celebrates Columbus' arrival in America with a mass in front of his statue in Turin Parc, on the corner of Jean-Talon E. and Chambord. June 2 is the anniversary of the modern republic of Italy, and June 13 is the feast of St-Anthony.

MEDIA

The first Italian newspaper was *Corriere del Canada*. It began in Montreal in 1895. Others, espousing the views of local community or the Italian government, sprang up during WWI and before WWII. The main Italian papers are **Corriere Italiano**, 4508 Jarry E. (376-8887), **Insieme**, 4358 Charleroi (328-2060), and **Il Cittadino Canadese**, 6020 Jean Talon E. (253-2332).

For something *vivace* pick up **ViceVersa** — "Le magazine transculturel." (847-1593). This may be the magazine of the future with articles in Italian, French and English. It's a well-designed magazine with essays on international politics, the arts and society, and writers reporting from Montreal, New York, Toronto, Paris, Warsaw, Brussels . . . everywhere.

There is extensive radio and television programming in Montreal. Cable TVs *Télé-Italia* (255-1045) and CFMB 1410 (483-2362) — both have daily Italian programs.

RESTAURANTS AND CLUBS

$ indicates that a lunch or dinner should cost under $10 (without taxes, tips, or wine). $$ is under $25 and $$$ above that. Credit cards accepted are listed. "BYOB" means that you can bring your own wine. Hours often vary with the seasons so please call ahead.

BISTRO UNIQUE $ VISA MC AMEX
1039 Beaubien E. (279-4433)
■ This used to be just Pizza Unique, but it's gone upscale since it changed into a bistro and opened up the menu with more Italian

dishes and a hefty array of imported beers. Still, the pizzas are thin and tasty and this has become a popular local place for a quick lunch or late evening snack.

CAFE VIA DANTE $
Dante and Alma

■ Daily from 6:00 a.m. to 3:00 p.m. Fresh orange juice, very good cappucino, and a large slice of panettone (sweet cake-bread) is under $4.00. Local hangout with a 1950s ambience and Mussolini's picture on the wall.

CAFE INTERNATIONAL $
6714 St-Laurent (495-0067)

■ The café has been operating since 1935, as it advertises, although much of that time was in Italy. Never mind. There's lots of room here, a good atmosphere and maybe the best espresso in town.

CAFFE ITALIA $
6840 St-Laurent (495-0059)

■ Great coffee, nice people, a good sporting bar with pool and table soccer in the back, lots of regalia in front. This is soccer central during the world cup. The film *Caffe Italia* was shot here.

CASA CACCIATORE $$$ VISA MC AMEX
170 Jean-Talon E. (274-1240)

■ The "House of the Hunter" seems as kitsch as can be with stuffed birds and animal-heads on the walls and an arbour of plastic grapes, but the food and service are great. The antipasto is enough for two, pasta dishes are quite good and the Florentine-style steak (the name seems to change with the waiter; last time it was Steak à la Joe) is thick and tender.

DA MARCELLO $$$ VISA MC AMEX
825 Laurier E. (276-1580)

■ Wonderful roasted meats and game-birds, true Tuscan cooking. The menu changes seasonally and the table d'hote offers reasonably priced choices. Going through changes since Marcello is no longer there.

PASTA CASARECCIA $ VISA MC
5849 Sherbrooke W. (483-1588) 1487 Macdonald, Ville Saint-Laurent (334-9262).
■ Each location combines an Italian grocery store with a small restaurant. The Sherbrooke street location is on the garish side. There's great home-made pasta, a good take-out selection, and roughly once-a-month $$ gourmet evenings which are usually reserved weeks ahead.

LA CASA $ VISA MC
505 Jean Talon E. (271-7465)
■ Inexpensive, popular Italian lunchtime buffet.

ELIO PIZZERIA $$ VISA MC AMEX
351 Bellechasse (276-5341)
■ In almost thirty years, this family-run restaurant on the fringe of Little Italy has grown beyond its pizzeria origins with veal dishes, steaks, freshly-made sausages, pasta and a good minestrone. Sauces are nicely blended and applied with a light touch.

FRANK RISTORANTE $$ VISA MC AMEX EN-ROUTE
65 St-Zotique E. (273-7734)
■ This part of the neighbourhood has become a little dowdy, but Frank is a class act. Good wine, large portions, but increasingly upscale prices. Frank has been on the same corner for 30 years. They've got to be doing something right. The daily specials are good value. Everything's fresh. Gnocci (velvety wee dumplings of potato pasta) are made on Thursday.

LE LATINI $$$ VISA MC AMEX EN-ROUTE
1130 Jeanne-Mance (861-3166)
■ The food is "genuino," the setting is Fellini, and the staff is from Venice and Calabria. The wine cellar alone is worth a visit. This

may be, consistently, the best Italian restaurant in Montreal. Classically simple, but uncommon dishes include porcini mushrooms with freshly made linguini and carpaccio — translucent slices of marinated steak. Enough good wines are available by the glass to afford a different selection with each dish.

MOMESSO $
5562 Upper Lachine Rd. (484-0005)

■ A huge snack-bar, open from noon to midnight, with one great dish: hot submarine sandwiches, made only one way: on a fresh crusty loaf with slabs of Italian sausage. Add onions, coleslaw and hot peppers, but that's it. There's hamburgers, pizza, beer, wine and espresso, and hockey star Sergio Momesso's pictures on the wall. But those subs, Mama mia!

PIZZEDELIC $$ VISA MC AMEX EN-ROUTE
3509 St-Laurent (282-6784)

■ Thin-crusted exotic pizzas with toppings like feta, blue cheese, artichokes, olives and dried tomatoes, escargots, shrimps, and anchovies.

PIZZERIA NAPOLETANA $ BYOB
189 Danté (276-8226, 495-0079)

■ The crowds at night indicate that Napoletana may have the best pizza in town. Thin crust, home made sauce, nothing too fancy. Try the vegetarian funghetto (mushrooms) and the marinara (clams, shrimps). The pasta is good too, especially pennini 'roman' (prosciutto, onions) and gnocci 'crema' (cream, parmesan).

ROBERTO'S $
2221 Bélanger E. (374-9844)

■ This is the place to come after the early evening movie. The pasta is good but save room for dessert and coffee, Italian ice cream and cakes. Want it all? Ask for Spaghetti ice cream with extra meatballs!

ROTISSERIE ITALIENNE $
1933 Ste-Catherine W. (935-4436)

■ The sign says this is 'cucina rustica' (country kitchen) and this small Italian bistro is a nice change from many more formal Italian restaurants in the downtown area. Nothing fancy, but generally quite tasty appetizers, pasta and pizzas. There's usually porchetta — a whole roasted piglet — by the counter, the clam sauce is good and the penne arabiata has a solid chili bite in the sauce.

TRATTORIA DAI BAFFONI $$ VISA MC AMEX
6859 St-Laurent, corner Dante (270-3715)

■ Times have been good since the DePalma family moved dai Baffoni (the mustache) here from its homey store front on St-Laurent. The food is average Neapolitain. It's great fun for a large group, particularly on the terrace in summer or near (but not too near) the wood burning fireplace in autumn and winter.

TRE MARIE $
6934 Clark (277-9859)

■ Two dining rooms surround a kitchen run by three women named Maria. This is the closest thing to a real trattoria in town. Five hearty Neapolitain specials change every day. Fish is served on Friday. In our fantasies, our aunts are probably Italian or Jewish. If we're lucky this is the way they would cook.

FOOD SOURCES

BOULANGERIE NDG, 5801 Upper Lachine Road (481-4215). Great bread and Italian pastries as well as imported cheeses, olive oils, pasta and meat. The whole neighbourhood seems to shop here on Sunday mornings and the ricotta-filled cannoli pastries can be sold out by noon.

LA FROMAGERIE HAMEL, 220 Jean-Talon E. (272-1161). Located next to the Jean-Talon Market, Hamel has a variety of

Italian cheeses, meats and fresh pasta. Good bread and croissants. There are a couple of stools and an espresso machine wedged into a window space overlooking the market.

M.G.G. PRODUCTS, 7130 Casgrain (270-1778). Tired of paying those SAQ wine prices? The Zanettis can help you spend less and enjoy more. Their Jean-Talon market location sells wine-making equipment. Come in mid-September, select from over a dozen varieties of California grapes, and enjoy your own house wine before winter is out.

MILAN BOUCHERIE INC., 176 Jean-Talon E. (273-1257). The sign says Italian and French cuts of meat, but the butchers, here, claim the difference is slight. ("A French man, he eats a French cut, an Italian, an Italian cut." "Yeah," says a customer, "and I guess a Chinese eats with chopsticks.") Never mind, this is a good Italian delicatessen with a butcher shop a cut above the ordinary. The charcuterie selection is excellent and there are lots of fresh sausages from mild leek and pork to spicy chorizo.

MILANO FRUTERIE, 6884 St-Laurent (273-8558). Much, much more than the fruit store it started out as forty years ago. Mama mia! this place is great: excellent antipasti counters, freshly made pasta, a good butcher counter, Perugina chocolates, a dozen olive oils from "no cholesterol or salt, milder-tasting 100% pure extra light" to "unfiltered cold pressed extra virgin" — perfect for dipping crusty Italian bread. Their fruit and vegetables are of the highest quality.

MOTTA BAKERY AND PASTRY, 303-315 Mozart E. (270-5952). Pizza, bread, pasta, tortellini, cannelloni and good baked goods.

POISSONNERIE SALERNO, 7020 Casgrain (273-5051). A small fish shop with good variety: octopus, squid, sardines, fresh and dried cod, locally-smoked salmon, even tasty uncultivated mussels

— and lots of helpful suggestions on preparing Mediterranean dishes.

RENATO BAR AND EQUIPMENT, 12 Danté (279-3540). A wide selection of coffee machines to try before you buy. Sip an espresso at one of the window tables while discussing the merits of various machines. Renato's has a good espresso blend to go.

ROMA, 6776 St. Laurent (273-9357). An old, established bakery with good pastry and excellent breads particularly white pizza — a delicious snacking bread made with olive oil and rosemary.

TRANZO, 1089 Girouard (488-7907). A good grocery and butcher shop much appreciated for fresh sausages and roast piglet; also, olives, sauces, fresh walnuts and imported pastas. Hard to find (at the junction of Upper Lachine and Girouard), Tranzo is at the beginning of NDG's Little Italy.

W. ZINMAN ENR., 7022 St. Dominique (277-4302). There are not many live poultry markets left in Montreal. Zinman's has been around for 60 years. Since 1974, it's been owned by Luigi Guarascio and Giuseppe Ferrarelli. They get their chickens from farms around Montreal and claim their free range chickens actually get to walk around. They also have live rabbits, ducks, and often geese and turkey.

SHOPS AND SERVICES

AQUARIUM ATLAS 6725 boul. St-Laurent (277-8220). Yes it's in Little Italy and the owner, Pierre Vinciarelli, is Italian. There's nothing particularly Italian about this place but it's a lovely store to stroll through. There are salt water fish swimming in huge, beautifully-designed aquariums. The clerks are knowledgeable and a toucan named Coco greets you at the door.

BIJOUTERIE ITALIENNE, 192 St. Zotique E. (279-5585). Gold jewelery imported from Italy.

LA CASA DI MODA TAVORMINA, 7060 boul. St-Laurent (277-0716) is one of the last remaining shops in Little Italy specializing in wedding dresses.

CYCLES BAGGIO, 6975 boul. St-Laurent (279-5655). You know you've walked into the right place when you see photos on the wall of superstar cyclists like Fausto Coppi. After 60 years, the Baggio family no longer owns the store, but there are still several lines of Italian frames: Torpado, Limongi, Alan, Miele, Fiori, Baggio, and Benotto. Also excercise bikes and a good selection of cycles for children.

FERRONERIA SIMONE, 5531 Upper Lachine (484-1848). Mammoth plates for pasta, espresso machines, knick-knacks, wine vats and sausage grinders, Italian vegetable seeds, key cutting, rifles, paint, you name it. An old-fashioned hardware store with a strong Italian flavour.

GIOVANNI GRIMALDI, 6758 boul. St-Laurent (270-2098). Mr. Grimaldi has been cutting and shaping men's suits for half a century. This is one of the few of the old style select shops left in Little Italy.

ITAL VIDEO, 5864 Jean Talon E. (255-5374). Rent Italian videos. They're brought in from Italy and Toronto.

ITALMELODIE, 274 Jean-Talon E. (273-3224). The Zeffiro family has owned this store and music school for a long time. Scrunched into a corner of the Jean-Talon market, the place looks small but the stock is huge. Guitars, accordions, keyboards, midi (computer assisted equipment), and percussion instruments.

LIBRERIA ITALIANA, 6792 St-Laurent (277-2955). Books, magazines, newspapers, music, videos and games imported from Italy. Particularly strong in popular literature, design and architecture. Board games such as Monopoly in Italian. *La Republica* and other newspapers arrive a few days after they're published in Italy.

The staff is friendly, particularly to Italophiles who can't get past *prego* and *grazie*.

MEUBLES NAPOLI, 7001 St-Laurent (271-3543). Italian designed and made furniture, including the Rougier line of contemporary styles designed in Italy and manufactured here.

QUINCAILLERIE DANTE FERRAMENTA, 6851 St-Dominque (271-2057). Helena and Maria run the cooking, hardware, and paint sections. Rudolfo takes care of the guns. There is a large selection of pasta machines and many nifty Italian culinary gadgets. As the sign says, "C'e' Tutto Per Tutti!" indeed. This is the place to come when you know what you want to do (make sausage, put up tomatoes, try wine making) but don't know where to start.

SACERDOTE MARBLE, 6382 Boul. St-Laurent (277-5796). There's inlaid marble tables from Brazil, mammoth pottery urns from Mexico and slabs of exquisite granite, marble, and quartz from 17 countries. Ask for Warna who designs the furniture and enthusiastically shares her knowledge.

LA STRADA, 7010 St-Laurent (274-9242). La Strada sells reasonably priced Italian-made shoes and bags.

VELLONE, 7092 St-Laurent (272-0344) and 1374 Jean-Talon E. (721-0082). Born in the area in 1967, nephew Ivano Vellone manages the family store. He runs for the Parti Québecois occasionally and is one of a group of young dynamos trying to create a renaissance of Little Italy. The store sells a large range of Italian records, cassettes and older Italian films. There's much popular music from opera to Italian soft rock. A good place to get records of current stars from Italy who are featured on Cable TV Channel 24.

MARCHE DE LA TOUR, 6660 Jarry E. Saint-Léonard (325-8510) (By car, take the Métropolitain expressway [Autoroute 40] east to the Langelier exit and then to Jarry; or take bus 193 from the Jarry Métro.) Pisa this isn't, despite the tower of structural steel leaning over the entrance. This shopping centre was supposed to have a distinct Italian flavour but it hasn't worked out that way. The Italian-style stores and restaurants have left but the market has a good selection of pastas and olive oils, the butchers make their own sausage, and the bakery has biscotti fresh from the oven.

A WALK THROUGH LITTLE ITALY

Start at the Casa d'Italia, 505 Jean-Talon East.
  (Métro Jean-Talon nord [north] exit)
End at the Marché Jean-Talon, near Métro Jean-Talon

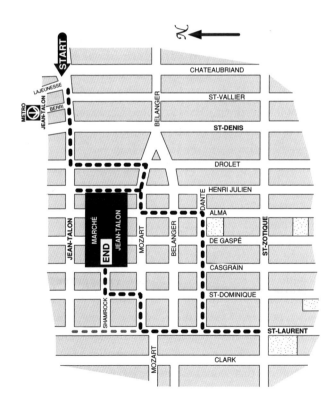

> *People are coming here because it's where everything started . . . I mean who didn't go to Notre-Dame-della Difesa Church, who didn't go to San Filippo Benizi or Notre Dame-de-la-Défense School. So now, it's kind of sentimental.*
>
> — Ivano Vellone, *Vellone's Music* on boul. St-Laurent.

This is a good neighbourhood stroll. Allow lots of time for going into stores and buildings and the occasional espresso stop. START AT THE CASA D'ITALIA, 505 Jean Talon E.

This building is a wonderful example of art-deco design and was built in 1936 under the direction of the Opera Nazionale Dopolavoro, the local chapter of an international workers association. The land was granted by the City of Montreal. The Italian community contributed to the building fund campaign and many Italian construction workers donated their labour to build Casa. The Italian government's financial contribution gave it effective control of the community centre until the Canadian army took over the building during WWII. The Canadian government returned it to the community after the war.

There are two plaques in the lobby which date from when the Casa was constructed. One is for those who helped build the Casa. The other sets out a code of ethics from the Italian government and admonishes newcomers to have "pride in your race; love for Italy, your homeland; and respect for your new land."

The word Fascism comes from the Italian word *fascio* meaning "to bundle together." The Fascist symbol — sheaves of wheat, bound together for strength, with an *àscia* (axe) jutting from the top — represents the union of a country that consisted of separate states only a couple of generations before. In the lobby are two versions of the symbol — one is held by an angel painted on the wall. The other, much larger, is inlaid into the floor but is partially covered by offices that were built in the lobby after WWII.

Today, the Casa houses several community organizations.

There's a small Italian library and an Italian restaurant with a good luncheon buffet.

CROSS JEAN TALON AND WALK WEST. Notice the three-storey greystone buildings with their magnificent wrought iron staircases on St-Denis. In 1852, a fire in Montreal left 10,000 people homeless and new wooden housing was banned. Fortunately the city had several quarries, including one north of Mont-Royal boulevard and stone from there was used for new buildings such as these which date from late 1800s.

Several reasons have been offered as to why builders put staircases outside, in a city with such severe winters. Aesthetically, French-Canadians, moving here from rural parts of the province, did not want homes which opened onto corridors; financially, it was cheaper to build three storey buildings with the staircases outside, since the hallways would not have to be heated; also, placing the staircase meant there was room for larger flats within. As elegant as they seem now, many at the time thought they were "tasteless paraphernalia." In any case, they are dangerous in winter and, by 1950, a municipal law stopped them from being added to new housing.

WALK WEST TO DROLET which is named for Chevalier Drolet, a 19th century Montrealer. By 1910, most of the streets running north-south in this part of the city had been opened and were linked by the east-west dirt road of Mozart. Open country lay beyond Jean-Talon. The streetcar took about thirty minutes to get downtown to Phillips Square.

This neighbourhood still displays its original enthusiastic construction. Some buildings are similar to the greystones on St-Denis; others feature balconies and the covered loggias of a more Mediterranean influence. Several are not much bigger than the original tar-paper and sheet-metal shacks built around the turn of the century.

Each home was separately erected and some still have a narrow strip of land between them. Several have small, attractive gardens in front.

TAKE A RIGHT AT MOTTA'S BAKERY. Go around the corner (or through the store) and turn north (right) on Henri-Julien. This is what most immigrants wanted when they left Montreal's downtown congestion and squalor — a new home with a courtyard and a garden. In summer, these backyards are sumptuous plots of land with grape arbours, squashes hanging from vines, sunflowers, and tomatoes. The Jean-Talon market is just across the street.

On the corner of Jean-Talon and Henri-Julien is Granato, the local funeral home now owned by a large Quebec chain.

RETURN DOWN HENRI-JULIEN. TAKE A RIGHT ON MOZART. Across, at 268 Mozart, E. is the National Awning company. The company has been here since the 1940s but the building is about 80 years old and is one of the few which give a sense of how homes were built. There is a veranda on the second floor and the house is set back from the street. In the 1950s, the awning company rented it to the city which converted it into a clinic to treat children with tuberculosis and polio.

TAKE A LEFT AT ALMA AND WALK DOWN TO DANTE. The church, La Madonna Della Difesa, sits on one corner. It is open for mass weekdays at 8:00 a.m. and 7:30 p.m. On Sundays and feast days, masses are at 8:30, 9:30 and 10:30 in the morning. When the church was originally built, in 1910, it incorporated the elementary school Notre-Dame-de-la-Defense, across the street, on Henri-Julien. By 1921, the school had 770 students but was too expensive for the parish. The Montreal Catholic School Commission took it over and kept teaching religion in Italian for several years.

Today the school has 400 students from 38 ethnic communities. 20% are Italian and there are large numbers of Haitian, Salvadoran and Vietnamese youngsters. This school was the Commission's last bilingual one (French and English) and French has been the language of instruction since the early 1980s.

Building of the church began in 1918. Much of the funding came directly from the community and even those who had only a few dollars to give, have their names engraved in marble, inside the entrance. The style of La Madonna Della Difesa is Roman and is typical of Italian church architecture. The architect and designer was Guido Nincheri, a native of Florence, who, because he was not then a Canadian citizen, submitted his plans through a local architect, Roch Montbriand.

Nincheri painted murals in many Québec churches, but he is best known for la Difesa's impressive fresco in the apse. There are hundreds of figures. Nincheri, himself, supports Pope Pius XI; and Nincheri's son is dressed as an altar boy. The fresco traces the history of the church from Adam and Eve through the patriarchs and into the twentieth century. Ecclesiastical and political figures include a Canadian senator in the cap and gown of the University of Ottawa. To the right is the fresco's most famous subject — Mussolini on horseback. During WWII, the mural was covered up by the RCMP. Nincheri was branded a fascist and left Montreal for Rhode Island but returned after the war and painted several other ecclesiastical works. The church's magnificent white Carrara marble altar and railing were installed in 1950.

When looking at the mural, remember that it was painted before WWII. Until he invaded Ethiopia, Mussolini was an internationally-popular statesman; the mural commemorates the Lateran Treaty of 1929 in which Mussolini created the modern Vatican State.

In 1984, a statue of a soldier was placed outside the church. It was to have commemorated Italian soldiers, but some community leaders felt this would be poorly interpreted. The inscription reads "Omaggio ai caduti di tutte le guerre" (honour to soldiers of all wars).

In 1920, the city named this street for Italy's famous 14th century poet, Dante Alighieri. A bust of him is in Dante Park west of the church. A bocci court is at the back of the park and Italian flags fly over the street during much of the year.

The Italian Canadian Social Club is across the street, at 209 Dante. It's open to members most afternoons, although anyone seems to be able to drop in. The Club has been there since 1936 and is decorated with pictures and statues honouring Mussolini and other WWII Italian heros. The club's owner, who fought in the Ethiopian campaigns, died in 1991.

CONTINUE ON DANTE TO ST-LAURENT. St. Joseph's, the Catholic church at 166 Dante, features a traditional mass, ostensibly to distinguish it from La Difesa's more Italianate orientation.

Dante retains an Italian neighbourhood flavour that has disappeared from much of the area. Espresso bars cater to people from specific regions of Italy, each with its own character and characters. Anyone can get coffee here, but these places cater to neighbourhood men; single women may find them a little uncomfortable.

Continue on to Little Italy's best-known hardware store — Quincallerie Dante at the corner of St-Dominque and Dante. It's been in the Venditelli family since 1956. It was originally a grocery store; but now sells rifles, gnocci makers, and paint; in fact, almost anything except food.

Trattoria dai Baffoni, at the corner of Dante and St-Laurent is a neighbourhood institution. Decades ago, when it was across the street on St-Laurent, it was a crazy small box of a restaurant with great food. Today, it is huge and less exotic, although more approachable for non-Italians. Waiters sport baffoni (mustaches). The Trattoria is owned by the DePalma family who are key organizers for soccer and cycling.

TAKE A LEFT ON ST-LAURENT. Walk down to St. Zotique and look up to see the city's large "Petite Italie" medallions above the street. They indicate Little Italy officially begins at this corner. Poke into Atlas Aquarium, at 6725 St-Laurent, to see an amazing variety of tropical fish. Cross at St-Zotique and go back up the other side. The food shops, in particular, reflect the area's newer ethnic communities. You couldn't have bought tahini here a dozen years ago.

Like St-Laurent further south, this area is becoming increasingly trendy. Rents are going up and many older stores have gone out of business. Those who have their own shops usually bought their buildings several years ago.

Many of the Italian shops that have remained are fairly successful. Libreria Italiana, at 6792 St-Laurent, has newspapers and magazines from Rome and Milan; Milano's supermarket, at 6884 St-Laurent, has taken over several adjoining stores; and Vellone, 7092 St-Laurent, stocks recent Italian videos and records. Leon Vellone, who manages the family store, is one of the younger generation of community leaders trying to create a renaissance in Little Italy.

The Fiducie Canadienne Italienne, at 6999 St-Laurent is the community's own financial institution and has helped strengthen the economy of Little Italy. There are several espresso bars and coffee shops between here and Jean-Talon.

TURN AT MOZART AND WALK ONE BLOCK EAST TO ST-DOMINIQUE. Zinman, at 8022 St-Dominique, between Mozart and Belanger, is one of the few live poultry markets left in Montreal. Across the street is the police station for the area, District 43. Built in 1931 by local architect E. A. Daoust, it is a superb example of local art deco, less squat but similar to the Casa. There is a small, complimentary building, originally built as the police chief's home, behind the station, at Shamrock and Casgrain.

THE WALK ENDS IN THE JEAN-TALON MARKET, the best and most diverse farmers' market in the city. It used to be called the Marché-du-nord and the narrow street running alongside the market stores is still named Place du Marché-du-nord. Earlier, this was the Shamrock Athletic Field which served the area's first immigrants, the Irish who arrived in the 19th century.

The market is divided into two parts. On the periphery are fruit stores, butcher shops, fish stores, cheese shops, restaurants, bakeries and other shops. The centre is for produce sellers. In summer, most of the fruit and vegetables are from farms near Montreal. There are sellers of local honey, maple syrup, double-yolked eggs, and cut flowers. Denis Lauzon, at stand #166, has over 20 varieties of fresh herbs. He also grows hard-to-find vegetables such as salsify and black radishes. The market is open throughout the year although specialized stands may not be open during the winter months.

WHEELCHAIR ACCESSIBLE PUBLIC WASHROOMS are on the ground floor of the main public building where Shamrock street meets the market. Most of this building houses a large bakery with a small café. It's a good place for a break.

SOME BOOKS, A PLAY, AND A FILM

Canadese: A Portrait of the Italian Canadians, Kenneth Bagnell, Macmillan, 1989.

Italian Canadian Voices, edited by Caroline Morgan Di Giovani, Mosaic Press, 1984.

Italians in a Multicultural Canada, Clifford J. Jansen, Edwin Mellen Press, 1987.

The Italians of Montreal: From Sojourning to Settlement 1900-1921, Bruno Ramirez & Michael del Balso, Les Édition du Courant Inc., 1980.

Les Italiens au Quebec, Claude Painchaud & Richard Poulin, Les éditions Asticou enrg. / Les éditions Critiques, 1988.

Voiceless People, a play by Marco Micone, Guernica Editions, 1982.

Caffe Italia, Montreal produced by Cinema Libre, is an acclaimed documentary film on the Italian community, much of it takes place in the boul. St-Laurent café of the same name.

Xenofolies, Michel Moreau, NFB 1992. Québecois and Italians fail at understanding each other in this documentary shot at a high school in the Montreal area.

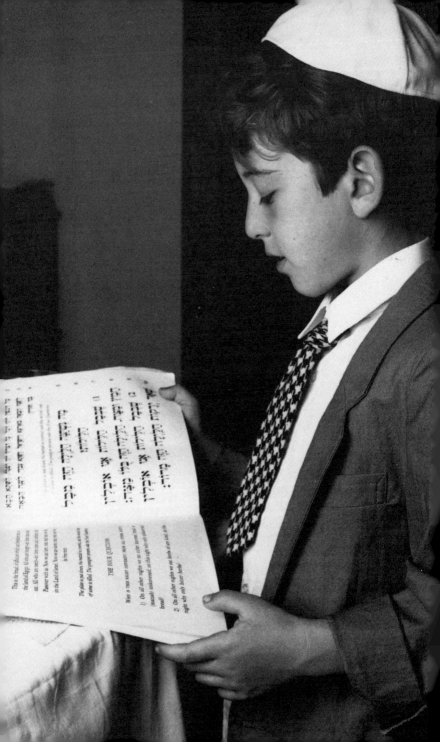

JEWISH MONTREAL

POPULATION: 96,000

COMMUNITIES: Mile End and Outremont, Snowdon,
Côte-des-Neiges, Côte-St-Luc, Chomedey, Dollard,
Hampstead, Ville Saint-Laurent

SHOPPING: Snowdon, Mile-End (St-Viateur and Fairmount
Avenue), Victoria and Van Horne Avenues

New France was a Catholic colony. Jews were only allowed to settle
here after the British conquest of 1760. The best known Jewish
figure was also one of the first to arrive: Aaron Hart, a Londoner
and a supplier to the British troops. He opened a trading business
in Trois-Rivières and became the town's first Postmaster. Hart's
children were raised with a traditional Jewish upbringing. His son
Ezekiel was elected three times to the legislative assembly of Lower
Canada but was not allowed to take his seat because he was a Jew.
One of Aaron Hart's descendants, Cecil Hart, was a manager and
coach of the Montreal Canadiens in the 1930s. The National
Hockey League's Hart Memorial Trophy, given to the most valu-
able player, is named after him.

By the late 1700s there was a trading company in Montreal
established by Jewish trappers, traders, and merchants. In 1768 the
community formed Canada's first congregation — Shearith Israel
(The Remnants of Israel). The congregation continues today as the
Spanish and Portuguese Synagogue in the Snowdon district of
Montreal.

Although Britain permitted Jews to enter, for more than 60
years Judaism itself had no legal status. This meant that marriages,
births and deaths weren't officially recorded and property couldn't
be inherited. (Other non-Anglican or non-Catholic communities,
such as the Methodists, also had this problem.)

In 1828, Montreal Jews petitioned the government to recognize their religion. The French-Canadian dominated Assembly supported the bill hoping it would weaken the Anglican establishment, and in 1832 Canadian Jews received full rights before the law, 25 years before this would happen in Britain.

By the 1880s, the small Jewish community was prosperous, mostly British-born and considered itself almost landed gentry. Its leader was Sir Mortimer Davis, founder of Imperial Tobacco and a descendent of the Harts. The community had a cemetery on Mount Royal and another near the "Back River" (Rivière des prairies). This was a contented, tightly-knit group totally unprepared for the inundation of impoverished, Yiddish-speaking Jews which began pouring into the city in the 1880s. These immigrants were Ashkenazim (Jews originating in North and Eastern Europe) fleeing anti-Semitism in Russia and Europe. They came by the tens of thousands and soon made Yiddish Montreal's third most common language.

Some of the newcomers settled in the Papineau area of northeast Montreal. Others moved into the growing factory town of Lachine, but most lived in the central immigrant strip along Boulevard St-Laurent, then known as St. Lawrence Main Street. These newcomers were disparagingly called "Yids" or "downtowners" by the Anglo-Jewish establishment (or "uptowners") who lived several blocks west between Dorchester (René-Lévesque) and Sherbrooke. The "uptowners" were merchants, doctors and professionals while many of the "downtowners" were also educated, but knew little English or French. In Eastern Europe, they had been skilled workers, musicians, photographers, writers, scholars, and artists. Now they worked the streets as pedlars, truck drivers, carpenters, and tinsmiths in the railway yards, and clerks and teachers in the community.

The garment trade drew these Jews like a magnet. Most worked 10 or 12 hour days in unventilated buildings, often renting their machines and chairs, cutting and sewing clothes alongside poor French Canadians newly arrived from rural Quebec. In 1893, men earned $10 for a 60-80 hour week with women getting from $3 to $5.

■■ WHAT'S IN A NAME?

People used to be known by how they looked (Eric the Red), their occupations (Shepherd, Goldsmith), where they lived (du Castel), or their parents (Son of John which became Johnson). Some names go back thousands of years. Joseph, for example, is derived from one of the twelve tribes that descended from Jacob's twelve sons.

Many Jewish names have changed slightly over generations, particularly when there was inter-marriage. For example, Levy, the biblical tribal name for Israel's priests, is also known in Quebec as Levee, Levay, Lévy, Levi, and Lévé.

For the most part, however, Jews had no tradition of last names and, when these were needed, many took them from their occupations. A Steiner was a stoneworker, a Schneider a tailor and a Bronfman a "man who makes something to drink" — a distiller! Some people had no choice. There is the story of the nervous man who couldn't remember what to say when he immigrated. Asked for his name, he slapped his head and muttered, in Yiddish, "Schöen Fargessen!" ("I've forgotten"). The immigration officer wrote down Sean Ferguson.

Despite the hard work, the garment business held certain attractions. The boss was likely to be Jewish and spoke Yiddish; Saturdays and other Jewish holidays could be taken off (even if the hours were made up late at night and on Sundays). A couple with a machine and some cloth could set up their own small shop, get work from larger companies, and dream of making a fortune.

It's hard to imagine the intensity and compactness of this world. Many of the workers had joined labour movements in Europe and stayed involved with socialist causes in Montreal. There were Zionists and anti-Zionists, socialists and Communists, Yiddishists, anti-religionists and Orthodox. Each proclaimed what was best for the Jewish people and the world.

Boulevard St-Laurent was the Main and it encapsulated this world. Here were Jewish bookstores, newspapers, libraries, push carts, pedlars, kosher restaurants, grocery stores, Yiddish theatres, Yiddish community clinics, Hebrew and Yiddish afternoon schools, synagogues, "mikvahs" for ritual baths, and "landsmanshaften" — mutual aid societies to help the newcomer adapt to Canadian society. It was a world in which a Jewish municipal party advocated such radical ideas as eight hour work days, no child labour, equal rights for all national groups, the creation of municipal libraries and art galleries, and the use of Yiddish in city regulations. To the uninitiated, the Main was chaos. To those who lived there, it was life itself.

But this was also a world fuelled by immigrants and the flow ended abruptly with the Great Depression. Previously as many as 400,000 immigrants had entered Canada in one year; however, by 1931, less than 28,000 were admitted with Jews specifically excluded.

Although Quebec lead most of the world in decreeing that Jews were equal before the law, attitudes changed as the Jewish community grew. The Church, besieged in Europe, decried Jews as supporters of reform, modernism, and liberalism. In 1898, the Montreal Chamber of Commerce refused membership to an applicant because he was a Jew. When the world-famous French actress Sarah Bernhardt (who was Jewish) arrived here, she was pelted with eggs and tomatoes and charged with "moral corruption against Christian society."

By the 1920s, Jews were put into a special immigration category, and the official church journal *Action Catholique* was telling readers "If we do not buy from the Jews, they will leave." McGill University limited the number of Jewish students it would accept and, in 1934, interns at Montreal hospitals went on strike rather than work alongside a Jew. In the Laurentian resort community of Ste-Agathe, signs went up saying "No Jews or dogs."

As wwii approached, Canada's immigration policy was further restrained. Refugees, particularly Jews attempting to escape Hitler's Germany, were not allowed into the country. Ironically, Jews in the Auschwitz concentration camp called the building in which their food, clothes, and jewellery were stored "Canada" because it represented luxury and salvation (and was as impossible to enter).

After the war, racism against Jews diminished and the establishment of the State of Israel in 1948 helped legitimize the cultural aspirations of the Jews as a people. Thousands of Jews arrived in Montreal from a war-ravaged Europe and a new kind of Jewish immigrant for Quebec began arriving too. These were Sephardi Jews, many of whom were fleeing anti-Semitism in Iraq and Egypt. They paved the way for a larger influx from Morocco that came shortly after that country became independent from France in 1956. Morocco's new government would not guarantee civil liberties and 300,000 Jews left. Most went to Israel but about 30,000 settled in Montreal. Many Quebecers were amazed to find that there was a large and growing community of Jews whose first language was French. Today, Sephardi Jews account for more than a quarter of the community and are a dynamic part of the Jewish community, partially replacing English-speaking Jews who continue to leave the city and province.

Since the mid-1970s, the Montreal Jewish community has

shrunk from about 120,000 to 95,000. However, it continues to be one of the strongest and most vital communities in North America. Hundreds of immigrants from the Soviet Union and even Israel choose to settle here every year and Montreal boasts one of the world's larger communities of Ethiopian Jews.

■■ WELCOME TO CANADA

A Modern Folktale

The Arabic word "wilkum" sounds like the English "welcome" but means "woe to you." André Elbaz, in his book Folktales of the Canadian Sephardim, *tells a story about a French-speaking Jewish couple from Morocco who arrive at Montreal's airport. A large sign on the wall reads "Bienvenue au Canada" and next to it says another, "Welcome."*

"Bienvenue, that's nice," says the man. "But," says his wife, "next to it, they warn us — wilkum! Woe to you! You'll soon find out what's in store here!"

ORGANIZATIONS

There have been Jewish organizations since the first group of Jews arrived in Montreal. The first would have been a burial society so that the Jewish dead could be properly put to rest. The first formal charity was The Hebrew Philanthropic Society organized in the 1840s when cholera epidemics struck Montreal. The Baron de Hirsch Institute, which still exists, was set up in 1863 to help settle Jewish immigrants and provide shelter for the poor and orphans. The first important umbrella organization was the Federation of

Jewish Philanthropies, set up in 1917 to cope with the massive wave of immigration from Eastern Europe.

Two unusual groups were also created: the Hebrew Free Loan Association provided interest-free loans to Jewish immigrants and on Ontario Street, the Volkskueche or People's Kitchen was set up "Where men and women may obtain a solid, comforting meal for five cents or nothing at all, when they have nothing."

Today the Jewish community continues the pattern of having a few large groups presenting common concerns and many small groups responding to specific needs.

The Cummings Building at 5151 Côte-Ste Catherine houses many important community organizations and institutions: **Federation of Jewish Community Services**, (735-3541) raises funds for Israel and for community services such as home-care, Jewish schools, and programs for seniors and immigrants. It increasingly deliberates on behalf of the community with government. In May, it holds a fundraising marathon walk, called the "March to Jerusalem," followed by an Israeli-style street festival. The **Montreal Holocaust Memorial Centre Museum** (345-2605) has guided tours and exhibits about Jewish life in Europe before and during its destruction by the Nazis. The **Jewish Public Library** (345-2627) is also located in this building. The library began in 1914 and has over 100,000 books and periodicals in English, French, Hebrew and Yiddish, in addition to a historical archives. A branch of the library is at 755 du Sablon, Chomedey (688-8961). The **Association for the Advancement of Jewish Day Schools** (345-2615) represents Montreal's Jewish day schools to government and other school commissions in Montreal. In 1903, the government decided that the Jews would be considered Protestant for the purposes of education. A brief attempt to set up a Jewish School Board did not work out. Instead, the community sent its children to Protestant Board schools or to its own private day schools. The first Talmud Torah (Students of the

Torah) was set up in 1896 and today there are more than 60 pre-school, elementary and secondary Jewish schools in Montreal, Dollard, Laval and Chomedey.

Canada-Israel Committee, 1310 Greene (934-0771) represents community views on Israel to government and advocates a pro-Israel policy within Quebec.

Canadian Jewish Congress (CJC), 1590 Docteur Penfield (931-7531). Founded in 1919, the CJC is primarily a political organization representing a variety of different community groups and organizations to all levels of government.

Canadian Zionist Federation, 5250 Decarie (Décor Decarie) (486-9526). There used to be numerous Zionist organizations, each propounding a different vision of the state of Israel. The federation represents many of these groups, and supports Israel through educational activities and assisting Aliyah (immigration to Israel).

Communauté Sépharade du Québec, 4735 Côte-Ste-Catherine (739-4998) is an umbrella organization for Montreal's growing Sephardi Jewish community. It works with synagogues, Sephardi day and afternoon schools and publishes the bi-monthly *La Voix Sépharade*. Every other year the Community holds a ten-day Sephardic arts and culture festival at the nearby YM-YWHA and Saidye Bronfman Centre.

The complex of community buildings at the corner of Côte-Ste-Catherine and Westbury include the **Centres Communautaires Juifs de Montréal / Montreal Jewish Community Centres,** 5480 Westbury (735-5565); the theatre, art programs, and gallery of the **Saidye Bronfman Centre** (739-2301); and the **Young Men-Young Women's Hebrew Association** (737-6551) with a nursery school, children's and senior programs, a gym, swim, tennis and weightlifting facilities. Members include many non-Jews and the legendary Wolf Pack joggers who have participated in charity runs and marathons for over 30 years.

Jewish Anarchists Group (844-3207). Many in the Jewish community think there's already too much anarchy, others know that Anarchism has been a political movement for more than a hundred years and this group is merely another manifestation; anti-authoritarian while adhering to Jewish religion and Jewish life. It meets regularly at the Alternative Bookstore at 2035 St-Laurent.

Jewish Education Program of Montreal, 3133 Van Horne (737-3086) is a learning centre for Jewish adults who want to learn more about Jewish culture.

Jewish Family Services, 5250 Decarie (485-1112) provides help and services for youth protection, adoption, care for the elderly and family counselling.

Jewish Genealogical Society of Montreal, 5787 McAlear (489-4093) helps trace Jewish family names.

Jewish Information and Referral Service (737-2221). Weekdays 9:30-4:30. Want to know when a Jewish holiday starts? Thinking of getting involved in a Jewish community volunteer program? Maybe you just want to learn how to make chicken soup! Lots of helpful advice, no question is too dumb.

Jewish National Fund (JNF), 1980 Sherbrooke W. (934-0313). Established in 1906, the JNF initially bought land in Palestine from Turkey and local landowners. Later, it reclaimed land and helped build new communities. Today, it raises money for land development, forestation and road building in Israel.

League for Human Rights of B'nai B'rith, 6333 Decarie, (Décor Decarie) (733-5377). B'nai Brith — "Sons of the Covenant" — is the largest Jewish fraternal organization in North America and has been a presence in Canada since 1875. It supports Hillel Jewish student clubs at universities and its League for Human Rights is a non-profit group combatting all forms of racism and bigotry.

Montreal Jewish Historical Society (489-8741). Regular lectures and meetings to discuss Quebec Jewish history.

Sir Mortimer B. Davis Jewish General Hospital of Montreal, 3755 Côte-Ste-Catherine (340-8222). The hospital was established in 1934 because Montreal needed more hospital beds and Jewish physicians and nurses found it difficult to get work or care for their patients in non-Jewish hospitals. Today it is a major research institute and the grounds, which extend from Côte-des-Neiges to Westbury, will soon accommodate the Jewish Hospital of Hope for the terminally ill.

■■ TO LIFE!

The word "chai" is Hebrew for "life." The numerical value of its Hebrew letters is 18 which is therefore considered a good luck number. People often give 18 (or a number that is a multiple of 18) to charity and the most common toast with a glass of wine or liquor is L'chayim, *"to life."*

Shalom Line (343-4343) is the Jewish community's listening service. People call to talk about loneliness, drugs, sexual problems, and other worries.

Vaad Ha-ir / The Jewish Community Council, 5491 Victoria (739-6363) certifies kosher establishments, authorizes Jewish divorces and acts as a rabbinical arbitrator for community disputes.

Yakhdav (487-2880). Yakhdav means "togetherness" in Hebrew and this group brings together gay and lesbian Jews to celebrate Jewish festivals.

Yiddish Committee of Canadian Jewish Congress, 1590 Docteur Penfield (931-7531). "Mameh Loshn" (Mother Tongue) activities and entertainment. There is a particularly active younger group, including those "learning Yiddish again for the first time."

Yiddish Theatre Troupe, Saidye Bronfman Centre, 5170 Côte-Ste-Catherine (739-2301). Classes in Yiddish Drama and plays and musicals maintain Montreal's tradition as one of the few cities in the world that has had live Yiddish entertainment for over a hundred years.

RELIGIOUS LIFE

While Judaism is the religion of Jews, it has many denominations most of which are practised in Montreal.

Jews often refer to themselves as Ashkenazi (when their origins are from countries in Northern, Central and Eastern Europe and Russia) or Sephardi (North Africa, Spain, and parts of other European countries bordering on the Mediterranean). These more accurately describe a person's ancestry than his or her religious orientation. The oldest congregation in Canada is the Sephardi Shearith Israel — **Spanish and Portuguese Synagogue**, founded in Montreal 1768, and now located at 4894 St-Kevin (737-3695). The **Ashkenazi Shaar Hashomayim** (Gate of Heaven), 450 Kensington, Westmount (937-9471), the second oldest congregation in Canada, was founded in 1846 and moved to this location in 1922. The building has a small library and museum and the congregation follows a "traditional" approach between orthodox and conservative practices.

HASSIDISM. Montreal has about 12,000 members of several Hassidic sects. The movement started in 18th century Poland under the Baal Shem Tov, a charismatic leader who preached that one should serve G–d (the name is never spoken or spelled) in joy, nurturing the sparks of holiness found in everyone. As disciples spread the message, different groups pursued their own orientation and took on the name of their spiritual leader's village or town.

Hassidism (literally "the pious" use Yiddish as their daily language and Hebrew for prayer and religious study. There are several Hassidic groups in Montreal. The largest in Mile End and Outremont are the Satmar and Belz. The Lubavitch, based in the Snowdon area, are unique in actively persuading less religious Jews to be more observant.

ORTHODOX Jews adhere to Jewish law; most wear yarmulkes (skullcaps) and keep kosher. Almost all synagogues in Montreal belong to the Orthodox movement and maintain separate areas for men and women to pray. Orthodox families often have many children since Orthodox rabbis frown on birth control and support the biblical injunction to "be fruitful and multiply."

CONSERVATIVE JUDAISM was originally called "historical Judaism." It originated in the United States near the end of the 19th century as a middle ground between Orthodoxy and the more rationalist approach of the Reform Judaism movement. It broke sharply with the Orthodox in allowing men and women to pray together and permitting observant Jews to drive to services on the Sabbath and holidays. Not surprisingly, suburban synagogues are often conservative, such as **Beth-El** (House of God), at 100 Lucerne Road in the Town of Mount Royal (738-4766).

RECONSTRUCTIONISM broke away from the Conservative movement in this century and sees Judaism as an ongoing civilization. It emphasizes equality between the sexes and a love of Hebrew culture. Many consider reconstructionism more of an intellectual movement than a religious one. The Reconstructionist Synagogue — **Dorshei Emet** is at 18 Cleve Road, Hampstead (486-9400).

REFORM began in Germany in the early 19th century with a liberal, less literal approach to Judaism. Much of the service is in English, men and women sit together during services, and both can officiate. Montreal's oldest Reform synagogue is **Temple**

Emanu-El Beth Shalom, 4100 Sherbrooke St. W. Westmount (937-3575).

The Rabbinical Council of Greater Montreal represents orthodox rabbis; while the Board of Jewish Ministers of Greater Montreal is a forum for rabbis from all denominations. Leadership in both groups changes every year or so. The **Grand Rabbinat du Québec**, 5850 Victoria (738-1004) oversees religious activities within much of the Sephardi community.

MEDIA

Jews, often called "the people of the book," were among the most educated of immigrant groups, and newspapers played an important part in the community's growth. In the first half of this century, several publications competed for loyalty and readership. The most important was the *Keneder Adler* (Canadian Eagle), founded in 1907 as a literate paper for the common man. Today, the prominent Jewish newspaper is the **Canadian Jewish News**, 6900 Décarie (Décor Decarie) (735-2612), a weekly published in Montreal and Toronto. Although privately-owned, its mandate is not to make a profit but to present the interests of the established community leadership.

La Voix Sepherade, 4735 Côte-St-Catherine (733-4998) is published bi-monthly for Quebec's Sephardi community.

Tribune Juif, 5505 Côte-Ste-Catherine, suite 14 (737-2666) an independent bi-monthly magazine strong on cultural and political issues both in Quebec and Israel.

Jewish programming can be heard on "The Jewish Hour" on CFMB Radio 1420-AM Sundays at 1:30 p.m. and the "Jewish Program" on CKUT 90.3-FM Thursdays at 6:00 p.m.

The **Jewish Media Foundation** (488-6599) produces several Hebrew, French and English television programs on Cable TV.

■■ THE JEWISH CALENDAR

The Jewish day goes from sundown to sundown with seasons determined by the sun, while months and festivals depend upon the cycle of the moon. Periodically, an extra month is inserted into the calendar to keep the holidays in their proper season. 1992 began three months into the Jewish year 5752.

The Sabbath *occurs every seven days and its personification as a bride is one of the most enduring images in Jewish tradition.*

Major holy days in the fall include Rosh Hashonah — *the Jewish New Year,* Yom Kippur — *the Day of Atonement, and* SimchatTorah — *the annual beginning of the reading of the Torah (the first five books in the Bible).*

In winter, Hannukah *(the festival of lights) celebrates the revolt, about 2,100 years ago, of the Jews against the Syrians. Its symbol, a candelabra called a Hanukiah, commemorates a 1-day supply of temple oil that miraculously stayed lit for 8 days.*

There are two important festivals of freedom: Purim *commemorates the liberation of Jews under the Persians and is celebrated with costumes, singing, charity and gifts of food to friends; the Spring festival of* Passover *or Pesach celebrates the end of Jewish slavery in Egypt and the return to Israel.*

Two significant days of observance have been added to the Jewish calendar in this century. Both are in the Spring: Yom Ha' Atzmaut *celebrates the establishment of the State of Israel, and* Yom Hashoa *commemorates the destruction of European Jewry during the Holocaust of WWII.*

Many festivals have traditional foods. During Passover bread made with yeast cannot be eaten because the ancient Jews fled Egypt without time to bake bread. Biscuits called matzohs are eaten instead, as well as delicious flourless cakes and cookies. During Hannukah, fried foods are eaten to celebrate the oil-lit lamp.

BOOKS AND FILMS

A.M. Klein: Short Stories, M.W. Steinberg, editor, University of Toronto Press, 1983.

A Coat of Many Colours: Two centuries of Jewish Life in Canada, Irving Abella, Lester & Orpen Dennys, Toronto, 1990.

Deemed Suspect: A Wartime Blunder (German Jews in Canadian prison camps during wwii), Eric Koch, Methuen, Toronto, 1980.

An Everyday Miracle: Yiddish Culture in Montreal, Ira Robinson, Pierre Anctil, and Mervin Butovsky, Véhicule Press, Montreal, 1990.

Folktales of the Canadian Sephardim, André E. Elbaz, Fitzhenry & Whiteside, Toronto, 1982.

Home Sweet Home: My Canadian Album, Mordecai Richler, Penguin Books, Toronto, 1986.

The Jewish Community in Quebec, Interculturel Institute of Montreal, 1987.

Le rendez-vous manqué: Les Juifs de Montréal face au Québec de l'entre-deux-guerres, Pierre Anctil, Institut Québécois de recherche sur la culture, Montreal, 1988.

Rendez-vous à Montréal: A Guide to Jewish Montreal, Allied Jewish Community Services, Montreal, 1990.

Feature films available on video include *The Apprenticeship of Duddy Kravitz*, *Falling Over Backwards*, *Lies My Father Told Me* and *Moïse*, a short, unusual film in which a Hassidic family finds a baby on its doorstep.

The **National Film Board Library** in Place Guy Favreau (283-4823) has several short documentaries on Montreal Jewish writers Mordecai Richler and Irving Layton, a dozen films on the Holocaust including *Dark Lullabies / Berceuse pourdes ombres* in which a Montreal filmmaker goes to Germany to understand what happened to her family, and *The Street*, an award-winning animation film based on a Mordecai Richler short story about family relations.

The **Archives of the Canadian Jewish Congress**, 1590 Docteur Penfield (931-7531) has a large lending library of film strips and 16mm films, in French and English, on Jewish culture, the Holocaust, Jews in other lands and intergroup relations.

RESTAURANTS AND CLUBS

$ indicates that a lunch or dinner should cost under $10 (without taxes, tips, or wine). $$ is under $25 and $$$ above that. Credit cards accepted are listed. Hours often vary with the seasons so please call ahead. Kosher restaurants and stores close for Jewish festivals and on the Sabbath, from Friday at sundown to Saturday at sundown.

BEAUTY'S $ AMEX EN-ROUTE MC VISA

93 Mount Royal W. (849-8883)

■ Good food, great style. Superb blintzes, bagels and lox, eggs, homefried potatoes, fresh orange juice, salads, soups, sandwiches, etc. All the basics done very well. This place is an institution, not merely because it has survived for over 40 years while the rest of the Jewish neighbourhood moved to the suburbs, but because it remains a classic diner. The fifties retro look was redone a little while ago as Beauty's assiduously maintains its image.

BROWN DERBY $ AMEX MC VISA

Van Horne Shopping Centre (739-2331)

■ Sure, the Brown Derby has nouvel-shmouvel cuisine: quiche, feta salad, tortellini, etc. Forget it. This is where you come to find out why your Jewish friends' eyes grow moist when they describe their mother's cooking (assuming she was from Eastern Europe, or at least the Main): stuffed cabbage, smoked carp, dumplings of gefilte fish, cabbage borscht with flanken (boiled beef), clear chicken soup with a matzoh ball rising out of it like the Taj Mahal, eggplant mashed and glistening under a sheen of oil and onions. The waitresses are just like Mom too. ("Take the Club Roll Special. It's cheaper, it comes with soup and you don't need the fries.")

BUBBY'S $$ AMEX MC VISA
1336 Greene (989-2225)
■ Looks like Mom's, if Mom had a half dozen tables in her living room. Old-fashioned European cooking with a "Yiddisher Tam" (Jewish taste): marinated herring, beef flanken, chicken in the pot, hearty desserts. Reservations recommended.

CHEZ BABA II $ KOSHER
5487 Victoria (341-8824)
■ This is the kosher, unaffiliated version of the Moroccan tea stand, downtown in Le Faubourg. Customers line-up for the home-made doughnuts and mint tea but it's the spicy merguez sausage sandwiches on a freshly baked roll and the outstanding loubia (white bean) soup which make Baba II a good spot for lunch or snacks. Baklava, mekroude (small rose scented cakes), and other pastries are better than in most middle eastern shops. Service can be agonizingly slow.

DELI SNOWDON $ MC VISA
5265 Decarie (488-9129)
■ The Morantz brothers started this delicatessen over 40 years ago, just as Snowdon's Jewish community was getting established. The place has gotten fancier to shmooze (gossip) at the counter. Still, it's great deli with several kinds of smoked fish and meats. The matjes (herring in wine sauce) and gefilte fish are made in the back. For lunch, try the bean and barley soup and a smoked meat or brisket sandwich on rye. Baked goods, particularly the apple and cherry strudel, are delicious.

EL MOROCCO II $$ KOSHER AMEX EN-ROUTE MC VISA
3450 Drummond (844-6888)

■ The setting is North African with divans and settees hugging the walls. Good grilled meat and fish dishes for the unadventurous, otherwise consider a full meal of appetizers such as harira (a Moroccan minestrone) and pastilla (a meat pie with almonds and raisins). Main courses include several kinds of couscous and chicken dishes with almonds, honey, and olives. Desserts are thick and sweet and go well with hot mint tea impressively poured from teapots held at arms length above the table. Do not try this trick at home.

FOXY'S $ KOSHER
5987 Victoria (739-8777)
■ Looks like a greasy spoon but makes great falaffel: spicy fried balls of ground chick peas, crunchy on the outside, warm and moist within. Served with a nicely spiced sauce, salad and hot pickles in pita bread.

GOLDEN SPOON $ KOSHER VISA
5217 Decarie (481-3431)
■ Homestyle kosher meatless, Middle-Eastern cooking ranges from mediocre to excellent. There is a fine hand with the pastries, particularly the vegetable stuffed, ultra-flaky bourekas and small honey-coated baklavas for dessert.

JERUSALEM $ KOSHER
4961C Queen Mary (344-4095)
■ A small snackbar that could have popped out of Tel Aviv. The place is spotless. The ingredients are fresh. There are salads, home-made soup, delicious bourekas (cheese or potato filling in a puff pastry) fish, eggplant, hummous (chickpea and sesame dip), and many other Mediterranean and Yemenite dishes.

MOISHES STEAK HOUSE $$ VISA MC AMEX EN-ROUTE
3961 St-Laurent (845-1696, 9545)
■ There are steak houses and then there is Moishes with regal

portions and a setting that is fancy (somewhat rococo actually) but comfortable. The trick is not to fill up on the pickles, coleslaw, rye bread and other nosherei (a little something to get your appetite in shape) that quickly cover your table before the meal arrives. Appetizers include a large selection of Jewish dishes. The daily specials are good value. Steep stairs but there's an elevator near the entrance. Reservations suggested.

MONTEFIORE CLUB
1195 Guy Street (934-0776)

■ This private club was established in 1880 and its Guy street building was completed in 1906. It began as the Montefiore Social and Dramatic Club and was named for the British-Jewish philanthropist, Sir Moses Montefiore. Excellent traditional Friday night Sabbath dinners for members and their guests.

SCHNEIDER'S FAMOUS STEAK HOUSE $$ AMEX MC VISA
5839 Décarie (731-3376)

■ There aren't too many of these old fashioned Jewish steak houses left anywhere. Schneider's is an original. You walk into what, 35 years ago, was somebody's home. You wait in the hallway and then sit at one of several family-size tables with the rest of the crowd. There's a television in the corner and the waitress calls you "dear." Homestyle cooking with a vengeance: chicken soup, Romanian sausage karnatzle, herring and eggplant, beef brisket, baked chicken, and of course, steak.

SCHWARTZ'S HEBREW DELICATESSEN $
3895 St-Laurent (842-4813)

■ Sets the standard for Montreal-style smoked meat heaped high on rye bread with a pickle, black-cherry soda, and a side of great fries. Those who don't worry about cholesterol and fancy something that "schmecks" (tastes good) might consider some "spek" (smoked spicy, paprikaed beef fat) on top. Also good rib steaks and combination platters. No desserts.

WILENSKY'S $

34 Fairmount W. (271-0247)

■ Famous for fifty years for the Special (fried baloney and salami on a toasted bun — *no* mustard is extra!) and hand-pumped sodas. Nostalgia for the old neighbourhood brings a lunch-time line-up and cars double-parked outside. Nice people those Wilenskys, with shelves of used paperbacks to read and sometimes a stock market or racing tip.

A WORD ON KOSHER

Kosher means ritually fit, wholesome and honest, and kosher laws are derived from the Bible. A kosher animal must be in good health and be killed quickly, with as little pain as possible. Shops and restaurants with kosher food are inspected by a council of the Jewish community and close during the Sabbath and Jewish festivals. Kosher products are marked with a "K" or "U" usually within a circle. Since the word kosher also means honest, it has lent itself to phrases not connected with food. If "everything's kosher" then it's all right. On the other hand, when something is "not strictly kosher" it's probably not the proper thing to do.

FOOD SOURCES

First there are Bagels — Many places in Montreal still make bagels the old fashioned way with a little honey in the water for sweetness and a wood fire that produces just the right kind of heat and flavour. The old standbys are the **Bagel Shop** at 263 St. Viateur W. (276-8044) and **Fairmount Bagel**, 74 Fairmount W. (272-0667) which makes raisin and cinnamon bagels in addition to the standard poppy and sesame seed. **Levine's** also has an old oven going at 16 Rachel E. (982-6072). Westenders can buy them at **Super-**

Carnival on St-Jacques west of Cavendish. Snowdonites can pick them up at **Real Bagel**, 4940 Queen Mary (737-8841), and downtowners can get them in **Le Faubourg** on St. Marc and Ste-Catherine.

HOME MADE KOSHER BAKERY, 6915 Querbes (270-5567). Enter. Inhale. Buy. Average bagels (the oven is gas fired instead of using wood) but few places have better baked goods. The seeds in the poppy seed cakes are rarely ground as fine as here. The breads and cookies are excellent.

MEHADRIN, kosher, 257 St-Viateur W. (279-6351). A good butcher store with superb smoked poultry.

KNICK-NOSH, kosher, 5206 Décarie (487-2618). Essential Jewish catered cooking (matzoh balls, chicken soup, roast brisket of beef, farfel (dry-roasted and cooked lumpy pasta), kasha (buckwheat) and mushrooms, salads and desserts) with a couple of gourmet items like duck à l'orange frozen to go. Place your order by phone first.

QUALITE KOSHER QUALITY DELICATESSEN, 5855 Victoria (731-7883). "Do you have any chicken today?" "We have everything." And they do. There's a small grocery store, full bakery, and a delicatessen with a huge take-out selection: beef spare-ribs, roast beef, roast chicken, chicken schnitzel, chicken in a chinese-style sauce, latkes (potato pancakes), apple strudel, cooked pepper salad, eggplant and several kinds of smoked fish and herring.

PITA TIKVAH, 274 St. Viateur St. (277-0931). Thyme, onion, sesame, and bagel pitas (the dough from the holes are punched out for mini-pitas). This is great bread for dips and sandwiches.

ST. LAWRENCE BAKERY, 3830 St-Laurent (845-4536). A fixture on the Main since 1912. Brick-oven baked bread such as Russian rye, challah (traditional Sabbath dinner egg-enriched bread), salt-sticks, onion rolls, and cheesecake by the pound.

SHOPS AND SERVICES

Many store owners keep kosher and close their shops Friday evenings, Saturdays, and during Jewish festivals, but are often open on Sunday.

BIBLIOPHILE, 5519 Queen Mary (486-7369). Large selection of Israeli fiction, Judaica, and a good selection of general literature.

BOOK CENTRE, 5007 Queen Mary (731-2677) and 3349 des Sources, Dollard-des-Ormeaux. Jewish history, religion and culture and books by local Jewish authors.

FOLKDANCING, Israeli-style, at Mount Royal's Beaver Lake during the summer and twice a week at the Snowdon YM-YWHA (735-5565).

GAN-EDEN GIFT CENTRE, 4705 Van Horne (733-1947). Despite its name, (it means "garden of Eden") this place is more like an attic: china, crystal, Moroccan dresses, Hassidic music tapes, cooking pots, religious articles, books, even an oriental carpet or two. If you can't see it ask; if they don't have it, you probably don't need it.

HYMAN'S BUS TO NEW YORK CITY (271-6627). $100 gets you a round trip to Brooklyn on Hyman's bus. Almost all on board are Orthodox; be prepared for praying, singing, and lots of babies.

KOTEL HEBREW BOOK AND GIFT STORE, 6414 Victoria (739-4142, 8839). Religious articles, books, and Hebrew educational toys like magnetic Hebrew letters for the refrigerator.

RODAL'S RELIGIOUS ARTICLES, 4689 Van Horne (733-1876). This shop has much more than suggested by the name. There are gift-items from Israel and Jewish music; a good place for browsing. The staff is helpful at explaining ritual items like Sabbath spice boxes.

WALKING TOURS. Stan Asher (681-9817) grew up on the Main and leads anecdotal excursions of Jewish Montreal for groups and the Jewish Public Library (345-2627).

WALKING TOUR OF THE OLD JEWISH NEIGHBOURHOOD

Start at the corner of Sherbrooke and St-Laurent
 (bus 55 north from the Métro St-Laurent)
 End at the corner of Parc and St-Viateur

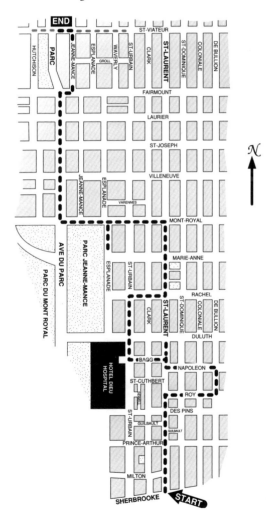

The Jewish community had its beginnings near old Montreal, where Pascal's hardware store used to be, at Craig (St-Antoine) and Bleury. The Jewish Talmud Torah school was nearby on St-Urbain near La Gauchetière. The Pascal, Reitman, and Steinberg families all started here as poor immigrants: glaziers, tailors and grocery store owners who, with their children, managed to build large retailing operations.

By the 1930s, the immigrant neighbourhood most think of as "Jewish" extended from the Monument National Theatre (often booked for Yiddish productions) on St-Laurent into the tree-lined streets of Outremont.

This street which divides the city into east and west has been known by several names over the past three hundred years: St. Lambert, Saint Lawrence, and St-Laurent but most commonly the Main. Much of this walk focuses on a Jewish community that had its greatest growth between two world wars, when 6% of Montreal's population and almost half the student body in the city's Protestant schools was Jewish.

Then, as one Jewish journalist described it, the Main was a thick ethnic ghetto "steaming and boiling . . . (with) assemblies, concerts, lectures of all sorts, banquets, resolutions, conferences, balls, tag days (for fundraising), suggestions, collections, protests . . . arguments, intrigues, circulars, handbills . . . dissension!"

START AT THE CORNER OF SHERBROOKE AND ST-LAURENT. Until the turn of this century, relatively few people lived north of Sherbrooke street.

Just below Sherbrooke, at 2115 St-Laurent, is the former Ekers Brewery, built in 1894 and owned by a former mayor of Montreal, Henry Ekers. It is now being renovated as Montreal's International Museum of Humour. The impressive group of buildings just east of the southeast corner of Sherbrooke and St-Laurent date from 1846 and are owned by the religious order of Notre Dame de la Charité du Bon Pasteur. Across the street, on the northwest corner of Clark and Sherbrooke, is the former home of William Notman, one of Canada's most important photographers. It was built in 1852. Much of his work is preserved in the Notman archives at the McCord Museum of Canadian History, near here at 690 Sherbrooke St. W. The gas station across the street is on the site of the old Molson family home. It was first built in 1819 and originally belonged to the Torrance family. The Torrance, Notman, Molson families were among Montreal's 19th century British-rooted 'aristocracy.' They built homes here, above the city, moving further away as Montreal's population grew.

The horsedrawn streetcar line, which climbed the Boulevard St-Laurent hill below Sherbrooke, went electric in 1880. Motorized trams began to travel as far north as Mont Royal. Industry could now move away from the slums near Old Montreal and onto higher ground. This innovation coincided with the late-19th century arrival of waves of European poor, including thousands of Jews, who immigrated to Canada and settled in Montreal.

WALK NORTH ON ST-LAURENT. The old Elysée movie theatre at the corner of Milton and Clark, visible as you walk up St-Laurent, was built in 1904 as the Shaare Tefilah, known as "The Austrian Synagogue." In 1960, the congregation merged with the Shomrim Laboker synagogue, now at 5151 Plamondon in the Snowdon district of Montreal.

By 1930, Montreal had a population of almost 900,000 people. Boulevard St-Laurent divided the city even more so than today, with the French to the east, and the English to the west. Immigrants travelled up the centre until they could afford to move elsewhere.

The Balfour Building, at 3575 St-Laurent, was once the centre of the clothing (or *schmata*) district, with offices for large and small manufacturers of mens and ladies suits, dresses and coats. It was recently renovated and now houses almost a hundred small businesses, architecture and design firms, arts associations, and community groups.

Levine Brothers Bakery, at 3670 St-Laurent, is one of the few Jewish-style shops left in the area and although the owners are now Portuguese. It still turns out traditional Jewish breads like raisin challah, along with Portuguese specialties. The Nusach Ho'aori Synagogue, around the corner at 100 des Pins E., is now the home of the Theatre de Quat' Sous.

Beignes Mickey, on the northwest corner of des Pins and St-Laurent, was Schaps where a malted milk or a smoked meat on rye cost 5¢. Everyone hung out at Schaps. Harry the Cheeseman was just up the street "Give me a good pound, Harry." "Why should I give you a bad pound?"

WALK UP ST-LAURENT AND TURN RIGHT (EAST) AT ROY. Waldman, the store with the huge fish sign, has been here for generations. Further down is Zinman's one of the few live poultry stores left in the city. Knowledgeable women would pick up a chicken and blow the feathers away from the rear to make sure the bird was fat and healthy. The orthodox would select birds to "schlog kapparot," a Yom Kippur custom in which a chicken is swung over the head as a symbol of expiating sins. The bird would then be slaughtered and given to the poor.

GO LEFT (NORTH) ON DE BULLION. The Beth Israel & Shmuel Synagogue was at 3732 de Bullion Street. A huge room ran the length of these buildings. Women would climb to the third floor and, leaning over the balcony, peer down at the service and the men, on the second floor. The "shammes" or caretaker lived on the first floor. This was one of dozens of similar synagogues in the area.

De Bullion used to be called Cadieux and was known as a red-light district. In 1918, a private citizens' commission into "vice in Montreal" released a report identifying several houses of prostitution on the street. The city went into action and closed down several houses and renamed the street de Bullion in 1927.

CONTINUE NORTH ON DE BULLION AND TURN LEFT ON NAPOLEON TO COLONIALE. The Colonial Turkish Steam Baths,

3963 Coloniale (285-0132) has been run by the same family for three generations. Fifty years ago, most apartments in the area had no hot water. The weekly father and son outing to the Baths was a necessity and the pummelling massage, with a birch branch rub-down, a rite of passage. Now, a steam bath, sauna, and a whirlpool costs $12.50 and the massage another $8.00 (plus tip). It's open to women on Tuesdays from 1:00 p.m. to 9:00 p.m.

Many of the buildings on this street have changed little since the 1920s. Some still have the same doors. The building at 4021 Colonial, was home to (*Ethnic Guide* co-author) Barry Lazar's father's family. Its large courtyard was used by the Levine Brothers Bakery to keep their delivery wagons and horses.

CONTINUE WEST TO ST-LAURENT. The block of St-Laurent between Napoleon and Duluth remains, for many Montrealers, the essence of The Main. Four generations of the same family have run Berson's Monuments, across the street at 3884 St-Laurent. On the second floor is the studio of sculptor Stanley Lewis. He is one of a several Jewish artists who were born in the area before WWII, moved out, and have returned to work and live.

"Delicatessen" is a German word for "good to eat" and there were a lot of them here. Each claimed the best method of trans-forming tough brisket of beef into delectable smoked meat. Schwartz's, formerly the Montreal Hebrew Delicatessen, at 3895 St-Laurent is the best known. Next door was Kravitz's with photos of famous Quebec wrestlers covering the walls. In the 1970s it moved across the street and became the Main Steak House (with Hebrew-style lettering) at 3864 St-Laurent.

The alley just south of Schwartz's should be designated a national historic site. This was the location of Montreal's first wood-fired bagel bakery where two friends — Meyer Lewkowicz and Jack Shlafman — sold bagels from a pushcart. Then they opened up a store several blocks north on Fairmount. After a while Meyer left and opened a new bagel bakery on St. Viateur. Eventually, Jack sold the Fairmount bakery and the oven was bricked up. In the 1970s, Jack's son bought the building and convinced the family to restart the bakery. But here, from a pushcart and an oven, is where it all started. At the very least, there should be a plaque!

Another landmark restaurant is Moishe's at 3961 St-Laurent, a Jewish-style (but not kosher) steak house, that has been at this location since 1937.

CROSS ST-LAURENT AND WALK WEST ALONG BAGG, named for Stanley Clark Bagg, a local landowner. The Schubert Baths (872-2587), at the corner of Bagg and St-Laurent, were built in 1931 and named for a Jewish municipal councillor. They are open to the public, admission is free, but men and women swim at different times because there is only one changing room.

At the corner of Clark and Bagg is Beth Shlomo (Temple Solomon). This small orthodox synagogue was built in the 1920s and is the only one in the neighbourhood still functioning. Services are held on Saturday mornings and on most Jewish festivals. The pews and carved wooden ark were transported by horse and cart in the early 1920s from the Shaar Hashomayim when that synagogue moved from McGill College and Cathcart downtown, to Côte St. Antoine in Westmount.

CONTINUE ALONG BAGG AND TURN RIGHT ON ST-URBAIN. Across the street, just south of Bagg, is Montreal's first hospital — Hôtel-Dieu (the House of God) — founded in 1645 by Jeanne Mance. Originally located in Old Montreal, the hospital has been here since 1854. Its chapel, around the corner on Avenue des Pins is an elegant neo-classical building designed by Victor Bourgeau who would later decorate the interior of Montreal's Notre-Dame Basilica.

In the 1930s, few Jews went to hospitals. The food wouldn't be kosher and patients weren't sure of the kind of welcome they would receive. (There were a few Jewish clinics, but most doctors made house visits.) Furthermore, few Jewish doctors were hired

Beth Schlomo synagogue, corner of Clark and Bagg, 1990.
PHOTO BY D.R. COWLES

to work in public hospitals. The Jewish community built its own, the Jewish General, in the Côte-des-Neiges area, in 1934.

CONTINUE UP ST-URBAIN. The Portuguese Association of Canada has been at 4170 St-Urbain since 1969. Previously this was a synagogue for the combined congregations of Beth Hamedrash Hagadol Chevra Shass.

Baron Byng, at 4251 St-Urbain, was built in 1921 as a public high school under the Protestant board. Throughout the 1930s and 1940s, over 90% of the students (but few of the teachers) were Jewish. Its alumnae include David Lewis, the first leader of the

New Democratic Party of Canada, and writers A.M. Klein, Irving Layton, and Mordecai Richler. It is now the headquarters of Sun Youth, an important community organization with a large food bank, immigrant counselling, seniors' assistance, help for victims of crime and fires, and many other services.

TURN RIGHT ON RACHEL and walk to St-Laurent. Pharmacie I. Labow, has been run by Isidore "Izzy" Lebowitz for almost 60 years. Mr. Lebowitz has never lived more than a 15 minute walk away and the phone booth, shelves, and scale were here when he opened the pharmacy.

Across the street was the Rachel street market where farmers from outside Montreal sold fruit, vegetables, eggs and chickens. It has been redesigned as Place des Ameriques, a park with a Latin American motif, reflecting the neighbourhood's growing Latin-American population.

A QUICK SIDE-TRIP DOWN ST-LAURENT TO DULUTH takes in several stores that are local institutions. Dominion General Store, at 4151 St-Laurent, still ships parcels of jeans, suits, shirts, and underwear to Russia. H. Fisher Tailor Supplies, further south at 4129 St-Laurent, has been in the area for 65 years and grew out of the needle trade supplying local tailors. Today most of its business is mail order to tailors across the country.

CONTINUE NORTH ON ST-LAURENT. The glitzy Crocodile restaurant at 4238 St-Laurent was once the Stotland Dress Company. Soulier Karls Chaussures (Karl's Shoes) has been at 4259-61 St-Laurent since the 1950s, and looks it. As Ludy Karl says "there has to be something you need here!"

Schreter Inc. is at 4356 Saint Laurent (845-4231). Joseph Schreter came to Montreal from Romania, started his first clothing shop in 1920 around the corner on St-Dominique and moved it to this location in 1958. Nothing much has changed. Nothing fancy, just racks and shelves of good quality, moderately-priced clothes such as Harris tweed jackets, down coats, silk shirts, as well as summer camp clothes, boots, leather jackets, and unusual "fashion accessories" like one-size-fits-all multi-coloured stretch gloves. This is a regular stop for former Montrealers looking for value and nostalgic for the old neighbourhood.

4423 St-Laurent is an important landmark. Here, in 1917, with $200, Mrs. Ida Steinberg opened up a small grocery store. Under her sons' direction, the store grew into one of the largest super-market chains in the country. For a sense of what that first store was like, go into Segals Grocery Store, 4437 St-Laurent. It's 75 years old and still in the family. Little has changed, it is still primarily a fresh produce store, only now there are stacks of dried cod for the Portuguese and Latins who have replaced the area's Jewish community.

For more than half a century, this section of the Main was the heart of a thriving clothing manufacturing industry. It prospered on the sweat of French Canadians from depressed regions of rural Quebec and women and men from Eastern Europe. Tens of thousands of Jews were employed here and several companies occupied entire buildings.

The Ideal Dress Company was at 4446 St-Laurent. If you stand south of the building and look up, you can still see the faded name on the wall. In 1911, workers often started at 6:00 in the morning and ended at 8:00 or 9:00 at night. Pay was $10 or $12 for a 60 hour week and "an all-wool, ready-made, fit-you-like-a-glove suit of clothes" could be bought for $9.99. Labour unions began in the clothing industry. In 1912, there was a general strike. It lasted nine weeks and the tailors were victorious, winning a 52 hour week.

TURN LEFT (WEST) ON MONT ROYAL AND WALK TOWARD L'ESPLANADE. In 1918 and 1919 fire destroyed three large hockey arenas in Montreal and Westmount. The city decided to build a new arena on a vacant lot, here, on the south side of Mont Royal avenue between St-Urbain and Clark. It was built within six months. The Canadiens won the inaugural game on January 10, 1920 against

Toronto 14 to 7. The Montreal Maroons also played here for a while. The Maroons were known as the English hockey team (with mostly English-Canadian hockey players) and the Canadiens as the team of French-Canadians. The Forum was built in 1924 and, although there were plans to renovate the Mont Royal arena, in 1938 the building was converted into manufacturing space and shops. The original roof of the arena is still visible just above the storefronts, particularly from St-Urbain and Clark. Arena Bakeries once had many stores in Montreal, however none are still in business, including the first one which was at 60 Mont Royal W.

Beauty's Restaurant, at 93 Mont Royal West, has been part of the neighbourhood since 1942. Owner Hymie Sckolnick still waits on tables and chats with everyone.

L'Esplanade south of Mont-Royal has several buildings which were important to the community as it grew. At the corner, was the Jewish Public Library, (established further south along the Main in 1914 as the Jewish People's Library and People's University). Now the library is in Snowdon and this building is an annex of the Bibliothèque Nationale, the provincial library.

The block of buildings based at 4373 l'Esplanade was the Hebrew Old People's Home and is now Chez Chanon, a refuge for homeless women that is affiliated with the Sanctuary of Mother Theresa, next door.

One of the most intriguing buildings on the street is recently renovated complex of apartments and condominiums on l'Esplanade south of Mont-Royal. In this labyrinth each apartment had its own address. The poet Ida Maze lived in number six at 4479B over-looking the alley.

Geyt in gass a regndl,
Geyt er zei antkegn;
Vaksn mayne kinderlach,
Vie blimelach in regn.

A little rain fell in the street
Back again it came;
But my children grow in it
Like flowers in the rain.

> — from "Flowers in the Rain" by Ida Maze,
> translated by Irving Massey and
> quoted in *An Everyday Miracle*

The ornate building at 4351 l'Esplanade housed the Rabinowich brothers, four doctors whose family immigrated to Montreal from Palestine in 1914. Several of their descendants are doctors in Montreal today.

FURTHER DOWN, AT THE CORNER OF RACHEL AND L'ESPLANADE, is the armoury of the 1st Regiment, known as The Grenadier Guards. It was built in 1912 and is still active, continuing to attract immigrant youth as members.

RETURN TO MONT ROYAL AND TURN LEFT (WEST) TO AVENUE DU PARC. The building at 265 Mont Royal W. was the first "Jewish Y" — the Montreal Young Men-Young Women's Hebrew Association (YM-YWHA), a gift from the head of Imperial Tobacco, Sir Mortimer Davis. It was built in 1926 to keep Jewish youth off the street, a situation few liked to admit was a problem. Today it is part of the Université de Montréal. The "Y" Florist, now across the street on Parc, used to be next door.

TURN RIGHT (NORTH) ON PARC. It's an interesting but long four blocks to Montreal's oldest Hassidic neighbourhood. Consider taking the 80 bus which has the most multilingual riders in the city and is usually worth the bus ticket (or $1.60 cash — the drivers cannot make change). If you take the bus, get off at Fairmount Avenue.

Hassidic men wear garb traditional to 18th century Poland, particularly on the Sabbath and Jewish festivals. Their costumes include long black coats, white stockings and fur-trimmed hats.

There are several sects of Hassidim. Two of the largest are the Satmar, many of whom live on Hutchison, and the Belz who live on Jeanne Mance. These communities were established after WWII when there was still a large orthodox Jewish community in the area.

WALK EAST ON FAIRMOUNT. 172 Fairmount W. is the former B'nai Jacob Synagogue. Today it is a private French school with the original Hebrew name legible below the roof. (Further down, at 74 Fairmount W. is the Fairmount Bagel Bakery.)

TURN LEFT ON JEANNE-MANCE AND CONTINUE NORTH TO ST-VIATEUR.

St-Viateur is a marvellous street and worth a stroll for a couple of blocks either east, to St-Lawrence, or west past Parc and into the suburb of Outremont. To the east, at the corner of St-Urbain and St-Viateur, is St. Michael the Archangel, a dramatic building originally constructed in 1916 for what was then this area's large Irish community. Celtic shamrocks are part of the interior design. The church has been a Polish parish for the past 25 years and a small Polish coffee shop has recently opened next door to it.

The Belz Boys School is at 5565 Jeanne-Mance. The Satmar synagogue and community centre is at 5555 Hutchison on the corner of St-Viateur.

The Bagel Shop at 158 and 263 St. Viateur W., used to be called the Fairmount Bagel Bakery. That was until the bakery on Fairmount was reopened. The original St. Viateur bakery is the one closer to Parc, the other tends to have shorter lines. Both have wood-fired ovens.

A few of the old Jewish neighbourhood stores have remained: Levine's green grocer has vats of pickles and sauerkraut in the basement; Mehadrin, the kosher butcher, at 257 St-Viateur W. makes the best smoked turkey on the planet.

TO LEAVE THE DISTRICT, take the number 80 bus north to the Park Avenue Métro or south to the Place des Arts Métro station.

LATIN MONTREAL

POPULATION: 62,000

COMMUNITIES: Côte des-Neiges, Ville St-Laurent, Lasalle, Villeray, Plateau Mont-Royal and Saint-Jean Baptiste

SHOPPING: Rachel and St-Laurent, Belanger and Jean-Talon

Imigrar e travar uma grade luta
To immigrate is to put up a big fight.
— from a booklet for Portuguese immigrants

Montreal's Latin community is spread throughout the city, bridging Europe and the Americas. A third originate in Central and South America; the rest have roots in Portugal and Spain. The first major community were Portuguese who settled north of Prince Arthur in the 1950s. They were joined first by Spaniards and then Latin Americans who moved into the Saint-Jean Baptiste district, between boulevard St-Hubert and boulevard St-Laurent.

More recently, Central Americans and South Americans have moved into inexpensive apartments in Côte-des-Neiges and duplexes in Villeray. Ville Lasalle and Ville Saint-Laurent are also popular because they have a large number of furnished apartments.

Latin Montreal has changed a lot in the last few years. Economic difficulties and political turmoil have encouraged about 20,000 Central and South Americans, almost half of whom are refugees, to immigrate here since 1986. These newcomers are infusing the older Latin community and the city with energy, adding new dishes to restaurant menus, publishing original work in Spanish, and bringing Andean music to city parks and Métro corridors.

ARGENTINIAN

Around the turn of this century, Argentina was one of the most industrialized and prosperous countries in the western hemisphere. But the country went into a long economic decline after a series of military coups in the 1930s and 1940s. Political stability returned in 1946 when General Juan Peron was elected president and ruled until another coup forced him into exile in 1955. Another series of military and civilian regimes lasted until Peron was elected back into power in 1973. He died shortly after and was succeeded by his wife Isabel who stayed in power until ousted by a military junta in 1976. Democratic rule returned to Argentina in 1983.

About a hundred people, mostly students and professionals, immigrated to Montreal in the 1960s. The community grew in the 1970s as political repression increased in Argentina.

In the 1980s, Argentina's economy was a disaster, with inflation reaching an incomprehensible 6,000% a year. Many who came to Montreal during this period, having little to start with, worked at cleaning and service jobs while taking courses to upgrade their education.

Although Argentina's economy has improved, a few hundred new residents still arrive in Montreal annually; the community now numbers about 1,800. Many young, single adults come from the economically depressed province of Cordoba.

École Argentine à Montréal (340-9296) organizes celebrations of Argentinian holidays such as La Semaine de Mai commemorating independence from Spanish rule in 1817. There's music, food, lectures, and Argentinian films. June 20th is Flag Day and is usually the last day of classes at the school. July 9th is Independence Day and there is a community barbecue on the West Island.

◆ ◆ ◆

BOLIVIAN

This land-locked mountainous South American country is named for the great Latin American independence fighter Simon Bolivar whose statue (without a head!) is in the rear of Percy Walters Park at Docteur-Penfield and Redpath streets.

Bolivia was a much larger country in the 1800s, but, as the result of wars, lost its coast to Chile and its oil and rubber tree areas to Paraguay and Brazil. Bolivians began arriving here in the mid-1980s while their country was under military rule. Many immigrants were students who remained in Montreal after they finished their university studies. Indians, who have lived in the area for more than a thousand years, are still the majority of Bolivia's population and make up a third of the 2,000 or so Bolivians now living in Montreal. Bolivians celebrate carnivale in February.

BRAZILIAN

"North America is like a movie," says a Brazilian consulate worker, "and many people want to be part of it, at least for awhile." The community is small; some Brazilians have married French Canadians and others have become part of the much larger Portuguese community with whom they share a common language.

Montreal has a lively Brazilian music scene lead by the Paul Ramos Group and the big-band of Vovo y Samarmanda.

CHILEAN

For most of the past 15 years, Chile was under military rule and thousands applied to live here as refugees. As Chile becomes more democratic, some plan to return. Most, however, have based their life here and feel Montreal is now home. Those who fled Chile were mostly from the middle-class and have been relatively successful in Montreal. Unlike other immigrant communities, there are few community welfare organizations.

Soccer (futbol) is a major sport and social event among many Latin Americans. In Montreal, Chileans probably have the most soccer leagues of any ethnic group. Most weekends throughout the summer you can catch a game at Centre Claude Robillard or Jeanne-Mance Park. Finals are held in September. September 18 is Chili's national day.

MEXICAN

Mexicans started immigrating to Montreal in the 1950s. Many were professionals who had been politically involved back home and frustrated with Mexico's one party system. (The Institutional Revolutionary Party has governed the country, uninterrupted, since 1929). Often these newcomers found that their qualifications were not recognized in Canada and remained stuck in restaurant or factory jobs.

Although there are only a thousand or so Mexican Montrealers, there are also about 500 workers who have come every summer since the 1930s to work on Quebec farms. They often work in the fields 15 hours a day, seven days a week, isolated and facing racism from local employers and non-Mexican workers. In 1990, five workers died. **Le Centre Mexicaine du développement social et culturel**, 3680 Jeanne Mance (844-3340) assists professionals looking for skilled work and tries to help Mexican seasonal farmworkers.

The big community day is Fiesta Mexicaine de Independiencia (Independence Day) on September 16th. The **Centre Mexicaine** (725-3725) has information. The "Days of the Dead" are Aztec festivals which celebrate the deceased (November 2 for children and November 5 for adults). Other important days are Mother's Day in May and Children's Day in April. These are often celebrated together with dancing, food, and piñadas (papier-mâché animals stuffed with candies and streamers).

SALVADOREAN

El Salvador's twelve-year civil war finally ended in 1992. Over 75,000 people died in the war and several thousand Salvadoreans settled in Montreal as refugees. The war ruined El Salvador's economy, with 80% unemployment in some regions and many Salvadoreans arrived in Montreal desperately seeking work. Many are women who are single parents between 25 and 35 years old; their first concern is getting their families into Canada.

PORTUGUESE

North American links to Portugal go back hundreds of years. Portuguese navigators and fishermen followed the massive eastern coast cod stocks; some believe Columbus had information from the Portuguese on the route to North America. In Canada, Portugal's legacy is in our cartography: for example, there's Portugal Cove in Newfoundland and the Bay of Fundy (from Rio Fundo which means Deep Bay) in Nova Scotia. In 1498 Jo o Fernandes mapped part of Canada's eastern coast for Portugal and was given title, becoming the *lavrador* or landowner. Today we call this area Labrador.

Most Portuguese arrived after WWII, but there are some illustrious early Portuguese Quebecers including Pedro (Pierre) da Silva who came from Lisbon in 1677. He was the first postmaster of the route between Montreal and Quebec City. Da Silva fathered 15 children, most of whom also had large families; his descendants carry the names Dasylva, Dasilva and Da Silva.

Montreal's 28,000 Portuguese are the city's largest Latin community. Post-WWII immigration to Canada began after Brazil, a former Portuguese colony changed its policies, making it more difficult for those from Portugal to emigrate there. Many went to France instead and then to Quebec. At about the same time, Canada was looking for farm workers and Portugal was trying to reduce the population in the Azores, a cluster of mountainous islands belonging to Portugal in the North Atlantic. While there was some farming done on these islands, it was nothing like the highly mechanized mono-culture farm business in Canada; nevertheless, tens of thousands of people were hustled onto boats for Halifax and then scattered by train to work on Canadian farms.

The scheme was a disaster. Azorean farms were far different from the Canadian ones to which they were sent. There was the loneliness, the inability to speak the language and even the food was different — with no fresh fish on the Prairies. Within a few years most had moved to Montreal and Toronto. In the cities, the culture shock was enormous. Azoreans had been tenant farmers and they were desperate to have their own land and build a house in Canada. Many of the men were bachelors who married women back home by proxy and then brought them over.

The nucleus of Montreal's Portuguese community started on de Bullion Street and Roy. It began with a Venezuelan who set up a contracting company and an Azorean who opened up a general grocery store on Saint-Dominique. Waldman, on Roy, was the largest fish company in the city and provided work for many while others often ended up as cleaners and unskilled workers.

By 1960 the farm program had pretty much ended and Portuguese newcomers were increasingly urban and better educated. Men who spoke English or French often got jobs as clerks while women usually worked in the garment industry. These families immediately started saving money to own their own home. Many took in boarders and sacrificed family privacy, often urging children to leave school and work — all to pay the mortgage. Several white collar workers got jobs in real estate and with travel agencies which became important for translation services and for making arrangements to bring relatives to Canada.

During the 1960s, when Portugal was trying to quell revolutions in its African territories of Mozambique, Guinea and Angola, many young men fled Portuguese military service and went to France where they found work and learned French. Within a few years they found themselves trying to escape compulsory military service in France and Montreal became the next logical destination.

Since 1974, when Portugal ended over 50 years of military dictatorship, emigration has slowed markedly. Still, about 1000 Portuguese a year immigrated to Quebec, leaving a crowded country of 10 million people in an area one-twentieth the size of Quebec.

Our province's strong Catholic heritage has also been attractive to Latins. However, theirs is a Catholicism infused with resignation and fate. Icons are important and many homes have statues of saints, or a crown with a flying dove symbolizing the holy spirit.

The most important icon is at the **Missao Portuguesa de Santa Cruz**, 60 Rachel W. (844-1011). It is a copy of an important Portuguese statue, Senhor Santo Christo dos Milagres — Christ of the Miracles. On the fifth Sunday after Easter, it is carried through the neighbourhood by children in costumes, men wearing red capes (opas), bands and contingents from community organizations.

A small park behind Sainte-Justine hospital, at the corner of Plantagenet and Saison, is named after the Portuguese WWII hero, Aristide de Sousa Mendes do Amaral e Abranches. While he was Portuguese consul in Bordeaux France, Sousa Mendes defied his government's orders and issued visas for more than 30,000 people, a third of them Jews. After the war, one of his sons moved here and married a Quebecer.

SPANISH

About 40 years ago Spaniards started settling around St-Dominique and Rachel alongside the Portuguese. The community grew during the 1960s when employment was scarce in Spain and pretty much ended after democracy was restored in Spain in the 1977. Today there are about 21,000 people with Spanish origins in Montreal.

Montreal has two monuments to Isabella — Queen of Spain and patron of Colombus' voyages to North America. One statue is in Snowdon's Macdonald Park, on the corner of Dupuis and Clanranald, a gift from the city's Latin American consulates. The other, a bust of "Isabella the Catholic," in Sir Wilfred Laurier Park on Laurier and Brebeuf, is from Madrid's Instituto de Cultura Hispanica.

ORGANIZATIONS

Association des immigrants latino-américains de Côtes-des-Neiges (AILAC), 5307 Côte-des-Neiges (737-3642). Signs of the times: AILAC is changing its acronym to ALAC, dropping the "Immigrants." Its work will continue as an information and referral centre for Latin Americans in Côtes-des-Neiges. It has language courses, programs in math and computers, literacy classes and helps immigrants in dealing with government officers. ALAC also tries to increase awareness about Latinos among Quebecers and organizes festivals and cultural evenings.

Associaç o Portuguesa do Canadà, 4170 St-Urbain (844-2269) is the largest Latin organization. It began in the 1950s as a social centre and helped start the newspaper *O Luso-Canadiano* (The Portuguese Canadian), the Filarmonica Portuguesa concert band and the folk group Sol de Portugal (Sun of Portugal) which performs traditional folk dance and music of the Ribatejo district of Portugal.

In the 1960s Portugal was facing a fourth decade under the repressive political regime of Antonio de Oliveira Salazar. There was fierce opposition both within and outside the country. In Montreal, Tavares Bello, the editor of *O Luso-Canadiano* formed the Casa dos Portuguêses (House of the Portuguese) as a gathering place for those opposed to the government in Portugal. It was particularly popular with Azoreans who felt that their islands had as much a right to autonomy as the colonies in Africa. For a while, it was common to see bumper stickers in Montreal with "The Azores are for the Azoreans." Attitudes changed after the Portuguese revolution of 1974 and the Casa became the Mouvement démocratique portugais.

Centro Português de Referência e Promoç-a-o Social, 4050 St-Urbain (842-8045) fights for workers' rights and acts as a clearing house for community activities. Programs include French classes and information sessions on judicial rights, unemployment insurance regulations, housing, and Quebec society. The centre also has a seniors group, a literacy project and a support group for Portuguese women.

Carrefour Latino Américain de Montreal (CLAM), 6837 St. Denis (271-8207). A Latin American information and referral service for immigrants and refugees providing translation services, language courses, orientation for new arrivals to Quebec and refugee counselling. Most clients are Salvadorans, Guatemalans and Peruvians.

Centre Culturelle Kallaseyo (668-0126). This Bolivian

cultural group attempts to keep Montrealers aware of issues in Bolivia. Since many local Bolivians are aboriginal (as are most in Bolivia), they often participate with Montreal's Mohawk community for some events.

Centre des femmes Salvadoriennes, 4261 Drolet (843-7540) helps women adapt to life in Quebec and runs a clothing and furniture bank, assisting many who are both refugees and single parents.

Consejo Chileno de Quebec (Conseil Chilien du Quebec), 8465 St-Denis (388-2866) brings Chilean and non-Latin Montrealers together and assists expatriates who hope to return to Chile.

Corporacion Cultural Latinoamericana de la Amistad (COCLA), 1600 de L'Eglise (748-0796) is an information and referral centre with translation and interpretation facilities and French classes. There is also a women's discussion group and a food service which provides weekly free meals.

École Argentine à Montréal, 1200 Laurier E. (340-9296). A Saturday school to teach children Spanish and Argentinian culture; also, adult education language classes and programs in electronics and mechanics. Members drop in for coffee, a lecture, use the library, and read Argentinian newspapers.

Instituto Español de Montréal, 485 boul St-Joseph E. (843-8210). Spanish language and cultural courses.

La Maisonnée, 6865 Christophe-Colombe (271-3533) focuses on integration and has legal assistance, French courses, employment, translation and social services, and a food distribution for poorer Latins in Montreal.

St. Guadeloupe, 1153 Alxandre de Sève (525-4312) is the Latin American parish. The Mission helps with immigration, employment, and housing, and provides food and clothing to thousands of people every year.

SOS Guatemala, 7387 St-Laurent (271-8343). Hundreds of

thousands of Guatemalans sought asylum outside their country and some have settled in Montreal. SOS Guatemala provides community services and referrals and helps with translation, visiting government offices and immigration.

MEDIA

Montreal's Portuguese community has published several papers. The most prominent, the anti-Portuguese government *Luso-Canadiano*, ceased publication in the early 1970s, after its publisher died. *A Voz de Portugal* (Voice of Portugal), 4181 St-Dominique (844-0388) began in 1961 by supporters of the Portuguese government but it has now become a paper orienting newcomers to the established Portuguese community. *Jornal do emigrante*, 4300 St-Laurent (843-3863, 288-8692), published since 1977, also focuses on new immigrants. *El Correo*, 211 St-Sacrement (845-5874) is a monthly with news and analysis from Latin America. *Presencia Latina*, 4148 Verdun Ave., Verdun (767-0171) is a progressive Latin American community newspaper with local entertainment news and information.

CFMB 1410 Radio Montreal has "Hispanolatino," a Latin American show in Spanish on the air almost every day. Radio Centre-ville (CINQ 102.3-FM) also has several hours of Spanish language programming. Their schedule varies seasonally and usually includes news and music programs "Brésil," "Pays de Braise," "Panorama Centro-Americano" (news from Central America and about Central Americans in Montreal), "Eventos comunitarios" (community listings), "Mujeres"for women and weekend music shows "Variedades Musicales," "Cocktail Musical," and "Musica Variada E Comentarios." CKUT 90.3-FM has "El Quero's Album" in Spanish, French and English with lots of Spanish music, a music show

"America Latina," and "Latin Time," a current affairs talk show in Spanish, French and English.

Latin television programs on cable TV include *Latino Vision*, Ici *Mexico*, and *Mundo Latin*.

RESTAURANTS AND CLUBS

$ indicates that a lunch or dinner should cost under $10 (without taxes, tips, or wine). $$ is under $25 and $$$ above that. Credit cards accepted are listed. "BYOB" means that you can bring your own wine. Hours often vary with the seasons so please call ahead.

BIJU $ AMEX EN-ROUTE MC VISA
935 Duluth E. (522-8219)

NEGA FULO $ AMEX EN-ROUTE MC VISA
1257 Amherst (522-1554)
■ Why should we assume that restaurants offering Brazilian, Créole, Cajun and Mexican cuisine should be more authentic than one with a sign up for "Mets Chinois, Canadien, et Italien"? On the plus side, the staff tries hard and the atmosphere is reminiscent of large stucco cantinas. The Brazilian chicken and fish are quite tasty perhaps because the owner is Brazilian. The ceviche (lime-marinated fish) is delicious and the margaritas are worth a second round. The pecan pie is extraordinary. The menu at both restaurants is pretty much the same since they have the same owner.

BISTRO EL GAUCHITO $
4245 St-Laurent (499-9755)
■ Good for lunch or a late night snack of large, freshly-made empañadas — chicken, beef, spinach, cheese and a few other varieties. They're cheap and filling, but a little plain; even the hot sauce is on siesta.

▮▮ FOUR BEATS OF FLAMENCO

In the beginning was the dance, always the dance, claq-claq-claq, claq-claq-claq, then came the song and finally the guitar. Ahh flamenco. Watch the face for expression. Good dancers may not hit their prime until over forty.

Flamenco comes from Spain, but its roots reach back over 700 years to the guitar of the Arab, the soul of the Gypsy, and the cantorial songs of the Jew. (In Synagogues, prayers are often sung by the cantor whose title comes from the Spanish verb "cantar" — to sing). Flamenco singing is usually either cante chico "lighter songs" or cante hondo "deep songs" which are less common and demand a strong, mature interpretation.

Catch flamenco at restaurants such as **Rancho Grande**, *2074 Clarke (842-6301) and* **Sancho Panza** *3458 Parc, (844-0558). Don't just sit and watch. If you like what you see, call out the names of the performers when they pause, shout out an occasional olé, and clap with the beat. This is passionate art and performers are at their best when the audience is hot.*

BRASILEIRINHO $$ VISA MC
4552 St-Denis (847-0088)
▮ Cajun meets South American at this evening eatery in the centre of the city's relocated Latin quarter. Fresh alligator and soft shell crabs are flown in weekly from Brazil and Louisiana. Reserve for Friday and Saturday nights, when there's a mini-bossa-nova show.

CAFETERIA LA PALMAS $
14 Rachel E. (987-1243)
▮ A small snack bar across from the new Parc des Amériques. Half a dozen main dishes and filling soups make for a satisfying meal of

unusual Columbian dishes such as bandesa paisa (eggs with a rich bean sauce), mondongo (a meat and vegetable soup), arroz con pollo (chicken with rice and plantains), chorizo sausages and rellenas (stuffed potatoes). The thinly-crusted empañadas (meat filled patties) are served with a fresh coriander and chili sauce. There's also over a dozen made-to-order tropical fruit drinks such as passion fruit, coconut, banana and mango.

CASA DE MATEO $$ VISA MC
440 St-François-Xavier (844-7448)
■ A lively Mexican restaurant, across from the Centaur theatre, with quick service near the bar when you've only an hour before curtain time. At other times settle back with serenading mariachis in the larger dining room. Daily specials are unusual, such as duck with green molé sauce. Dishes prepared with jalapeño peppers are quite spicy but pair off well with imported Mexican beer or frosty margaritas.

CHAMPS
3956 St-Laurent (987-6444)
BAR LA CABANNE
3874 St-Laurent (844-4717)
■ How do they get those giant satellite dishes on top of those buildings? If a tornado hits, there will be flying saucers landing in Brossard. Champs receives sports broadcasts from everywhere, and the hand-lettered signs get a little bigger when Portugal is fielding a team. Good drinking in both. Champs looks like it got lost on the way to Crescent Street. La Cabanne is more of a neighbourhood hangout with decent luncheon specials and micro-brewery beer by the pitcher.

CHEZ LISBONNE $$ MC VISA
156 Roy E. (844-9874)
■ Good, inexpensive luncheon specials. The main menu is pricier but has a good variety of Portuguese-style steak and pork dishes

and fish including good cod, squid, and sardines. On weekends, there's live fado — Portugal's traditional music of sad, sweet songs of fate and unrequited love.

CLUB ESPAGNOL DE MONTREAL $$

4388 St-Laurent (849-1737)

■ Draft beer, excellent homestyle Spanish cooking includes fresh rabbit and chicken dishes, paella, and a superb tripe stew. This is more a community centre than a restaurant but don't be intimidated. Look for the small serving bar and ask for the owner, Chuchu Blanco, or his son, to go over the menu. Call first, this place can close anytime between 9:00 p.m. and 3:00 a.m.

COCO RICO

3907 St-Laurent (849-5554) closed by 9 p.m.

■ Great fast food: corn bread and large crusty buns, pork chops, ham, and roast chicken sandwiches, even a whole suckling pig if you order in advance. It's all done to a turn in large rotisserie ovens. If you want the same and more without the curbside service, try their restaurant — *Jano* (see below).

DON QUIXOTE $$ VISA MC AMEX

1224 rue Drummond (393-8980)

■ Spanish cooking and a pleasant ambience; most come for the tapas — Spanish snacks — served from 6:00 p.m. to 10:00 p.m. In Spain, the tapas are laid out on the bar for patrons to pick and choose with perhaps a dry sherry or wine. At Don Quixote, you order from the menu: sautéed artichokes and ham, ali-i-oli potatoes (potatoes with garlic and mayonnaise), Spanish omelette (cold potato omelette), shrimps swimming in a garlic sauce, fried squid, chorizo sausage, and mussels.

FIESTA TAPAS $ MC VISA

479 St. Alexis (844-5700)

■ Reservations are recommended for this faintly-Barcelonian

hideaway in Old Montreal. The tapas menu includes broiled dates wrapped in bacon, fried squid morsels, chunks of garlicky coated potato, clams, mussels, empañada pastry stuffed with the daily special. Portions come in two sizes, small is ample. Flamenco occasionally on the weekends.

ISAZA
5149A Parc (276-4240)
■ Easy to miss, if you open a door and don't hear any salsa rhythms you're probably about to enter someone's apartment. The club has been around for awhile and has many regulars. It's a friendly crowd with plenty of partners for dancing and no pressure if you just want to lounge around with a drink.

JANO $$ AMEX DINERS MC VISA
3883 St-Laurent (849-0646)
■ Portuguese charcoal grill with very tasty quail, barbecued pork steak, chicken, squid, fish, and plump grilled sardines. The boneless pork steak is recommended. Look for the brightly painted rooster (Portuguese symbol of love) perched over the door.

KISSES
5384 St-Laurent (278-1832)
■ An upscale hideaway. Dress up (women in heels, men with jackets). A good club with Latin music and some very impressive dancers.

LELE DA CUCA $ MC VISA BYOB
70 Marie-Anne E. (849-6649)
■ Lélé da Cuca (which means crazy in the head) is really nice and quiet. Maybe the name comes from trying to combine two fiery Latin cuisines. The Mexican side is cheaper and has the standard dishes: tacos, quesadilas, burritos and frijoles. Frijoles con arroz (black beans and rice) is tasty and includes nachos, melted cheese and salsa. The table d'hôte samples Brazilian cooking. The feijoada

— a stew of beans, pork, beef, sausage with rice, vegetables and grains — is quite ample.

PUPUSERIA EL MIGUELEÑO $ BYOB
7805 St-Laurent (276-0182)

■ There are a few pupuserias in the city: small El Salvadorean restaurants which make thick tortillas with a variety of fillings. El Migueleño also has a fair selection of main courses, hearty soups and fresh fruit juices.

LA PLAYA $
4459 St-Laurent (843-6595)

■ The murals were done by local artists and there are fishnets and traps hanging from the ceiling. The place is unpretentious, lively and a lot of fun. Latino bands play here on weekends, often to raise funds for community organizations.

RESTAURANT UNIC $
167 Sauvé West (389-5541) 11:00 a.m. – 8:00 p.m. closed Monday and Tuesday.

■ Unic rightly calls itself "modesto" and it does look the average burger-and-fries joint in this north-end industrial part of town. However this is also a good pupuseria with freshly-made tortillas and several El Salvadorean daily specials. Not worth a trip-out-of-the-way but great if you're in the area.

RIO DE LA PLATA $
163 Villeneuve E. (845-2341)

■ An Argentinian eatery for late night carnivores. Nothing fancy, just lots of meat on the grill and good chorizo sausage. Ask for a dish of jalapeño pepper sauce on the side. For dessert, try the chajá, a superb Uruguayan sponge cake. There's Latin music and the waitress has been known to give dance lessons.

LA SALSA $

4306 St-Laurent (982-9462)

■ California-based chain with cheap eats for people who think they might like Mexican snacks: soft corn flour tortillas, crispy wheat flour cheese-filled quesadillas, black beans, guacamole, and meat and cheese stuffed burritos. Nice menu but it lacks oomph! No desserts, but try harchata, a milky drink that soothes with the taste of a mild-mannered rice pudding.

FOOD SOURCES

EL REFUGIO, 4548 St-Laurent (845-1358). Chilean flat breads, home-made chorizo sausage, excellent empañadas, good shop for information about events in the Latin community.

LA CHILENITA, 4348 Clark (982-9212). Several kinds of freshly made empanadas and pastries.

MARCHE SOARES ET FILS, 130 Duluth E. (288-2451). Imported goods include Portuguese flan mixes, salt cod, stickle-back fish, goat cheese, olive oil and black olives.

MARCHE ANDES, 432 Bélanger E. (277-4130). Foods from Central and South America; beans, meal for tortillas, frozen foods, fresh empañadas and burritos; Latin videos, books, cassettes, magazines and newspapers. Next door is **Boucherie Andes** with beef, goat, pork and veal. This is also a good place to find out what's happening in the community, fundraisers for people back home, dances and festivals.

MEX CAN TORTILLAS, 301 Aurel Fortain, Ste. Rose (963-0633). Wholesale tacos, cornflour and wheatflour tortillas (42 to a box).

PADARIA COIMBRA, 191 Mont-Royal E. Portuguese bakery that seems to turn out bread every hour. Tasty pastries and delicious custardy "pasteis de natas" tartlets.

PANADERIEA EL REENCUENTRO, 5021 St-Urbain (270-7369). Chilean bakery making empañadas filled with spinach, eggs, cheese, or spicy beef, sandwiches, and fresh baked bread. As the name says. This is an amiable meeting place for Latins in the neighbourhood.

PANADERIA EL SALVADOR, 428 Bélanger E. (277-0014). Fresh quesadillas, tamales, bread, fruit pies and pastries made in a very small shop, often sold out by the afternoon.

STRELLA ESTRELLA, 22 Duluth E. (843-7012). A pastry shop with good coffee that opens at 6:00 am! Fresh and delicious, particularly the tiny pastelles nata, a thimble of pastry filled with sweet custard.

SUPER MARCHE ANDES, 4387 St. Laurent (848-1078). This store has everything: stuffed piñadas hanging from the ceiling, Latin American music is on cassette, and videos from Spain fill the back wall. It's also a full range Latin grocery store with refried beans, green and brown molé sauce, and tortillas imported from Guatemala. The staff is very helpful, especially to gringos who don't know their tortillas from their tacos.

SUPER MARCHE NASCIMENTO, 67 Prince Arthur E. (845-5751). The only Portuguese store left on the block. Step inside for dried cod and imported foods, the butcher counter features fresh and smoked Portuguese sausages.

SHOPS AND SERVICES

THE BOLERO DANCE TROUPE (858-0578) performs traditional styles such as Escuela Bolera, Classical Espagnole and the Flamenco. Escuela Bolera grew out of classical ballet in the 18th Century and mixes Flamenco and ballet. The dancers use castanets, but don't wear the character shoes used in Flamenco. Classical

Espagnole is refined version of the Flamenco. Dancers have classical training which they add to the Flamenco elements of the dance. The troupe gives an annual public performance in Montreal and the groups director, Ms. Casapovas, occasionally dances the Flamenco in Montreal's local Spanish restaurants.

BOUTIQUE ANA MARIA, 4409 St. Laurent (849-6619). Portuguese women's clothing store particularly good for nice and frilly maternity clothing and baptism outfits.

BOUTIQUE BACHUE, 78 rue Rachel E. (843-6430). Simple, elegant Columbian pottery and Latin American archaeological reproductions.

BOUTIQUE INCA, 4094 St-Denis (843-8751). A wonderful selection of wool clothing imported from Peru and Bolivia, with a large selection for children; inexpensive jewellery from Guatemala and Mexico.

BOUTIQUE LISBONNE, 4083 St-Laurent (849-6619). Women's clothing store with specialties imported from Portugal.

BOUTIQUE SUD-AMERICANA, 1005 Bernard W. (277-3391). Imports from South America include Bolivian wood and clay woodwinds, Guatemalan woven belts, vests, bags and jewellery.

CASA LATINA, 4551 St. Laurent (845-5645). Mexican videos, casssettes, newspapers, tortillas, nachos, enchiladas and lots of imported foods.

DANCE PARTY, (279-6838). Air conditioner technician by day, Latin dance D.J. by night, Ishmael Magaña, tours the city performing at private parties. Dance to a hot and quick salsa, slow and sexy merengue or something in between like the cumbia from Colombia.

DA PAULA'S TEXTILMODES, 4275 St-Laurent (849-0814).This small linen store stocks embroidered napkins, place mats and table cloths from Portugal.

DISCOTECA PORTUGUESA, 4003 St-Laurent (843-3863). A multi-enterprise Portuguese party store. There are the Portuguese records, knick-knacks, gifts, T-shirts, newspapers, magazines and videos. Then, there's the really big show: Isaias Lopes and his son, who run the store, are also local impressarios for entertainers from Portugal. They put on three or four shows a year. Check the posters in the store for forthcoming events. Finally, Discotecta Portuguesa has a Balkan flair. There is a substantial elderly Yugoslavian population in the neighbourhood and the store stocks lots of "old country" magazines, records and cassettes.

FLOR DO LAR, 3979 St-Laurent (The Cooper Building) (843-8909). A gift shop and news stand with Portuguese newspapers and news magazines like Sa'bado and the food magazine Tele Culina'ria. The terra cotta pottery, cassettes and records come from Lisbon.

FOLKLORE 1, 4879 Sherbrooke St. W. (486-8852). Quirky, exuberant taste combines crafts, silver jewellery and folk art from Mexico with Japanese farm jackets or central American pottery. The most spectacular pieces are displayed during Christmas, Easter, and the Day of the Dead.

INCA INTL., Le Passage Place Bonaventure (861-5326). Mexican ponchos sweaters, wool sweaters, flutes, and dolls imported from Latin America.

JACHA MARKA (272-5959). A Latin native group whose name means "Great People." Hear them at community gatherings and other events.

LIBRERIA ESPAÑOLA, 3811 St-Laurent (849-3383). Once this shop was famous as Oberman's Kosher Meat Market. Now it's practically a community centre for the growing Latin neighbourhood. Libreria Española is more than a bookstore. There are Spanish tapes, groceries, piñadas, empañadas, cakes, coffees, cheese and several Spanish and Portuguese newspapers. The book department has the latest Spanish language works, established authors such as Isabel Allende and Gabriel Garcia Márquez, and Spanish-language editions of books by John le Carré, Henry Miller, Colleen McCullough and Harold Robbins.

LIBRAIRIE LAS AMERICAS LTEE, 2075 St. Laurent (844-5994). Literature, dictionaries, reference books, language courses and a small section for books by Central American authors now living in Montreal.

LA MAISON DU HAMAC, 2003 St. Denis (982-9440). Beautiful hand-made hammocks, hand-woven bags, belts and cloth from Mexico and Guatemala.

PASCAL $5 AND $10, 4059 St. Laurent (844-0979). Traditional Portuguese pottery, hand woven rugs and touristy 'Portugal' t-shirts.

PONCHO VILLA, 139 St-Paul W. (845-4873). Imported clothing from Guatemala, Peru, Thailand and India.

REPRODUCTIONES LATINAS, 7807 St-Laurent (277-3774). Rodolfo Flores knows the neighbourhood well and his small print-ing operation is a good place for information about new com-munity organizations, Latin restaurants, and newspapers. He also does get quick Spanish translations for flyers, wedding invitations and business cards.

VOGA DRAPERIES, 17 Mont-Royal W. (843-6262). Linen, car-pets, blankets, curtains and fabrics from Portugal and Spain.

VOYAGES ESTORIL SOL, 60 Duluth (842-9611). A neighbour-hood agency specializing in travel arrangements for Portugal.

YAYO, (284-6510). Colombian satirical artist now living in Mon-treal. His work has the kind of off-the-wall bite we associate with Eastern-European cartoonists or Latin authors. Catch him in local magazines *L'Actualité*, *Croc*, and *MTL*.

LATIN WALKING TOUR

Start on St-Denis,
  near the Mont-Royal Métro
End at Square St-Louis
  across from the Sherbrooke Métro

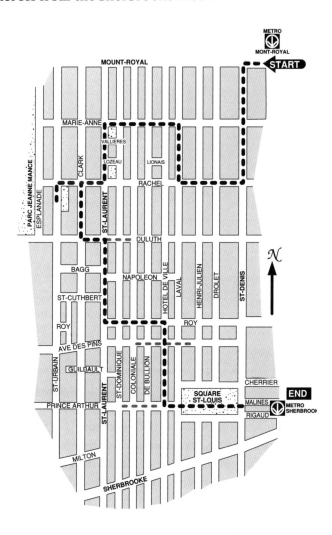

The tour of Latin Montreal STARTS AT MT-ROYAL AND ST-DENIS, NEAR THE MONT-ROYAL MÉTRO STATION.

"The Latin Quarter" was once the common name for a part of the city below Sherbrooke street. This wasn't for any large community of Portuguese or Spanish-speaking people, but for its bohemian atmosphere and large student population. The area north of Sherbrooke, which we'll cover in this tour, was originally the French village of St-Jean Baptiste and was settled in the 1870s.

This entire area is part of Plateau Mont-Royal, the flat plain of land east of the mountain which extends north from the escarpment at Sherbrooke St. The Plateau was originally developed in the late 18th century for its limestone quarries. Serious housing and commercial development began only in the last half of the 19th century, after horse-drawn street-cars were able to climb the hill from Old Montreal and travel above Sherbrooke St. By 1880 electric street cars went as far north as Mount Royal and the older buildings still remaining in this part of Montreal date from then as well.

Jews, Germans, and Eastern Europeans moved to this part of the city in the first half of this century. In the 1950s, by the time Portuguese immigrants began settling here, longer established residents were moving to the suburbs. The Plateau deteriorated as absentee landlords did little to maintain buildings. The Portuguese community renovated their homes and the Plateau gradually began to attract others. Today the area still has a sizeable Portuguese community as well as increasing numbers of people from Spain, Mexico, and Central and South America. It's also become popular with younger English and French-speaking families who appreciate the central location, varied housing, and good shopping in one of Montreal's most cosmopolitan neighbourhoods.

WALK DOWN ST-DENIS TO RACHEL. St-Denis has become one of Montreal's choicest streets, famous for its elegant curved staircases and, since the 1960s, row upon row of trendy boutiques and restaurants.

TURN RIGHT (WEST) ON RACHEL. In turning the corner, one walks from a street of bistros and fancy shops into a bustling Latin neighbourhood. There are fish stores, the Notre-Dame-de-Rosaire bakery, travel agencies and community associations. Often several generations live in one house. Many of the parents work at more than one job and grandparents care for the children at home.

St-Jean Baptiste church, at 309 Rachel E., was originally built in 1874 when this was the village of St-Jean Baptiste, named after Quebec's patron saint. It has a magnificent Baroque interior which can be seen during regular services and occasional organ recitals. There have been three fires and the current church was built in 1912 with a section dating from 1899. Santa Teresa de Avila — the Spanish Catholic Mission — is housed in the basement with its entrance around the corner at 4200 Drolet. It offers counselling and information and has a large bulletin board with notices of Latin community events. Across the street, is the a branch of the Spanish Consulate is at 360 Rachel.

TURN RIGHT ON LAVAL. In the 1970s, Portuguese bought and renovated houses, painting them in vivid colours. Many attached religious tiles or statues to the facades of their homes. The neighbourhood was transformed and the Portuguese community received a Montreal Society of Architecture award of excellence for the improvements.

Several of the houses on the west side of this street, such as 4270 Laval, are "in-fill" construction — houses built to "fill in the space" between other buildings.

Across the street is École St-Jean Baptiste, a French elementary school with a majority of Portuguese students. In early November, all schools in the Montreal Catholic School Commission are open, for one day, to parents of prospective students and others who wish to visit.

TURN LEFT ON MARIE-ANNE. As you walk west, there are several small shops catering to the Latin community. Casa

Aveirense, at the corner of Hôtel de Ville, is a Portuguese grocery store and cafe. Chez Doval, at the corner of de Bullion, makes great chicken and is typical of the many small Portuguese restaurants still in the area.

*Parc Portugal, corner St-Laurent
boulevard and Marie-Anne.*
PHOTO BY NEAL DAVID HÉBERT

The unusual three-story building at the corner of Marie-Anne and Coloniale is the home, office, and studio of Jacques Rousseau, an award-winning architect. He built it as an organic lesson in architecture emphasizing construction materials, beams, and unfinished walls both outside and within.

Diagonally opposite, at 4348 Coloniale, is *Jornal do Emigrante*, one of two local Portuguese newspapers. Next door is Lelé du Cuca, a Brazilian restaurant where customers can bring their own wine.

AT THE CORNER OF ST-LAURENT AND MARIE-ANNE is Parc Portugal. When the Park was inaugurated, one of the guests was Maurice da Silva, a descendent of Pedro da Silva who came to live in Quebec in the 17th century. Parc Portugal, rebuilt in 1990, has new tiled grounds and a bandstand with a terra-cotta roof. Rui Dias, a young Portuguese Montrealer, designed the mosaic pattern around the drinking fountain. The large pedestal monument is called a padr o. Explorers traditionally erected them when they claimed a new land for Portugal. This one is a gift from TAP — Air Portugal.

Across the street at 4256 St-Laurent is the Caisse d'Économique Portugais de Montréal. The building houses a bank, medical clinic, travel agency and real estate firm, all of which offer services in Portuguese. There are several Portuguese stores and restaurants along this stretch of St-Laurent. For a quick snack, try El Gauchito's empañadas, at 4245 St-Laurent.

The northeast corner of Rachel and St-Laurent was once the Rachel Market, a large farmers' market, now it is Parc des Amériques. The designs in the arcade use Aztec and Latin American motifs. Maps of the Americas created with mosaics are the work of Jules Lasalle, a Montreal sculptor who did much of the art along rue de la Gauchetière in Chinatown.

JUST BEHIND THE PARK, a former fire station at 4247 St-Dominique, is the Centre des Arts Contemporains du Québec à Montréal. In 1986, the interior was rebuilt for offices and a gallery. It promotes contemporary, frequently lesser-known, local and international artists.

FROM ST-DOMINIQUE TURN RIGHT AT RACHEL. Labow's pharmacy has been at this location for over 60 years. Notice the sign on the building. Faded, but readable, it tells of another era, when this part of St-Laurent was the centre of Canada's clothing industry and this building was the home of The British Mfg. Co.

Ltd. Men & Boy's Pants Men & Ladies' Sportswear. Times have changed and it's now Le Club Steel Monkey!

St-Laurent, and the area around it, still has some clothing manufacturers. Portuguese, Latin American and Vietnamese workers have replaced the Jews, French Canadians and others who worked in the unventilated factories, then justly called "sweat shops." Working conditions are better today, but it's still poorly-paid hard work dependent upon immigrant labour.

WALK ALONG RACHEL TO THE CHURCH OF SANTA CRUZ, between Clark and St-Urbain. The bell tower with the rooster on the weathervane has a whisper of Portuguese architecture. Although the church was designed by a local Portuguese architect, many in the community think its modern style is incongruent with the neighbourhood. The statue to the left of the door is the "Miracle Christ" — Santo Christo do Milagre. There are only two in Canada, both copied from the original statue in the Azores.

Across the street from the church is the Associaç o Portuguesa do Canadá (Association of Portuguese in Canada) at 4170 St-Urbain. Until 1971 this was a large synagogue — Chevra Shaas Adath Jeshurun — the name, in Hebrew, is still visible above the doors.

A great sidetrip, on a weekend, is a block further west to the soccer field at Jeanne Mance park. There is almost always a local Portuguese or Latin American team playing.

WALK BACK TO CLARK AND TURN RIGHT. 4160 Clark, built in 1905, is the former Protestant School Board's Mount Royal School. It is now a Portuguese senior citizens home. The three-story building at 4151 Clark still has the large door that once led to stables at the back.

WALK SOUTH ON CLARK AND TURN LEFT (EAST) AT DULUTH. Duluth Street dates back to the 1890s and honours Daniel Greysolon, sieur du Lhut (later spelled Duluth), an illustrious coureur des bois (trapper) and explorer who travelled to the headwaters of the Mississippi and built forts on Lake Superior, where the city of Duluth, Minnesota was named for him.

Twenty-five years ago the heart of the Portuguese community was further south, around Prince Arthur street. Now it is on this street. There are Portuguese associations, billiard halls and restaurants. The Café Portugal is the first stop for newly-arrived immigrants. Here they can find out about jobs, get a room, and hear the latest information from home. Strella Estrella opens before 8:00 a.m. and serves excellent Portuguese pastry and coffee. Palace Duluth serves Portuguese food and features lyrical Portuguese singing, known as fado, on Friday and Saturday nights. It's worth taking a little time to stroll east, at least a for a couple of blocks down Duluth, particularly on warm summer evenings.

CONTINUE SOUTH ON ST-LAURENT TO ROY. Many of the Latin stores offer more than is apparent. The Discoteca Portuguesa at 4003 St-Laurent, claiming a mixed clientele, has broadened its offerings to include Yugoslavian and Portuguese selections. Flor do Lar at 3981 St-Laurent is in the renovated Cooper building which once housed dozens of small and large clothing manufacturers. The Librarie Española (once Oberman's Kosher Meat Market) at 3811 St-Laurent sells food, groceries, music cassettes, and Spanish and Portuguese books, magazines and newspapers. The Banque Nationale on the corner of St-Cuthbert and St-Laurent has staff who "falamos Portugues," "parliamo Italiano," and "hablamos Espagñol." Jano, at 3883 St-Laurent, specializes in the barbecue cooking of the Ribatejo district of Portugal. The gift shop at 3981 St-Laurent carries Portuguese newspapers, inexpensive imported glazed-pottery, records from Portugal, and the latest European soccer scores in the window.

Further south, at 3650 St-Laurent, is Chez Barateiro, a small tailor shop that doesn't seem to have changed its window display in twenty years. Don't ask for Mr. or Mrs. Barateiro. That's Portuguese for bazaar.

TURN LEFT ON ROY. Waldman at 74 Roy E. (842-4483), is one

of the oldest and largest fish sellers in the city with a huge variety of fresh fish. This store was important to the first Portuguese newcomers to Montreal. They were from the Azores; they knew fish and the Waldman brothers needed workers who knew the product. It was an agreeable combination and induced many Portuguese to settle in this neighbourhood.

Once Roy was a major shopping street for the Jewish neighbourhood. Mr. Liebovitch and Mr. Tucker sold live chickens and there were a dozen other fish, produce and kosher butcher stores.

Today the corner grocery store — Marché Centrale Craveiro — is Portuguese and Manila sells Asian products at 20 Roy E., and Waldman's is now part of a chain of fish stores run by Greek Montrealers. Tucker's still sells chickens, but the sign says Zinman's, the workers are Portuguese and the owners are Italian! All these places are worth poking into.

The Restaurant Chez Lisbonne, at the corner of Hôtel de Ville, has good espresso and an inexpensive three-course Portuguese luncheon special with meat or fish. There is frequently live fado music on weekends.

TURN RIGHT ON HÔTEL DE VILLE. Several residents have lived here since they arrived from Portugal twenty or thirty years ago. A few have their names prominently displayed outside. One house has a Mediterranean-style, orange tiled roof, another has a statue common to those from the Azores.

The area has changed and the local schools reflect this. St-Jean Baptiste, on Laval, is mostly Portuguese and Spanish. Here, while most students are Portuguese, other nationalities include Italians, East Europeans and Vietnamese.

TWO BLOCKS EAST, AT THE CORNER OF DES PINS AND HENRI-JULIEN, is the French elementary school Jean-Jacques Olier. Olier was the founder of the Sulpician Order which held all of Montreal's land until the English conquest in 1759.

This school reflects the diversity of the area. The principal says "we encourage mutual respect, not assimilation."

THE CORNER OF DES PINS AND HÔTEL DE VILLE is a micro-cosm of so much that is changing in the area. On one corner is the Baha'i Information Centre, on another Sankt Bonifatius, Montreal's German-language Catholic parish, which conducts a German mass each Sunday. The Shalimar Depanneur, across the street has fresh samosas.

Across from it is St. Patrick's Elementary School, one of twenty-four English language schools in the Montreal Catholic School Commission. It was built in 1971 and has room for 600 students. Now there are just over 200 pupils and the principal worries about further decline since new students can only attend if their parents had an English language education in Canada.

Two blocks west of Hôtel de Ville, at 119 des Pins E., is Salon Central Portugais. Joaquim Sousa has been the neighbourhood barber for almost a quarter of a century. He learned his trade in Portugal, perfected it in France and ended up in Montreal. When he started, his shop kept three barbers going. The Portuguese community thinned and now there's only Mr. Sousa and a half-dozen customers a day. The shop is full of old magazines and Portuguese newspapers. Bottles of Resdan, Vitalis and Eau de Quinine stand against the wall. A basic haircut costs $10.

CONTINUE DOWN HÔTEL DE VILLE. Casa Micaelense Dias is at 3635 Hôtel de Ville. A quarter century ago, this grocery store was in the middle of a vibrant community. Now it is a shadow of itself — lots of wine and beer on the shelves and a back room for napping. The colourful lights outside are lit all year round. The wall plaque honours Santo Christo do Milagre. Notice the grape vines in front of the houses just north of the store — plentiful with clusters of grapes in late summer.

CONTINUE TO PRINCE ARTHUR. This street is named for Queen Victoria's third son who was Canada's Governor General from 1911 to 1916. Prince Arthur was originally Bagg street, but when the Prince first visited Montreal, a decision was made to name it after him. Bagg, the name of a local landowner, went to the small street three blocks north.

During the 1960s when 10,000 Portuguese lived in the area, Prince Arthur was important to the community. It had a fishmarket and many shops surrounded by an active Portuguese neighbourhood. As nearby Square St-Louis became attractive to younger, affluent Québecois, Prince Arthur changed. In the late 1960s and 1970s, hippies made the street their own, more stores and restaurants opened, rents rose steeply and many residents left. Today, there are perhaps 5,000 Portuguese living around here, mostly seniors and immigrant families. The Super Marché Nascimento, at 63 Prince Arthur E., is the only Portuguese store on the block. It still has dried cod stacked in the corner and home-made sausages hanging above the butcher counter.

In 1981, the city transformed Prince Arthur east of St-Laurent into a pedestrian mall. In warm weather, there's a carnival atmosphere with outdoor dining, musicians, jugglers, street vendors and artists. The fountain sculpture, called "Fleurs de Macadam," is by Gaétan Bilodeau.

TURN LEFT TO SQUARE ST-LOUIS. (Yes, the proper French word is "square.") This is one of the most elegant neighbourhoods in the city and is named for two brothers who were local businessmen. The land was originally intended for a reservoir but was turned into a park in 1876. The French speaking elite made the streets around it a discrete residential area with lovely Victorian houses. The fountain in the Square is by Armand Vaillancourt, who created many of the Montreal's monumental sculptures.

Square St-Louis has long been home to artists and writers such as the revered poet Émile Nelligan who lived at 3686 Laval at the end of the last century. For a long while, the area drifted into genteel dissipation but it has again become a favourite part of town for well known Quebecois artists. Singer Pauline Julien and poet and politician Gérald Godin have lived here, and musician André Gagnon has a home around the Square. The political poem, written in *joual*, on the side of 336 Square St-Louis, has been there for over a decade. It refers to the era when Jean Drapeau was mayor. Drapeau tried to have it removed by court order and lost.

The black and grey building across from the Square, on St-Denis, is the Institut de tourisme et d'hôtelerie du Québec. It has provincially-run programs in hotel management, tourism, and food and includes a moderately-priced hotel and restaurant open to the public. The SHERBROOKE MÉTRO STATION is just behind it, at the corner of Cherrier and Berri.

BOOKS AND FILMS

There are several Latin authors living in Montreal. *De Ausencias Y Retornos* (Daniel Indostrosa, Ediciones CEDAH, Montreal 1989) is poetry in Spanish by a Chilean expatriate living in Montreal. *La presence d'une autre Amérique* (Les Éditions de la Naine Blanche, 1989) brings together eleven Montrealers who write in French while identifying with Latin-American culture. Marilú Mallet is a Chilean writer and filmmaker living in Montreal. A collection of her short stories have been published in English as *Voyage to the Other Extreme* (Véhicule Press 1985).

Recent films on Latins in Montreal include *Les Noces de Papier / Paper Wedding* (Verseau and TV Films Associates) about Chilean political refugees who marry French Canadians to get into Canada; *Steel Blues / Jours de fer* (NFB) about a Chilean professsor who tries to adjust to life in Quebec while working in a steel plant; *La Familia Latina* (NFB) about Latin immigrants adapting to life in Montreal; and *Cher Amérique* (NFB) a prize-winning film about a Portuguese woman who leaves her children to make her fortune and her friend, a native Montrealer, who dreams of having children without giving up her career.

MIDDLE EASTERN MONTREAL

POPULATION: 50,000

MAJOR COMMUNITIES: West Island, Ahuntsic, Villeray, Cartierville, Ville St-Laurent, Côte-des-neiges, NDG, Chomedey and the South Shore.

SHOPPING: Boulevard St-Laurent between René-Lévesque and Ontario, chemin Côte-Vertu and boulevard Décarie in Ville St-Laurent.

It's taken a long time for Montreal to be thought of as a Middle Eastern city but we're getting there fast. Although there has been a Syrian-Lebanese community here for a hundred years, until recently, immigration from that part of the world was limited. Wars and continuing political upheaval in the Middle East encouraged many to consider settling in Canada, but it wasn't until regulations changed in the 1960s, putting more emphasis on qualifications and less on race, that serious immigration began. Although census figures show only about 50,000 people from Middle Eastern countries, community leaders say this figure may represent only half the real number now living here.

Montreal is an attractive city for those from the Middle East. Where others may have a myopic view of Montreal as tempestuous and fragile, Middle Easterners see a welcoming home with tremendous potential, far removed from the chaos of political oppression or the constant threat of war. Immigrants from the Middle East are often better educated and more prosperous than newcomers from other countries and working and living in French is a positive element for people educated in countries that were at one time French colonies such as Syria, Lebanon, Egypt, Morocco, and Tunisia.

ARABS AND ARABIC

"Seeking knowledge for one hour is better than praying for seventy years."
— the prophet Mohammed.

Most Middle Eastern countries are Arabic and the Arabian influence on western culture has been profound. Arab philosophers gave the world a scientific understanding of music, perfected instruments like the guitar, lute, tambourine and drum and created prototypes of the piano and organ. A thousand years ago Arabs developed the basic principles of mathematics, trigonometry and the concept of the number zero. Hundreds of years ago, Arab doctors were the first to identify chicken pox and measles, and to describe the bloodstream.

After the coming of Mohammed, in the 6th century, Arab influence spread from Northern India to Spain. But not all Arabs in the Middle East are Muslim — the only common denominator is the lyrical Arabic language. A few English and French words derived from Arabic are:

aj-jabr • algebra • algèbre
al-kharshuf • artichoke • artichaut
banana • banana • banane
naranj • orange • orange
qahwa • coffee • café
sifr • zero • zéro
sukkar • sugar • sucre

◆ ◆ ◆

ARMENIAN

The source of Armenian culture is an ancient land-locked nation divided between the countries of Turkey and Armenia (formerly part of the U.S.S.R.). The Armenes, an Indo-European people, migrated onto the rich plains between the Caucasus mountains and the Black Sea. Mount Ararat, which now lies in Turkey just across from Armenia, is the symbol of Armenian identity. According to legend, here was the Garden of Eden and the resting place for Noah's Ark.

Armenia was first conquered by Alexander the Great in 328 B.C. and has at times been under Roman, Persian and Turkish control. In modern times, an Armenian republic existed briefly after WWI. During WWI, more than a million Armenians were slaughtered by the Turkish army on a forced march from their homes through the desert.

Armenians speak, write and pray in Armenian, an ancient language related to Greek; most belong to the Armenian Orthodox church. A split in the church began in the 1930s over whether the religious leader (the Catholicos) based in Armenia had real power or was a puppet of the Soviet Government. This political division was formalized in 1956 with two Catholicos, one based in Armenia and another in Lebanon. In Montreal, Sourp Hagop (St. James) church at 3401 Olivar-Asselin represents the authority of the Lebanese Catholicos while the church of St. Gregory the Illuminator at 615 Stuart in Outremont adheres to the Catholicos in Armenia. (St. Gregory is revered for converting an Armenian king to Christianity in 301 A.D. which subsequently made Armenia the first country to adopt Christianity as its state religion.) St. Gregory the Illuminator has one of the finest Armenian choirs in North America, it can be heard Sundays at 11:00 a.m.

The 12,000 member Armenian community have several particularly strong institutions apart from the churches. Many are on

Manoogian street in the south-east corner of Ville St-Laurent, named in honour of an Armenian-American philanthropist. The **Armen-Québec Alex Manoogian School**, 755 Manoogian (744-5636) is under the jurisdiction of the French language Montreal Catholic School Board); the **Tekeyan Cultural Centre**, 825 Manoogian (747-6680) has cultural activities and publishes a weekly newspaper in Armenian, French and English; and the **Armenian General Benevolent Union** (AGBU) at 805 Manoogian (748-2428) has Golden Age activities, an Armenian boy scout troupe, and publishes *Norayk a* monthly in Armenian, French and English.

The **Armenian Community Centre**, 3401 Olivar Asselin (331-4880) has a youth organization, relief society, the weekly *Horizon*, and offices for several community organizations.

Ensemble de Danse Nayiri of the Tekeyan-Armenian Cultural Association of Montreal, 825 Manoogian, Ville Saint-Laurent (747-6680) performs at Armenian and other cultural community events and the Drummondville Folk Festival.

EGYPTIAN

Most of Montreal's Egyptian community arrived in the 1960s. They were often businessmen and professionals who saw a poor future when president Gamal Abdel Nasser began his program of nationalizing the country's industries. This well-educated group included both Jews and Christians, they easily integrated into suburban communities in the West Island, Ville Saint-Laurent, the South Shore and the Town of Mount Royal.

Recently between 500 and 1,000 Egyptians a year have chosen to reside in Montreal and many of this new group are Moslems. Uniquely Egyptian, however, is the Coptic Church. According to tradition, Copts were descended from the Pharoahs and were converted by St. Mark. The Patriarch is based in Egypt and the liturgy is in Greek, Arabic, and Coptic.

Most Egyptians became Moslems as the country was absorbed into various Islamic empires, but the Coptic church remains the largest Christian religion in Egypt and the ancient Coptic language is preserved only in the church's liturgy. There are about 1000 Coptic families in Montreal and new churches are being built on the South Shore and West Island. St. Mark's, the oldest one, at 7395 Garnier, has Sunday services at 9:00 a.m.

The **Egyptian Cultural Centre for North America Tut-Ankh-Amun** is at 132 Kingsley (683-2527) in Dollard des Ormeaux. It has meeting rooms and rents out Arabic videos. The organization produces a television program of entertainment from Egypt and local news in Arabic, French, and English broadcast on the Vision TV cable network.

IRANIAN

The country known as Persia for more than two thousand years became Iran in 1935. The Pahlavi dynasty ruled from 1925 until the abdication of the Shah Mohammed Reza Pahlavi in 1979 when fundamentalist leader Ayatollah Ruhollah Khomeni returned from exile in France and established a Shiite Islamic republic.

Shia, which means "sect" broke away from Sunni ("the way") Islam during the Middle Ages. Shia has a strong clerical hierarchy with the Immam interceding as a spiritual guide.

The Montreal Iranian community is divided by the 1979 revolution. Most who immigrated before were professionals or students from middle class families. Many of them had immigrated here after several years in Europe or other parts of North America. When the Shah fell, they decided to stay. Those who came after 1979 were fleeing their country and were generally much younger and poorer than the first group.

In 1986 there were about 3,500 Iranians in the Montreal area. By 1990 there were an estimated 10,000 of which almost a third hoped to enter Canada as refugees.

In the past decade, Iranian Montrealers have seen their community appreciated or deprecated depending on western attitudes toward Iran. When the Shah was removed from power, many Iranian restaurants suddenly found they had no customers; several closed. Today, particularly since American-Iranian relations have improved somewhat, Iranians have felt more at ease; one video store lists its phone number as 483-IRAN. Some say that Montreal has a similar "feel" to Teheran, which is also a city with a mountain in the centre and where French is commonly spoken.

The Association Iranienne du Québec, 3519 Jeanne-Mance (289-9639) organizes community celebrations and holds Farsi (Persian) language classes. Moslem community events include feasts on March 21 to celebrate the spring solstice and Shabe Yalda held before winter to celebrate the longest night of the year.

BAHA'I

As in Iran, the community in Montreal is a diverse one with Moslems, Armenian-Christians, Jews, and Baha'is. Baha'i is a world-wide faith which started in Iran in the second-half of the 19th century. Followers preach tolerance, equality of men and women, and a universal language. The Baha'i world court is frequently asked by non-Baha'i organizations to adjudicate important matters. Although it began in Iran, it's followers have been intensely persecuted and its leaders martyred there. Today there are about 30,000 Baha'is in Iran, and perhaps four million throughout the world.

Although there are only a few hundred in the Montreal area, this city is an important one for believers. In 1912, the son of Baha'u'llah, the founder of the faith, stayed in a private home on

Pine avenue during a tour of North America, while staying in hotels in other cities. The home is kept as a shrine and is not open to the public. The **Baha'i Faith Information Centre** is at 171 Pins E. (849-0753).

IRAQI

In the last few years, a third of Montreal's small Iraqi community has applied to stay here as refugees. Ironically, many have settled in Côte-St-Luc among one of Montreal area's larger concentrations of Jews. The **Centre Communautaire Irakien** is at 5733 Sherbrooke W. (489-0114).

LEBANESE

For much of this century, Lebanon was known as a mountainous, beautiful country. Modern Lebanon became an independent country in 1946 and Beirut a sophisticated city, was called "the Paris of the Middle East." However, Lebanon's many religions made for a volatile mixture, easily ignited by outside forces. Civil war has raged intermittently since the 1970s. It's not surprising that while Lebanese yearn for the day there will again be peace in their land, they choose to live elsewhere in the meantime.

Montreal has had a Lebanese community since Abraham Bounadière arrived here in 1882 and an Eastern Orthodox church was built 10 years later. These first immigrants were Christians escaping the harshness of an Islamic regime under the Ottoman empire. Many worked as peddlers, in stores, in construction and in garment factories. The community stopped growing when the Canadian government uniformly grouped Middle Easterners with Asians in its early immigration legislation and ended new migration. The objective was to stop further Chinese immigration, but by 1923, all immigration from Asian and Middle Eastern countries lands had ended. Legislation changed following WWII and a new wave of immigrants arrived from Lebanon. These were often professionals or students who finished degrees here and stayed on.

As war made Lebanon increasingly unliveable more Lebanese have immigrated to Quebec, often simply to have a piece of paper giving them permission to be here, while they hope for conditions to improve back home. Several Lebanese who made money in Arabian countries have invested in Quebec. Many live in the Town of Mount Royal which some refer to as Petit Liban.

Quebec recently placed staff in Nicosia to facilitate immigration and in the past decade has annually accepted about 8,000 Lebanese a year. In the last few years almost half of those applying to enter Quebec as refugees have come from Lebanon. One of the community's most distressing problems is raising children who have grown up knowing little-else but war. Their acute perception of the world can be a problem for them and for their teachers.

The Lebanese community's strengths have been its churches. The Greek-Melkite church of St-Sauveur was established in 1892 when the Lebanese Christians were given access to Notre-Dame de Bonsecours in Old Montreal for services. In 1923 the community took over an Anglican church on Viger near St-Denis and renamed it Saint-Sauveur de Montréal. Melkites, while part of Roman Catholicism, have their own language and culture; most are from Lebanon.

St-Sauver opened a community centre in 1974 with daycare, community activities, and services for new immigrants. The church publishes *Trait d'Union* linking Melkites across Canada.

The first Orthodox church offering services in Arabic was St-Nicholas Antiochian Church. Founded in Montreal in 1905, the community soon divided over the appointment of a new priest. Dissidents set up their own church, with the same name. The case went to court and, with the wisdom of Solomon, the judge decided that one would be called Saint-Nicholas of the Syrian Orthodox Community of Canada and the other, the Church of Saint-Nicholas of the Syrian Orthodox Community of Montreal which, in 1939, changed its name to Saint-Georges.

Members of a third substantial religious group, Maronite Christians, originally assimilated into the Montreal's Roman Catholic parishes. The Maronite sect of Christianity dates to the 4th century and became part of Roman Catholicism in the 13th century. During the 1960s a large number of newer, wealthier immigrants came to Montreal from Egypt. Many in this group were descendants of Lebanese who had settled in Egypt in the 19th century. This group set up its own church, Saint-Maron of Montreal.

The first major lay organization, the **Association canadienne libanaise-syrienne du Québec**, 40 Jean-Talon E. (274-3583) was established in 1924 to assist new immigrants. It is still involved in local affairs and has an active social club. More recent groups include **Carrefour des Cèdres**, 2376 Quesnel (932-3961) which focuses on development programs in Lebanon and education programs to increase public awareness about the situation in Lebanon. The **Société libano-canadienne de Montreal**, 1087A St-Denis (499-1585) assists Lebanese in Montreal and petitions governments to condemn Syria and Israel for invading Lebanon and interfering in that country's affairs.

An unusual community group is the **Council of Lebanese Christian-Muslim Religious Leaders of Montreal** (chairmanship changes regularly, for information contact Father Joseph Shaheen, 270-9788). "We are unique, clergymen, all idealists saying this is what Lebanon should be," according to one clergyman. The group includes Moslem, Christian and Druze religious leaders in Montreal and lobbies government on behalf of Lebanese immigrants.

The radio program Liban-Outremer is heard Friday mornings at 9:00 on CKUT 102.3-FM.

PALESTINIAN

The small Palestinian community is fairly well integrated into the larger Arab community, with many living in the South Shore town of Brossard. The community has several organizations.

Medical Aid for Palestine, 356 Sherbrooke E. (843-7875) is linked to the Palestinian Red Crescent Foundation and raises money for medical relief for those in Gaza and the West Bank.

General Union of Palestinian Students, 5687 Park (398-6290) tries to ensure that Palestinian students in Canada don't forget the suffering back home. The union holds public lectures on Palestinian issues, exhibitions on the Intifada, and the culture of Palestinians.

The **Canadian Palestinian Foundation**, 4030 Cote Vertu, Ville St-Laurent (956-1685) promotes Palestinian culture with social events organized for all Arab communities. It operates an Arabic language school on Saturdays in Pierrefonds, sponsors Arab festivals, lectures, exhibitions and demonstrations for a Palestinian homeland and helps newcomers adjust to life in Montreal.

■■ LEILA'S STORY

Leila Marshy Eid is a 30 year old Montreal film-maker and staff member of Medical Aid for Palestine (MAP).

In 1948, the year Israel became a state, my father moved from Nazareth to Lebanon. In 1956 he emigrated to Newfoundland to work at the U.S. airforce base and that was where he met my mother. They moved to Montreal in 1959 but the rest of the family still lives in Nazareth and Beirut.

. . . *LEILA'S STORY* . . .

I was born here and really wasn't that conscious of my Arab background until the Six Day War broke out in June 1967. My father wrote newspaper articles, letters to the editor, spoke at churches and tried to present Canadians with the Arab point of view. Our family was harassed and eventually, my father stopped expressing his political views. As an Arab in Montreal, he was received negatively and even called anti-Semitic. My father never pushed our Arab background. Like many immigrants of his generation, he tried hard to fit in, to interact with the larger Canadian society.

Although our family was part of the Arab community in Montreal. Most of my friends were Jewish and I used to be very embarrassed about being Arab and even told people I was Jewish. It was only when I started working in film that I began reflecting on my background. I was directing a film about the racist policies of the Canadian government and most of it centred on Black and Jewish experiences of racism. The film made me look at my own racism and the racism I had experienced. During the filming process the Arab experience was never discussed.

The project upset me and soon after I jumped at the opportunity to win a scholarship to study in Cairo. I went there in 1987 and became involved in the Egyptian arts world. People accepted me for the first time as an Arab in Cairo and this was a very creative, happy time for me. I also began working with the Palestinian Red Crescent Society and, when I came back here, I stayed involved through . The city is changing. In Montreal, today, you can speak Arabic all over. In every third store, there seems to be someone speaking Arabic.

The *kaffiyah*, a scarf or head-covering worn throughout North Africa and the Middle East, has become a symbol of the Palestinian struggle. The scarf's colours may indicate a person's political or religious orientation: black is favoured by those supporting the Fatah wing of the Palestinian Liberation Organization (PLO), red is often worn by socialists and communists, and green by Palestinian Muslims.

TURKISH

Turkey, a primarily Moslem but not an Arab country, has had a profound influence upon the Arab world. The Ottoman Turks conquered much of Eastern Europe and almost all of the Arab world, reaching their greatest power in the 16th century with Suleiman I, called the Magnificent by Europeans and *Kanuni* or lawgiver by his subjects. Suleiman brought Turkish culture to its zenith and Turkish armies into Hungary and Austria. Legend has it that Viennese bakers, working through the night, heard Turkish soldiers trying to tunnel under the city walls. Their alertness saved the city and they were permitted to create a new bread roll — the crescent or croissant — in honour of the victory.

The Ottoman Empire took centuries to lose its power and finally collapsed after Turkey sided with Germany, the losing side in WWI. In 1923 Kamal Ataturk became the first president of the modern Turkish state.

Until recently, relatively few Turks have immigrated to Canada. Those who did come were usually Armenians who joined Montreal's large Armenian community. In 1989, several thousand rural Turks arrived in Montreal as refugees. They had been told by travel agents in Turkey that Canada wanted immigrant workers. While many returned home under demands by Ottawa, hundreds remain in an immigration backlog, hoping that they will be able to remain in Canada as refugees.

ISLAM

Not all Arabs are Muslims.
Not all Muslims are Arabs.
Not all Muslims are Shiites.
Not all Shiites are for Khomeini.
Islam is not the only religion involved in politics.
    — Fatima Houda-Pepin, Director, Centre Maghrebian

A Muslim, Moslem, Mohammedan or Mussulman is a "believer" in the faith. The word Moslem comes from the Arabic "aslama" which means to submit and Islam means "submission to God."

The Imam has studied the Koran and leads religious services. Outside the mosque the Imam usually is an ordinary citizen with a non-religious job.

Islam counts almost a billion followers and the countries with the greatest number (Indonesia, India, Pakistan, Bangladesh and China) are not in the Middle East. However, Islam did grow out of Arabia and the language of Islam's sacred book, the Koran or Quran, is Arabic.

Islam was founded in the 7th century by Mohammed, a successful businessman in Mecca. At the age of 40 he was inspired by a vision of the angel Gabriel and began denouncing idolatry and preaching the worship of one God (Allah). For Moslems, Mohammed was the last in a long line of prophets which includes Abraham, Moses and Jesus Christ so that Islam is considered the ultimate faith. Islam sparked almost a millennium of Arab creativity and conquest which ended when the last Moslem dynasty was defeated at Grenada, Spain in 1492.

There are 350,000 Moslems in Canada; at least 50,000 in Montreal, most of whom arrived after 1970. Moslem families in

Canada tend to be younger, better educated and have more children than is the average for this country. In Montreal, the Islamic community is fairly evenly divided between South Asians (particularly those from India, Pakistan and Sri Lanka) and Arabs.

Montreal has several mosques and Islamic schools. They are spread throughout several municipalities in the Montreal area with many modest mosques located in apartments. (Remember to remove shoes before entering a Mosque; women should cover their heads and wear long dresses.)

The oldest Mosque is the **Masjid-ul-Islam** (Islamic Centre of Quebec) at 2520 Laval, Ville Saint-Laurent (331-1770, 5582). It was set up in 1965 and has plans to expand its building. **The Sunni Grand Mosque** is at 1590 St-Laurent.

École musulmane du Québec, 7435 Chester (484-8845) is a primary and secondary school with about 250 students. It was established in 1985. The curriculum is standard for the province and religious classes are on the Koran, however students don't have to be Moslem to go to the school. Next door is the mosque for **Communauté musulmane du Québec**, 7445 Chester (484-2967).

Other groups include **L'Association Musulman de Montreal Nord**, 4675 Amiens (325-7322, 322-6043), **Markaz-ul-Islam**, 1885 Nielson, St. Hubert (443-3482) and **Masjid Fatima**, 2012 St. Dominique, which is frequented by Moslems from Syria and Lebanon.

The Islamic calendar is lunar, with each month having 29 or 30 days. It began when the Prophet Mohammed left Mecca for refuge in Medina, in 622 A.D. The New Year is celebrated in mid-summer. Ramadan, which commemorates the revelation of the Koran, is usually in the Spring and entails a month of fasting between sunrise and sunset.

Centre d'Information sur l'Islam, 2054 St. Denis (844-2029) has classes in Arabic, English and French with instruction for those interested in Islam, and a reading room with information on Islam and the Moslem world.

Centre maghrébin du recherche et d'information, 3285 Cavendish, suite 340 (487-6488) helps others to understand Islam, the role of women in Arab lands, and Maghrebian (North African) and Moslem communities. It's documentation centre has books, journals, clippings, audio and video tapes. Under Mme. Fatima Houda-Pepin, the Centre has brought together Moslems, Jews and Christians and become an important multi-cultural group.

MEDIA

CFMB radio has an Arabic language program, Sunday evenings at 10 and Cable TV broadcasts several programs including *Télé-Égypte*, *La voix du Liban*, *Horizon Arménien*, *Arménorama*, and *Baladie Syrie*. *Al-Mirat*, 775 Mistral (388-7169) is an Arabic weekly. *Abaka* is a weekly in Armenian, French and English. *News and Views* (289-1907) covers Third World issues in Islamic countries and is published every other month.

RESTAURANTS AND CLUBS

$ indicates that a lunch or dinner should cost under $10 (without taxes, tips, or wine). $$ is under $25 and $$$ above that. Credit cards accepted are listed. Hours often vary with the seasons so please call ahead.

AIDAS $
2020 Crescent St. (842-3473)
■ Tasty Middle Eastern fare at reasonable prices. Good, spicy sujeck (Armenian sausage), tasty falafels (pita-bread stuffed with with balls of ground up chick peas deep fried with onion, parsley

and lots of spices) topped with fresh parsley, tomato and onion; and Lebanese-style pizza with cumin, sesame seed and vegetable oil on a thick wavy crust.

ALEXANDRIA $

373 Ste-Catherine W. (987-1700)

■ Great lunch or late night Middle Eastern street food: kebabs, eggplant, chicken in pita, falafel and pastries. Ask for what you don't see, like thick, pungent "Egyptian" coffee. There are a few tables in the back.

AU COIN BERBERE $$ VISA

73 Duluth E. (844-7405)

■ The restaurant itself like the menu is small, but appealing particularly for those fond of couscous — the Middle Eastern fine grained version of pasta. There are a dozen versions available served with a hearty vegetable stew plus additional dishes such as spicy sausage, broiled chicken, beef or stewed lamb. Servings are large and the couscous can be heavy. Consider side orders of chickpea salad or the Berbère house green salad. Desserts are limited but the mint tea and Turkish coffee are good.

AUX LILAS $$ MC VISA

5570 Parc (271-1453), 1285 de Maisonneuve E. (527-4109)

■ Small, family-run restaurants serving freshly made Lebanese dishes. Appetizers are extremely good here; consider ordering several small dishes rather than any individual meal. Coffee and pastries are excellent.

AZAR $ EN-ROUTE MC VISA

5672 Monkland (489-2468)

■ Falafel with hummos, lahmadjoune (ground lamb and tomato sauce on a very thin pizza dough) and tabbouleh (parsley salad), and fager bi sabankh (spinach pie). Small portions and a helpful staff. An outdoor terrace makes for lovely summertime dining.

CHEZ BABA $

Le Faubourg 1616 Ste-Catherine W. (937-4877)

■ Men from Morocco, Tunisia and other North African countries like to lounge at Chez Baba's counter for an energetic discussion and strong mint tea. There's couscous and a few meals, but this sub-sidewalk hideaway is known for its delicious selection of sfenj (Moroccan donuts) and other pastries.

CAFE ATLAS $

5155 de Maisonneuve W. (369-2447)

■ A basement-level Iranian restaurant in a spot where several other cuisines have failed. This place should succeed because it caters to the Iranian-run Atlas cab company whose drivers are based at the Vendome Métro station across the street. The restaurant can seem a little intimidating: many men taking a quick break and the menu is a billboard in Farsi. Ask — the staff tries hard. Daily specials may include lamb stew served with dilled rice, braised sheep brains, koo koo (a thickly sliced spinach and parsley omelet), or marinated beef and chicken kebabs. There are a few simple, sweet desserts and the homemade yogurt is as thick and rich as sour cream.

DAOU $$ AMEX DINERS EN-ROUTE MC VISA

519 Faillon E. (276-8310)

■ Good Lebanese food like this deserves to be savoured leisurely and lunch at Daou can easily take a couple of hours if you're not careful. Excellent marinated grilled chicken, baba ganoush (grilled eggplant purée), and salads. Main dish portions are large; it's best to go with a group to sample everything. Leave room for katayeff. These are thin, rose water-flavoured crepes filled with ricotta cheese and pistachios — the aristocrat of blintzes. Weekend diners should reserve a day or two in advance.

DIMA $$

1575 Dudemaine (334-3876)

■ A spacious Armenian restaurant with outstanding vegetarian specialties like mouhamara (an incredible combination of pomegranate juice, walnuts, hot peppers and bread crumbs), metabol (smoked puréed eggplant), and felafel. The fatouch salad and kibbeh nayé (steak tartar with bulgar) are also good. The ambience is a little haphazard with both a lunch counter and more formal table settings.

FATTOUCH $

3673 St-Laurent (499-9093)

■ Light lunches and evening snacking with a good Greek and Middle Eastern selection: falafel, souvlaki, moussaka, Lebanese omelettes, good salads like tabbouleh (parsley salad) and the fattouch (cucumber, lettuce and tomato salad in a rich, garlicky dressing). Mint seems to be in everything but baklava.

KHAYYAM $$ MC VISA

2170 St-Catherine W. (939-1565)

■ An Iranian restaurant with paintings of desert scenes, Arabic caligraphy and Iranian table cloths. The buffet or the platter for two is a good introduction to Iranian cooking. There are ample portions of several dishes including marinated sirloin, ground beef and chicken kebobs, two kinds of rice pilaff and appetizers like eggplant spiced with dried red peppers. Among the rice dishes the red 'pearl' one stands out with its sprinkling of slightly sour, imported Iranian berries. Meatless dishes are excellent and, for desert, the Iranian ice creams are superb. An unusual beverage is doogh, a salty yogourt drink topped with cumin seeds.

PATISSERIE ELARJA $

750 Décarie, Ville St-Laurent (744-6765)

■ A pastry shop that is not quite a restaurant. Unusual snacks such as candied carrots. This is a good place for a light meal. Try a combination plate with dishes such as kibbeh (ground meat balls), hummos (chick pea dip) and salads. There's even a small butcher stand and grill turning out kebabs and cutting steaks to order. The makanèk (small, spicy Lebanese sausages) are outstanding. For dessert try bilawrieh, a warm cheese filled pastry with rose water syrup.

PHARS $$

5594A Sherbrooke W. (484-4087)

■ The name is Farsi for Persia. Phars serves a representative variety of dishes for the growing Iranian community in this part of Montreal. It's a large, comfortable restaurant that's just opened as we go to press. Initial impressions are good, particularly fish dishes and appetizers. It has a liquor license and should accept credit cards soon.

RESTAURANT & PATISSERIE D'ORIENT $ AMEX
(at Norgate) VISA (at Ste-Catherine)

1091 Décarie, Ville Saint-Laurent (Norgate Shopping Centre) (747-7283), 1376 Ste-Catherine W. (875-9269)

■ A classy cafeteria with a long steam table buffet with dozens of dishes and pastries. The poisson-fort is tasty and not too spicy, the beef shwarma is freshly made and the felaffel is among the best in town. There are several kinds of salads, meat and vegetable stuffed vine leaves and mountains of mouth-watering multi-layered filo-dough pastries.

LA TENTE $$$ AMEX DINERS EN-ROUTE MC VISA

1125 Décarie, Ville Saint-Laurent (Norgate Shopping Centre) (747-7876).

■ The Middle Eastern food is good; but the place is really known for its lively shows, belly dancers, and music late Friday and Saturday evenings. The shows start around 10:00 p.m. and, while there is no cover charge, there is a minimum of $25, not at all hard to do with a glass or three of raki (a potent Middle-Eastern anis liquor similar to arak or Pernod).

FOOD SOURCES

ATLAS, 1051 Bernard W. (274-8685). Homemade Turkish-delight candy, delicious boregs (small triangular pastries filled with spinach, meat, or cheese), honey-saturated tulumba cakes and other pastries. Sesame seed covered madnakash (a large Armenian flat bread) is made a few times a week.

DEGUSTATION HAROUT, 5727 Park (273-5883). This small grocery store, next to the Rialto Theatre, is a nibblers delight. There are fresh fruits and vegetables and a good selection of Middle Eastern spices and canned goods. Browse through the bins of imported dried fruits, stacks of nut brittle and a counter tiered with Middle Eastern pastries. Ask about Harout's Armenian specialties, particularly the sausages and thinly sliced smoked meat which is much closer to a Swiss-style air dried beef than a pedestrian pastrami.

HALEL MONTREAL, 916 Decarie, Ville St-Laurent (744-0006). A small store with locally-produced and imported Middle Eastern groceries, particularly spices, and brined and fresh cheeses.

LAHMADJOUNE BEYROUTH-YERVAN, 420 Faillon (270-1076). A small bakery making good Middle Eastern breads and pastries. Excellent Lahmadjoune — small, spicy Armenian pizzas, cooked in a wood oven.

MARCHE AKHAVAN, 5916 Sherbrooke O. (485-4744). This is a small jewel of an Iranian dried foods store. There are Middle Eastern coffee makers, gold rimmed glasses for mint tea, gilt wrapped sugar cones for weddings, imported dried limes, Iranian nuts, Turkish jams, lots of herbs and spices and a small selection of fresh Iranian breads, cheeses and pastries. (When visiting a home on a happy occasion, such as a wedding or the birth of a baby, Iranians bring a gift of something sweet, such as the traditional foil-wrapped sugar cones. On the other hand, putting salt in someone's shoes means you don't want them to come back.)

MAIN IMPORTING GROCERY INC./ALIMENTS ORIEN-TALE, 1188 St. Laurent (861-5681, 5682). Spices sold in bulk, frozen foods imported from Egypt, Lebanese lemons marinated with curry, turnips in beet marinade, imported canned specialties, cheeses, olives, and pickles.

MARCHE ROSE, 1406 St. Laurent (849-2111). A good source for Middle Eastern food and spices as well as some imported cooking utensils, rugs and cloth.

PROVISIONS BYBLOS, 175 Côte Vertu, Ville Saint-Laurent (334-1010). A good market, with helpful staff; great for those of us aspiring to be competent Middle Eastern chefs. There are crates of loose tea, spicy salted string cheese, several kinds of pita, fresh herb breads and Armenian pizza. The butcher section has fresh organ meats like brains and lamb testicles, as well as marinated chicken and beef ready to be put on your own shish (skewer) and kebabed (barbecued) at home.

SAYAT-NOVA 7151 Alexandra St. (277-0889). Come here for Lahmadjoun, small, luscious, pita-thin Armenian pizzas. Sayat-nova's Park Avenue restaurant and bakery burned down several years ago but the bakery, the best part of the operation, opened up on this small street off Jean Talon W., two streets east of Parc Ave.

SHOPS AND SERVICES

ARABIC VIDEO CENTRE, 7629 St-Hubert (274-3245). Hundreds of Arabic videos, and Arabic language newspapers including *Al-Akhram* the semi-official Cairo daily which is printed in Washington, D.C. (via satellite) and delivered to Montreal.

CENTRE D'ETUDE ARABES POUR LE DEVELOPPEMENT, 1265 Berri, (843-7872) is a documentation centre with journals, newspapers and books on the Middle East. The Centre also produces analytical papers on Middle East issues.

INAAM HAMMOUDI speaks Arabic, French and English. She taught in Lebanon and now teaches reading, writing, and spoken Arabic to small groups in the afternoons and on weekends. For private lessons call 973-4280.

MIDDLE EAST BOOKSTORE, 877 Décarie, Ville St-Laurent (744-4886). Books on the Middle East in English, French and Arabic. Good selection of cookbooks, dictionaries, Arabic newspapers, music tapes, calendars, and postcards from Lebanon (including snapshots of bombed downtown Beirut).

MIDDLE-EAST IMMIGRANT AID SOCIETY OF CANADA, 10024 l'Acadie (332-2210), under the jurisdiction of the parish of St-Sauveur, assists Christian Middle-Easterners new to Montreal.

NAZEMI VIDEO, 5897 Sherbrooke W. (483-6017) and 1399 St-Jacques (483-IRAN). Iranian videos, of course; but the Sherbrooke St. store also carries Spanish, Greek, and Italian films.

TROUPE FOLKLORIQUE EGYPTIENNE DE MONTREAL LES PRINCESSES DU NIL, (388-0517). Hélene Smolens has been teaching traditional veil, folk, and peasant dances for 25 years in Montreal. Her group performs regularly and she conducts classes on Tuesday and Friday evenings at the Centre Communautaire Bois-de-Boulogne, 2025 l'Acadie.

VIDEO CAIRO NOURI, 817 Décarie, Ville St-Laurent (747-5635). Arabic videos and music tapes, mostly from Egypt; some of the older ones may have English or French subtitles. Also, inexpensive overnight transfers of PAL and SECAM videos to North American standards.

A DRIVE THROUGH MIDDLE EASTERN MONTREAL

Start at L'Acadie and Côte-Vertu
End on Décarie south of Côte-Vertu

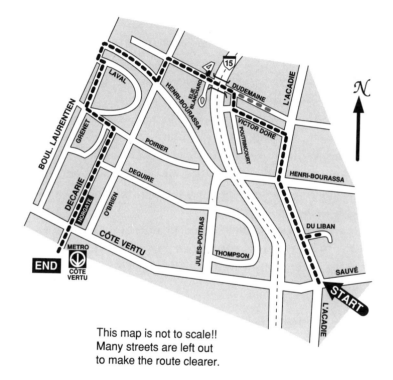

This map is not to scale!!
Many streets are left out
to make the route clearer.

Until about 25 years ago Montreal's Middle Eastern community was pretty much comprised of fairly small groups of Christians from Lebanon and Egypt, Armenians from Turkey and Lebanon, and Jews from Egypt, Iraq and Morocco.

Most of those who arrived during the 1950s and 1960s had belonged to Orthodox churches back home and, once here, attended Greek Orthodox churches and lived in areas where the much larger Greek community had settled, particularly in Park Extension and L'Acadie. The more prosperous moved to better homes in the adjacent New Bordeaux and Cartierville districts and to the nearby suburbs of Town of Mount Royal, Chomedey and Outremont.

Since the 1970s the Middle Eastern community has grown by tens of thousands. An average of 8,000 a year are still arriving, mostly from Lebanon, but increasingly from many Arab lands between the Arabian Sea and the Atlantic Ocean.

A substantial number of these recent arrivals left their countries after establishing careers in business or as professionals and academics. In Montreal they are unlikely to start, as other immigrants have, in Côte-des-Neiges, along St-Laurent, or in Park Extension. Many newcomers have settled further west and north in the suburban communities of Ville St-Laurent and the Montreal districts of Cartierville and New Bordeaux with tree-lined streets and better houses.

This tour is best travelled by car, but ardent cyclists can do it in a couple of hours. MAKE YOUR WAY TO THE INTERSECTION OF L'ACADIE AND CÔTE-VERTU/SAUVÉ, which is just north of the Métropolitain (highway 40) and east of Autoroute des Laurentides (highway 15).

There are several butcher shops and grocery stores catering to a Middle Eastern clientele in the area. Joe Haddad's butcher shop is at 733 Côte-Vertu. Byblos at 175 Côte Vertu has a large variety of cheeses, pastry, groceries and prepared and marinated meats such as Shish Kabob. Adonis is another popular market south of Côte-Vertu at 9590 de l'Acadie.

DRIVE NORTH ON L'ACADIE, two long blocks, to rue du Liban, on the right. This is a small street with duplexes on the right, many with decorative Mediteranean roof-tiles. The six storey building at 1855 du Liban is a residence for retired nuns of Our Lady of Providence. The building on the corner of L'Acadie and du Liban is the Centre Communautaire Bois-de-Boulogne, owned by the Parish of St-Sauveur.

St-Sauveur, at the corner of Viger and St-Denis near Old Montreal, was this city's first Greek Melkite Catholic and celebrates its centenary in 1992. Based in Lebanon, Melkite was an early Christian religion that has been part of the Roman Catholic church for almost 800 years. The Centre is used almost exclusively by Christian community groups from the Middle East, particularly by recently arrived immigrants and refugees. There is a daycare, scout troop, and regular community events.

CONTINUE NORTH ON L'ACADIE AND GO LEFT ON VICTOR-DORÉ. This street is a microcosm of changes in the larger neighbourhood. Only a generation ago most of the families around here were Jewish and attended the Young Israel of Val Royal orthodox synagogue is at 2855 Victor Doré. Their children would go to the Protestant School Board's English language Glencoe school across the street.

Today, there are only a few Jewish families in the area. The synagogue was sold to the Society of Armenians from Istanbul who rent back part of the space to the Jewish congregation and use the rest for cultural activities for the Armenian community. Glencoe is now a multi-ethnic French language school.

TURN RIGHT ON POUTRINCOURT AND TRAVEL ONE BLOCK TO DUDEMAINE. Turn right for a short sidetrip past several Armenian restaurants and stores east of l'Acadie, such as Dima at 1575 and Zahle at 1465 Dudemaine. Across the street from Dima is Epicerie Dudemaine with a good selection of books (in English, French and Armenian). Turn around after Zahle and go west on Dudemaine.

CONTINUE OVER THE BRIDGE ACROSS THE LAURENTIAN AUTOROUTE. On the left, is École Arménienne Sourp Hagop (Saint James). This was formerly Malcolm Cambell High School, under the public Protestant School Board; it is now a private school

Dinner at the home of Hoda and Anise Jubaili.

under the direction of the Armenian community. The name of the school is on the wall in Armenian and French.

SLOW DOWN BECAUSE THERE IS AN IMMEDIATE RIGHT AT THE FIRST STREET, ELIE-BLANCHARD. As the road curves, the first large buildings on the right is the church Sourp Hagop and the Armenian Community Centre. Next is St. Michael's Greek Orthodox church. Compare the roofs and architecture. St. Michael's has a classic bell tower and, if it was in stucco, the church would fit into any Greek village. Sourp Hagop's impressive solidity is almost like a fortress protecting its parishioners and reminiscent of a traditional style of church building common in Armenia. The small patch of green in front of the centre is Parc de l'Armenie.

CONTINUE WEST ON DUDEMAINE. Take a left on O'Brien and a right on Henri Bourassa. Go left at Boulevard Laurentian and take the first left onto Laval.

The Islamic Centre of Quebec is at 2520 Laval. Built in 1965, it is the first of the city's many Mosques and is open during most of the day. (Please remove your shoes in the small vestibule just beyond the door.) The Centre has a community kitchen, does much work with recent immigrants and refugees, acts as a burial society, and has a religious school.

TURN RIGHT ON GRENET AND LEFT ON POIRIER. This small commercial avenue is becoming filled with South Asian stores and small restaurants. TURN RIGHT ON DÉCARIE. The local branch of the YMCA is at 1745 Décarie and is involved in local housing projects and works with new immigrant groups, particularly Asians and Latin Americans.

Parkdale elementary school is at the corner of Deguire and Décarie. It was opened in 1952 within an almost exclusively white, middle-class Christian community. Today, it's 250 students come from every continent and the multi-ethnic staff is proud of the school's programs in inter-cultural education. Parkdale's principal, Horace Goddard, was born in the Caribbean and is a locally-published poet.

The Norgate Shopping Centre at the corner of Côte-Vertu and Décarie has several Lebanese owned stores. Rossy is one of a chain of discount stores started by one of Montreal's first Syrian-Lebanese families. Salim Rossy began here as a peddler and in 1910 opened a small general store on boul. St-Laurent. Today, his descendants own almost a hundred Rossy stores in Quebec and Ontario. Restaurant & Patisserie d'Orient features a buffet of freshly prepared traditional Lebanese dishes and mounds of baked-in-the-back middle eastern pastries. La Tente is a popular restaurant with a Lebanese chef and, on Friday and Saturday nights, Middle Eastern entertainment including singers and belly dancers.

YOU CAN STOP HERE; BUT IT IS WORTH CONTINUING SOUTH ON DÉCARIE. Phoenicia Video at the corner of Côte-Vertu and Décarie, rents videos in Arabic, French and English, the Middle Eastern Bookstore is at 877 Décarie, Chocomax — a Lebanese-European chocolate maker — at 814 Décarie, and Patisserie Elarja at 750 Décarie is a good place for a snack.

BOOKS, FILMS AND MUSIC

Non-fiction books about the Middle Eastern community include *An Olive Branch on the Family Tree: The Arabs in Canada*, Baha Abu-Laban, McClelland and Stewart, Toronto, 1985; *La presence arabe au Canada*, Baha Abu-Laban, Le Cercle du Livre de France et Secrétariat d'État du Canada, Ottawa, 1981; and *The Muslim Community in North America*, Earl H. Waugh, Baha Abu-Laban, and Regala B. Qureshi, The University of Alberta Press, Edmonton 1983.

When Words Burn: An Anthology of Modern Arabic Poetry (1945-1987), Cormorant Books, Dunvegan, Ontario, 1988, is edited and translated by Montreal poet John Asfour. *Orphaned by Halley's Comet*, Willams-Wallace, Stratford Ontario, 1992, is a book of short stories about immigrants and Montreal by Turkish Canadian Yeshim Ternar.

Two Middle Eastern cookbooks are by local authors: *Authentic Mid-East Recipes* by Suliman Chaderji and *Lebanese Cuisine and Middle Eastern Recipes* by Noha Bitar.

Films and videos include *Carnes du Maroc I*, (NFB) made by Canadian film makers who returned to Morocco 26 years after they had left it; *Foreign Nights*, (Mahaba Films), a story of the clash of traditional and contemporary values in a Canadian-Palestinian family; and *Short Change / Une fille impossible* (Cinegraphe), a humorous film about marriage involving a Koranic scholar, his less religious nephew, and a non-Moslem woman. *Batiya Bak!* (Aquilon film) is an award-winning documentary about a young Turkish girl's expulsion from Canada and her successful return.

In Montreal, traditional Middle Eastern styles are merging with world-beat music through acoustic instruments and a driving beat. Local performer Cheb Dino and groups Gil El Ghiwane and Anoosh have all produced records and appear regularly, particularly at **Club Balattou**, 4732 St-Laurent (845-5447).

ACKNOWLEDGEMENTS

THIS BOOK COULD NOT HAVE BEEN WRITTEN WITHOUT THE help of people who took us through their neighbourhoods: Sam and Lilly Capozzi, Vincenzo Galatti, Bud Jones, Larry Lazar, Sheila Moore, Amadeu De Moura, Norman Spatz and George Vogas.

All those who helped with comments and support: Lahssen Abasse, Silvana Anania, Jennifer August, Valentina Barbarosa, Rita Bauer, Deborah Bonney, Margaret Caldbick, Arturo Calventi, Kalpana Das, Helge Dascher, Diane DiCosta, Malcolm and Anne Douglas, Leila Marshy Eid, Felix Atencio Gonzales, Fatima Houda-Pepin, Isa Iasenza, Gordana Jovanovich, Cynthia Lam, Brenda Lee, Rob Macfarlane, Maria De Grandis Marrelli, Samantha Peeris, Maria Peluso, Suzanne Perron, Pierre Ramet, Elaine Randolphe, François Remillard (co-author of *Montreal Architecture — A Guide to Styles and Buildings*), Linda Rutenberg, Martine St-Pierre, Julie Samuels, Maureen Thompson, Frank Vivent, Joshua Wolfe (co-author of *Discover Montreal*), Ian Wong, and Paige Woodward.

Special thanks to Steve Parks and Jane Devine of the National Film Board's FORMAT Canadian Film and Video database. Multiculturalism and Citizenship Canada contributed financial assistance to make the writing of this book possible.

Rita Bauer, Marjorie Dewitz, and Celina Segal were superb proofreaders. Simon Dardick was an exacting editor and became a good friend.

They all did their best, any errors that remain are ours.

And just to note — Julius Schneller, Berel and Rivka Lazar, and Malcolm and Anne Douglas — without their determination and courage, we too would not be here.

CREDITS: Walking tour maps and "Mike's Music Rap" by Rita Bauer; Métro map courtesy of the STCUM.

PHOTOGRAPHS: ASIAN MONTREAL — 22 *Sri Lankan dancer, St-Jean Baptiste Day* courtesy of South Asian Women's Community Centre; 61 Linda Rutenberg. BLACK MONTREAL — 66 Linda Rutenberg; 89 Emile of Montreal, courtesy of the John Gilmore Fonds, Concordia University Archives. CHINESE MONTREAL — 98 *Resting in Chinatown, Harvest Moon Festival 1991* by Linda Rutenberg; 129 courtesy of the John Gilmore Fonds, Concordia University Archives. EUROPEAN MONTREAL — 134 *Ukrainian Egg Decorating* by Linda Rutenberg; 157 Neal David Hébert. GREEK MONTREAL — 164 *Students of Socrates School* courtesy of the Communauté Hellénique de Montréal; 178 courtesy of Canadian Pacific Archives. ITALIAN MONTREAL — 182 *Two Carabinieri on Mozart Street* by Linda Rutenberg; 192 Nereo Lorenzi, courtesy of the Casa d'Italia. JEWISH MONTREAL — 212 *Passover Seder* by Linda Rutenberg; 241 D. R. Cowles. LATIN MONTREAL — 248 *San Salvadorean Festival April 1991* by Linda Rutenberg; 274 Neal David Hébert. MIDDLE EASTERN MONTREAL — 282 Linda Rutenberg; 308 courtesy of Hoda and Anise Jubaili. PHOTO OF THE AUTHORS by Linda Rutenberg.

▮ ▮ THE FINAL WORD *is yours. Please let us know how the next edition can be improved. Write to us at THE GUIDE, Véhicule Press, P.O.B. 1 2 5, Place du Parc Station, Montréal, Québec, H2W 2M9. We thank you in advance in many of the languages of Montreal.*

Arabic   *shoukran*

Armenian   *shnor ha galian*

Chinese   *sheh sheh*

Czech   *dekuji*

Danish   *tak*

Dutch   *danke*

Finnish   *kiitos*

German   *danke*

Greek   *efharisto*

Hebrew   *todah*

Hungarian   *kösönöm*

Indonesian   *termia kasih*

Italian   *grazie*

Japanese   *arigato*

Norwegian   *takk*

Polish   *dziekuje*

Portuguese   *obrigadao*

Romanian   *multumiri*

Russian   *spasíbo*

Serbo-Croatian   *hvala*

Swahili   *asante*

Turkish   *tesekkür*

Yiddish   *dank*

ABOUT THE AUTHORS

BARRY LAZAR is a former executive producer for CBC Radio and was National Director of Communications for the Canadian Jewish Congress. He is a member of the board of Chinese Family Services in Montreal and founder of the Montreal YMCA's Minority Rights Committee. Barry Lazar presently works in Montreal as a freelance writer and broadcaster, and has worked on several films. His articles appear regularly in the *Montreal Gazette*.

TAMSIN DOUGLAS is a writer who has published feature articles in the *Montreal Gazette*, *The Mirror*, the *McGill Reporter*, and other publications. She was Communications Co-ordinator for International Programs of the Montreal YMCA and worked on the Y's Community and Ethnic Minority Dossier. She holds a degree in anthropology from McGill University with an emphasis on cultural anthropology and research on international development issues.

MARQUIS
Montmagny, Qc
juillet 1992